# Economics, Real Est
# and the Supply of La

# Economics, Real Estate and the Supply of Land

## Alan W. Evans

Centre for Spatial and Real Estate Economics
The University of Reading

**Blackwell**
Publishing

© 2004 Alan W. Evans

Blackwell Publishing
Editorial offices:
Blackwell Publishing Ltd, 9600 Garsington Road, Oxford OX4 2DQ, UK
  Tel: +44 (0)1865 776868
Blackwell Publishing Inc., 350 Main Street, Malden, MA 02148-5020, USA
  Tel: +1 781 388 8250
Blackwell Publishing Asia Pty Ltd, 550 Swanston Street, Carlton, Victoria 3053, Australia
  Tel: +61 (0)3 8359 1011

The right of the Author to be identified as the Author of this Work has been asserted in
accordance with the Copyright, Designs and Patents Act 1988.

First published 2004 by Blackwell Publishing Ltd

Library of Congress Cataloging-in-Publication Data
Evans, Alan W.
  Economics, real estate and the supply of land/Alan W. Evans. – 1st ed.
     p.   cm. – (Real estate issues)
  Includes bibliographical references and index.
    ISBN 1-4051-1862-8 (pbk.)
  1. Real estate development   2. Land use–Economic aspects.   3. Economics.
    I. Title.   II. Series: Real estate issues (Oxford, England)
  HD1390.E93   2004
  333.33'7–dc22

                                                                          2003022897

ISBN 1-4051-1862-8

A catalogue record for this title is available from the British Library

Set in 10/13pt Trump Mediaeval
by DP Photosetting, Aylesbury, Bucks
Printed and bound in India
by Replika Press Pvt. Ltd, Kundli 131028

The publisher's policy is to use permanent paper from mills that operate a sustainable forestry
policy, and which has been manufactured from pulp processed using acid-free and elementary
chlorine-free practices. Furthermore, the publisher ensures that the text paper and cover board
used have met acceptable environmental accreditation standards.

For further information on Blackwell Publishing, visit our website:
www.thatconstructionsite.com

To
Christopher and Adrianne,
Stephen and Denise,
and their children

RICS **FOUNDATION**

The **RICS Foundation** was established by the Royal Institution of Chartered Surveyors to promote and highlight the importance of the built and natural environment. The RICS Foundation supports and develops programmes of research to explore the key issues relevant to the way in which we manage, finance, plan and construct our built and natural environment, to make best and most effective use of the resources available to us.

## Real Estate Issues

**Series Managing Editors**
*Stephen Brown* RICS Foundation
*John Henneberry* Department of Town & Regional Planning, University of Sheffield
*David Ho* School of Design & Environment, National University of Singapore

*Real Estate Issues* is an international book series presenting the latest thinking into how real estate markets operate. The books have a strong theoretical basis – providing the underpinning for the development of new ideas.

The books are inclusive in nature, drawing both upon established techniques for real estate market analysis and on those from other academic disciplines as appropriate. The series embraces a comparative approach, allowing theory and practice to be put forward and tested for their applicability and relevance to the understanding of new situations. It does not seek to impose solutions, but rather provides a more effective means by which solutions can be found. It will not make any presumptions as to the importance of real estate markets but will uncover and present, through the clarity of the thinking, the real significance of the operation of real estate markets.

## Books in the series

Guy & Henneberry *Development and Developers*
Adams & Watkins *Greenfields, Brownfields and Housing Development*
O'Sullivan & Gibb *Housing Economics and Public Policy*
Couch, Fraser & Percy *Urban Regeneration in Southern Europe*
Allen, Barlow, Léal, Maloutas & Padovani *Housing and Welfare in Southern Europe*
Leece *Economics of the Mortgage Market*
Evans *Economics and Land Use Planning*
Evans *Economics, Real Estate and the Supply of Land*
Byrne & Matysiak *Real Estate Investment*
Seabrooke, Kent & How *International Real Estate*
Ball *Markets and Institutions in Real Estate and Construction*
Dixon, McAllister, Marston & Snow *Real Estate in the New Economy*
Adams, Watkins & White *Planning, Public Policy and Property Markets*
McGough & Tsolacos *Real Estate Market Analysis and Forecasting*

# Contents

# Preface

This book brings together work on the economic theory of the land market which I, and others, have carried out over the past twenty years or so. Bringing it together, systematising it, shows the way in which the parts interrelate, and presents a picture of the way in which the market operates.

My own thinking has developed over a long period. An early recognition was that the theory of urban location, the topic of my doctoral thesis (Evans 1973), emphasised the demand side at the expense of the supply side, indeed there was no theory of the supply side. My first attempt to try to remedy this using neoclassical growth theory (Evans 1975) failed to deal with the problem. But at that time, working at the Centre for Environmental Studies and teaching at University College London and the London School of Economics, I had considerable contact and argument with radical colleagues and radical students. The radical view was that landowners and landlords could and did exploit their position. Accepting that this might be true meant putting the arguments in terms of mainstream economics. So from a neoclassical thesis and radical anti-thesis came, I hope, a synthesis which is an improvement on both. So I am indebted to former colleagues, Michael Ball, Alex Catalano, and Doreen Massey among these, and to many students, for the arguments which led to the development of a number of the ideas presented in this book, and, usually, published earlier in article form, mainly in *Urban Studies* (Evans 1983, 1995, 2000a, 2000b), but also *Land Economics* (Evans, 1991) and the *International Journal of Urban and Regional Research* (1992).

This book is largely concerned with the economic theory of the land market. Some empirical evidence is referred to, where it is necessary to support and advance the argument. But the book could not have been written without the knowledge of the operation of the land market which other, more empirically oriented, researchers have set out. For their work I particularly have to thank Goodchild & Munton (1985), Bramley (1993a, b), Adams (1994/2001), and Kivell (1993).

The length of time during which the book has been in preparation has one advantage for the reader. There are far fewer rough edges than there might have been. For their help in smoothing the edges I chiefly have to thank the students in the Department of Real Estate and Planning (formerly Land Management) at the University of Reading. When I first gave the course of lectures on which this book is based, many of the lectures developed ideas which, at the time, were unpublished in any form. Maybe this sharpened people's minds, but students asked numerous questions, forcing me to simplify, amplify, or rethink. Some contributed suggestions as to examples and development and these are incorporated here with grateful thanks and acknowledgement.

At the time the lectures were initiated, I was awarded a Nuffield Social Science Research Fellowship to develop the research of which this book is the result, and of which the direct result was a series of journal papers, amongst them those cited above. I thank the Trust for this help. Colleagues have also helped in discussions and criticisms. Whilst a full list would become over extensive I would wish to thank Paul Cheshire (LSE), Lin Tzu-Chin (National Taipei University, Taiwan), Geoff Keogh (Aberdeen), the late Max Neutze (Australian National University, Canberra), and my colleagues at Reading, Mark Andrew, Graham Crampton, Éamonn D'Arcy, Alessandra Faggian, Phil McCann, Geoff Meen and Mike Stabler.

Finally, in preparing the lectures and the book for publication I have to thank Abi Swinburn for dealing with all those aspects of word processing and diagram preparation which I have never learned, as well as, with unfailing cheerfulness, acting as the lynch pin of the Centre for Spatial and Real Estate Economics at the University of Reading, a group with which I am proud to have been associated.

# 1

# Introduction: The Market for Land and Property

*'We can work it out'*

## The supply of land

It seems, at first sight, rather strange that over the past two hundred years and more of progress in the development of economic analysis, no theory of the supply of land has been constructed. In the case of the two other primary factors of production, capital and labour, there has been substantial work both on the supply of labour and on the supply of capital. The cause would appear to be the dominance of the mode of analysis introduced by Ricardo at the beginning of the nineteenth century with its assumption that the supply of land is fixed. This appears to be true in the most obvious sense, for the world is divided between the land and the sea, and the extent of any change in the total amount of land, through coastal erosion for example, would appear to be negligible. The assumption has therefore been accepted and scarcely questioned.

Nevertheless, although it appears to be obvious at a global level, it is not obvious, and not true, at a less than global level. In the case of some small countries it is very obviously false. Five per cent of the area of the former British colony of Hong Kong is land recovered from the sea, and the percentages are even higher in the cases of the former colonies of Singapore (10%) and Macao (33%) (Glaser *et al.* 1991). And the assumption ignores the fact that the use of land can be changed, particularly through urban development. Even with respect to the supply of land for agricultural use, the assumption ignores the extent to which the use of the land which exists can be changed, for example by the draining of marshland, as in the English Fens in medieval times, or by the irrigation of semi-desert, as in the American south-west in the twentieth century, or by the clearance of land of rocks and trees, as has occurred throughout the world throughout the centuries.

It is as though the theory of the supply of labour considered only the total population of the world, and failed to look at, say, what proportion of the population might work in any country, or what might be the supply of labour into particular kinds of employment, on the grounds that the world population could be taken as fixed in the short run.

In this book I try to set out a theory of the supply of land and to set it within an analysis of the economics of the property market. Primarily we will be concerned with the supply of land for a particular use, in particular, the supply of land for urban development. If we consider the nature of land, without being prejudiced, indeed blinded, by the Ricardian assumption, then it is very evident that land has characteristics which differentiate it from other factors of production and which will affect its supply for some particular use. The most obvious, the most important, is that land is fixed in location. The price or value of a piece of land, its relative advantages and its relative disadvantages, have to be considered together with, and indeed are virtually inseparable from, its location. And in the theories of land rent developed by Von Thunen with respect to agriculture, and by Alonso with respect to urban uses, the location of a piece of land relative to other sites is the crucial factor determining relative rents.

With respect to the supply of land for a particular use at some location the important factor is that of contiguity. The spatial relationship of sites, their size, and their configuration if they are put together may not merely be important but crucial. Moreover, there is nothing equivalent to contiguity in respect of other factors of production. One can advertise for capital to build a railway and merely accept those cheques which are cleared, one may advertise for labour and be only slightly more selective in accepting what is offered. But one cannot just advertise for sites on which to build a railway. The sites which would be acceptable are few and have to have specific spatial relationships, in particular those of contiguity and quite specific relative location. It is because of this problem that countries have laws which allow the state and some public utilities powers of compulsory purchase, powers which would be regarded as impermissible, except in wartime, in relation to labour and capital.

Finally, the ownership of land is important, the reasons for ownership, who owns it and how it is owned. It is evident that land and property are different from other kinds of assets. In English history, for example, the ownership and acquisition of land has given political power and social status in a way that the ownership of other kinds of asset could not, and this special position is explored in much of English literature. So although, in *The Importance of Being Earnest* Lady Bracknell is dismissive of the importance of land in her celebrated verbal duel with her prospective son-in-law, the exchange, and the epigram, is indicative of the special importance of land (*Lady Bracknell* 'What between the duties expected of one during one's lifetime, and the duties expected of one after one's death, land has ceased to be either a profit or a pleasure. It gives one position, and prevents one from keeping it up.' Wilde (1899) Act I, p. 224). And because of the special position of land it follows that the owners of land and property may sometimes act in what appears to be an economically irrational manner, choosing to sell, or not to sell, property when the alternative would appear to be more financially profitable. To choose an example a century later than Wilde, a possible landowner's position is given in Michel Frayn's *Headlong* – 'I happen to own this estate ... I didn't ask to own it. I just found myself with it, in exactly the same way as people find themselves landed with a big brain, or a weak heart, or big tits... I propose to go on owning it. Owning this estate is what I was put into the world to do. Nothing wrong with that. Everything has to be owned. That's what gives it life, that's what makes it mean something, having a human face attached to it. If we've learnt nothing else from the Communists we've surely learnt *that*' (Frayn 1999, p. 30).

A peculiarity of the land market is that different owners of land may have differing objectives and be described in different ways. The independence of the English yeoman farmer and the American homesteader who own and farm their own land is part of their respective countries' culture and folklore. The landed gentry in England derived their income from the rents obtained from their tenants and this gave them independence and political power. The holding together of the estate was regarded as of primary importance, as the eldest son inherited the estate and younger sons went into the church or the army, but some concern was expected for the condition of the tenants. There were responsibilities as well as rights, and because of both of these a landlord's behaviour may differ from that of an investor pure and simple whom an economist would expect to maximise the income from the estate. Their behaviour will also differ from that of the speculator buying a piece of land in the expectation that it can be sold within a short time for a higher price. Each of these terms – yeoman, homesteader, landed gentry, investor, speculator – implies differing attitudes to the land owned with respect to the present and to the future. As we shall try to show these differing attitudes will affect the process of change and development. In turn the process will also interact with and affect the views and role of the owner.

## The demand for land

The economic analysis of the theory of rent was one of the central concerns of classical economics. Adam Smith devoted a number of chapters in his *Inquiry into the Causes of the Wealth of Nations* to the topic, as did Nassau Senior, John Stuart Mill, Karl Marx, and others and at various points these authors did sometimes suggest that the owner of land might have an independent role to play. But, in the English tradition at least, it is David Ricardo who is primarily regarded as having sorted out the main themes of rent theory, and indeed, it would sometimes seem, who is regarded as having settled the subject. A consequence has been that the demand for land has been regarded as the primary, perhaps, the only determinant of land rent and land values while the perceived role of the land owner has been to use the land, or to allow it to be used, for the activity which will yield the highest current income.

The classical economists were, of course, almost wholly concerned with analysing the determination of the rent of agricultural land, rather than with the value of urban land. Ricardo's analysis, in particular, was based on the twin assumptions, first, that all of the (fixed) supply of land was used for agriculture, land in any urban use could be, and therefore was, ignored, and, second, that there was only one agricultural product, corn. A justification for this, in his case, was that he was primarily concerned with the analysis of the distribution of income between classes in society and the price of land in general, rather than with the rents of particular pieces of land.

The development of a theory to explain differences between the rents and values of different pieces of land is primarily credited to Johann Von Thunen in his book *The Isolated State*. In a study which is widely regarded as the first major piece of research in applied microeconomics, he set out to understand and explain the pattern of agricultural land values in the region of his landed estates in East Prussia. There he found that rents and land values were highest close to any major town which was a market for produce and declined rapidly with distance from this market. Moreover, the kind of agriculture found close to the major town was different to that found further away where the cost of transport of the product was higher. The same pattern of different kinds of agriculture arrayed in concentric zones around a major market centre was found elsewhere during the nineteenth century (see Chisholm 1968). It was obvious that differences in transport costs affected the rents that could be charged at different locations. The demand for sites further from the city was lower and so the rents which could be charged were also lower. Note, however, that in the Von Thunen analysis as in the Ricardian analysis, it is the demand for land which determines the rent which will be paid. Land owners have no role other than to try to obtain the highest possible current rent for the land which they own.

When the economic analysis of urban areas began to be developed in the twentieth century, it was the Von Thunen approach which was used, particularly in the initial analyses of residential location within urban areas, by Alonso (1960, 1964) and Wingo (1961). In these analyses the central business district of the urban area replaces the urban area in the Von Thunen analysis as the destination of all travel. Instead of the transport of agricultural produce to the city, however, the concern is with the daily movement of people to their workplace in the city centre. Through this analysis the decline in land values with distance from the city centre could be explained, and, as the analysis was further developed, the patterns of location of different social groups explained (Muth 1969; Evans 1973). The approach has been very fruitful, and much of the urban economic analysis which has been carried out over the past forty years or so has depended on it, in one way or the other.

But, as we have already stressed, both the Ricardian and the Von Thunen approaches have as a feature in common that it is the demand for land which determines the rent to be charged. The supply of land is unimportant. In Ricardo's case this is because he assumes that there is a fixed supply of land which cannot be altered. In Von Thunen's case it is because he assumes that the land surrounding the city is all available for agricultural use so that, if the demand is high enough, the land will be used by the owner or rented by a tenant. In each case the owners of the land have no particular role other than to maximise the income that they obtain from the land which they own, either using it themselves or renting it to a tenant.

This assumption might have been reasonably realistic in the case of agricultural land where the choices to be made are few, merely whether one crop is grown or another. The problem is that it continued to be made when the analysis was extended to urban areas and urban development where it may be, and often is, considerably less realistic. Over the last few years, however, the situation has changed as a number of contributions have been made to the economic analysis of land markets which make the point that the owner of a piece of land does have a choice – that he or she may choose, for one reason or another, not to rent out the land to yield the highest current income, and in turn may choose not to sell the land to the highest current bidder.

These contributions together define a topic which may be called a theory of the supply of land, or, as Max Neutze has suggested, more accurately, the supply of land for a particular use. It may have been that Ricardo, Von Thunen, Alonso and others were correct in assuming that the role of the land owner is usually slight in its effect on the general pattern of land values even around or within a large urban area. But in the analysis of the use of particular sites, and in the analysis of the use of land in smaller urban areas, the role of the owners of land cannot be ignored.

There is a further factor which increases the necessity for a proper understanding of the land market and that is the need to understand the economic effects of the system of land use planning which is in operation. The British system, in particular, sets out to prevent development in any form over large swathes of the countryside, and tends to restrict development elsewhere. As a result there may be relatively few areas where development is permitted and the behaviour of the owners of the land there needs to be understood. For example, some years ago a student thesis explored the Edinburgh land market in the 1950s (Kaucz 1976) finding that the planners had largely designated the land holdings of builder A for development in the first five years, and the holdings of builder B in the second five years. A and B accounted for some 70% of the residential development in the Edinburgh area. Kaucz found that the planners seemed surprised that development did not occur in the way that they had planned, surprise which can only result from implicitly assuming that land owners, even builders, exercised no independence but merely responded to demand. Perhaps such a simple assumption would not be made now, but an understanding of the role of the land owner is still sought. For example, David Adams (1994) has carried out a number of empirical studies of the role of land owners in the development of derelict sites and vacant land.

An increased understanding of the operation of the planning system is therefore an important reason, possibly the most important reason, for better understanding the role of the land owner and the nature of the supply of land. Nevertheless the discussion in this book is generally based on the working assumption that there is no planning system in operation. This is because we can only find out what the effects of a planning system might be if we know what the position would have been if it had not existed. If we know that then we are in a better position to understand the economic and physical effects of the system which is in operation. The reader who is interested in pursuing the subject can do so with the author in his book, *Economics and Land Use Planning* (Evans 2004). The aim of *this* book, however, is to bring together various approaches to the analysis of the supply of land for development into a coherent whole.

## The development of a theory of the supply of land

The approach taken is to build up an understanding of the economics of the land market, starting at the simplest level with demand-oriented rent theory and adding to it. It is as though we start with the outline of a picture, a few pencil strokes, and progressively add more colour and detail until the picture becomes, we hope, a reasonable representation of a recognised reality. So in the next chapter we set out the basic demand-oriented theory of rent and land value, as it was developed by the classical and neoclassical economists. In Chapter 3 we try to integrate the theory of land value with the theory of the supply of real property, showing the way in which, within urban areas, higher land values will tend to result in a more intensive use of land. To allow this, more capital has to be invested in the construction of more space on a site, and we show that this intensification of use can take several forms, from the extension of the existing buildings to their total demolition and the construction of new, differently configured buildings.

Consideration of this process indicates that it can be haphazard in nature as some sites are redeveloped while other, adjacent, apparently identical sites are left untouched. In part this may be because of differing attitudes and motivations of owners, to which we have already referred. In part, however, it may be because the information about the market, about prices, about alternative uses, which would be necessary for the property market to be 'efficient' in economic terms is not available. The conditions necessary for a perfectly competitive market would be that, with respect to the sale of any property, there were many buyers, many sellers, full information, and similar properties also on the market. The implications of the fact that these conditions are not fulfilled are discussed in Chapters 4 and 5.

Having established the imperfect nature of the land and property market, we turn specifically to considering the motivations of land owners and the supply of land for a particular use. In Chapters 6 and 7 we look at the main reasons why the owner of a piece of land may choose not to use their land, or to sell or rent it to someone else, for the activity which yields the highest current income. In Chapter 6 we suggest two reasons for this. First, the owner may be speculating that a higher return may be obtained in the future and that it is worth while giving up a marginally higher return in the near future for a much higher return later. Second, the future may be very uncertain and what is likely to be the most profitable form of development may not be clear. The expense and permanence of development closes off other options and an owner may therefore prefer to delay development in order to keep these options open.

In Chapter 7 we show that owners, particularly occupiers, may be attached to the land that they own, as home owners may be attached to their homes. This 'attachment' may cause them to be reluctant to sell their property unless they are compensated for having to give up the property, and the compensation they require may be large or small depending on their degree of attachment. The implication of this, and of the analysis in the preceding chapter, is that the supply of land for a particular use is an upward sloping function. Land is not different. As with the supply of any other good, the higher the price that is offered the greater will be the quantity that is supplied in any period. Thus the owners of land do have a role to play. They do not simply allow their land to be used for the current 'highest and best use'. It will become evident in the rest of the book that the existence of this upward function for the supply of land for a particular use is crucial to an understanding of the land market.

In Chapters 8 and 9 we consider various features of the land market associated with ownership. First, we argue in Chapter 8 that the process of development will differ if land is owned by landlords who let to tenants from what it would be likely to be if its ownership were split and it was occupied by users who were more attached to the land. The rate of development would be faster and the price of land for development would be lower in the landlord/tenant case than in the owner/occupier case.

Second, looking at ownership in a different way, US evidence shows that, in a relatively unplanned land market with continuing urban growth, as the probability of urban development increases, so the ownership of land passes from users – primarily farmers – into the hands of investors, who, after holding the land for a period, sell it on to the actual developers. We also show that in other contexts, with more restrictive planning systems, different processes of transition will occur.

In Chapter 9 we look at the land market from a more political viewpoint arguing first that the ownership of land and property has always been associated with political objectives and, often, political power. But we also show that land can be owned in common provided there is agreement as to the aims of the group. And finally we look at the libertarian view that land should be owned free of any constraint on the owner with respect to rights, responsibilities, and duties.

The fact that landowners may sometimes not simply accept the market determined rent but may set out to obtain a higher rent on some of their land or choose, apparently, to forgo income on some of their land, even agricultural land, by not letting it to the highest bidder, was not missed by

one classical economist, Karl Marx. He noted that landlords may sometimes be able to extract an increased rent from their land if it produces a
monopolisable product. In Chapter 10 we show that to do this they have to
restrict the uses to which their land can be put. We also show that the
theory of 'monopoly rent', as Marx called it, is applicable to some kinds of
urban development, in particular shopping centres. In Chapter 11 we consider the concept of what Marx called 'absolute rent'. He argued that
landlords will not let their land at less than some minimum 'absolute' rent.
We show that this view can be justified in terms of modern economic
analysis, in particular transaction costs and risk and uncertainty, and can
also be applied to explain some features of development in the present day.

In Chapter 12 we return to an analysis of the consequences of the imperfection and inefficiency of the land and property market. We have established in the previous chapters that the owners of land and property may not
simply accept the price offered for their property. In the first place the price
isn't determined by and in the market, as we established in Chapters 4 and
5. In the second place property owners may, for one perfectly valid reason or
another, choose to hold on to their land or property, either in an active
fashion, knowing the alternatives available, or, more passively, because
they have no thought of selling. Because of its characteristics the land and
property market is not only imperfect and inefficient but the participants in
the market lack knowledge of the alternatives available, in particular, of the
price they might be able to obtain or the price that they may have to pay.
Indeed, as we have suggested, many owners of land may be unaware of its
value, since most of those owning land and property are primarily interested
in using it and continuing to use it, whether farming the land or occupying
the property as a residence, office, or factory. The result is that anyone
wishing to buy or sell has to recognise the extent or their lack of information, or uncertainty by searching the market for those who might be willing
to trade, and the price at which they would be willing to do so. It is the
economic consequences of this uncertainty which is the main topic of
Chapter 12.

Given the lack of certainty about the availability of land, the fact that it is
not available 'off the shelf' and has often to be sought out and always to be
negotiated over, it is inevitable that developers will start looking to buy
land before they actually need it. In Chapter 13 we show why developers
engage in land banking – the purchase of land some time ahead of development, and why this process too will be affected by the nature of the
planning system in operation.

In Chapters 14, 15 and 16 we consider explicitly the problem of contiguity.

We argue that contiguity is demonstrably important and show it affects the process of site assembly. The problem of contiguity, a problem which does not arise in other product and factor markets, explains why governments intervene in the land market in a way which would be unacceptable in democratic countries in other markets. In particular governments use powers of compulsory purchase to put together sites for public development. Moreover, in some countries where the land holdings of peasant proprietors may be small and scattered, for example in Germany, Taiwan, and Japan, governments have devised systems for the reallocation of land ownership so that sites can be rearranged into more easily developable patterns.

Finally, in Chapters 17 and 18 we consider the economic effects of the taxation of land and property. From their analysis of the land market the classical and neoclassical economists concluded that taxing the rent of land or profits arising from the development of land would not distort the land market in any way. The rate of development would continue unchanged and the price of land would be unaffected. Our analysis demonstrates that this conclusion is wrong: the taxation of land, in particular the taxation of profits arising from development, will be passed on in higher prices and slow down the rate of development. Thus a view widely held and even occasionally acted on since it was first put forward by the classical economists in the nineteenth century is actually wrong. If nothing else I hope that this book will lay that idea to rest.

# 2

# Land Values, Rents and Demand

*'Fixing a hole'*

---

## Introduction

The basic theory of rents and land values as it was developed by the classical economists, and set out in this chapter, implied that these were wholly demand determined. In the classical theory of Ricardo it was assumed there is a fixed supply of land and that it has a single use which is to be used to grow 'corn', in other words food. From these assumptions follow certain conclusions. First, that the imposition of taxes on land will neither increase rents nor alter the use of land, and, second, that 'the price of land is high because the price of corn is high and not vice versa'. The basic neoclassical analysis which is also set out here assumed that land had alternative uses and these conclusions did not necessarily follow.

We argue here that although the neoclassical theory would appear to be more generally relevant than Ricardian theory, nevertheless restrictive planning systems can lead to situations where the Ricardian assumptions apply and Ricardian theory is the more relevant. The planning system may fix the amount of land available for a particular use, and may permit only this amount of land, and no more, to be used in that way. It has therefore been argued in England where the planning system does operate in this way that therefore the Ricardian conclusion follows, namely that the price of land is high because the price of [housing] is high, and not vice versa. Following on from this it has also been argued that it follows that the price of land and housing is wholly demand determined so that the supply of land for housing is irrelevant. As we shall show, whatever might be the merits of the first conclusion, the second certainly does not follow from it. This is because it ignores the fact that the supply of land is under the control of the planning authorities and can be changed. The Ricardian conclusion depends, on the other hand, on the assumption that the supply of land is fixed and unchangeable. An increase in the amount of land allowed by the planning system to be used for housing can therefore result in a fall in the price of land and housing, and this conclusion is consistent with Ricardian theory when this is correctly understood.

At the end of the chapter we go on to try to explain why many people, including many economists who should know better, can misremember, misunderstand and misrepresent basic rent theory. We conclude that it is, first, because students of economics spend very little time on the subject, including, possibly especially, those who go on to become professional economists. Second, it is because the concept of 'economic rent' which is widely used in economics is thoroughly misleading. It is meant to indicate a payment for a factor of production surplus to that required to transfer a factor from one use to another, but students assume, wrongly, that all land rents are in principle economic rents.

## Ricardian rent theory

The assumptions of Ricardian rent theory are that the supply of land is fixed, and that a single product is produced from this given supply of land. In the original analysis this product was called corn. The economic analysis is represented diagrammatically in Figure 2.1. Rent is indicated on the vertical axis and the quantity of land on the horizontal axis. The fixed supply of land is therefore indicated in the figure by the vertical line SS' in that OS hectares will be supplied whatever the rent offered or paid (above zero). The demand for land is derived from the demand for corn and is represented by the

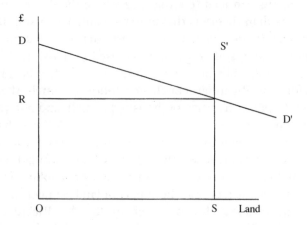

**Figure 2.1**

downward sloping demand curve DD'. Equilibrium in the land market in the form of equality between the quantity demanded and the quantity supplied fixes the rent which is paid at OR on the vertical axis.

Two conclusions follow from this analysis. First, the rent of land is solely demand determined; since the supply of land is fixed variations in rents can only occur through shifts in the demand curve DD'. Thus the rent of land is high because the price of corn is high and not vice versa, since the demand for land is derived from the demand for corn. Second, taxes levied on rents will not affect either the rent paid or the quantity of land supplied. The latter is fixed no matter what the price paid for it and the rent paid will be OR, as determined by the demand for land, no matter what proportion of this is taken in tax. From these conclusions follow the various proposals which have been made over the years for discriminatory taxes on land or the rent of land. Prominent examples are the single tax movement founded by Henry George in the nineteenth century, and the 100% Betterment Levy imposed under the UK Town and Country Planning Act of 1947 (on which see Prest 1981).

As Buchanan (1929) clearly shows, the Ricardian analysis takes the form that it does because it arose out of a particular political controversy – the debate over the Corn Laws in the early nineteenth century. The price of corn had risen during the Napoleonic Wars and the landed interest wanted duties on imports to continue in order to maintain the high price. The labouring classes and the new urban entrepreneurs wanted the price of corn to come down, the former to reduce the cost of living, the latter so that wages could also come down. Ricardo, and other economists of the time, were therefore interested in the effect of the Corn Laws on the distribution of incomes. The question at issue was whether the price of corn was being pushed up by the high rents demanded by land owners or not, and the Ricardian answer was that it was not. In the terms of the problem defined by the Ricardian assumptions, rent did not enter into the cost of production.

## Neoclassical rent theory

Marginalist or neoclassical rent theory was developed in a different political context. The controversies over the Corn Laws had raged 50 years or so before. So far as the neoclassical economists were concerned, the rent of land was merely another aspect of a general price theory rather than a question of the distribution of income. The simplified mode of analysis used by Ricardo with one land use and a fixed supply of land was set aside. Land had alternative uses and it followed that, like any other factor of production, it must receive its due remuneration. 'A potato field should pay as well as a clover field and a clover field as well as a turnip field, and so on' (Jevons 1911, p. xviii).

Further, since each piece of land had an opportunity cost – the rent that could be obtained in the most profitable alternative use, it followed that the rent of land *did* enter into the cost of production. 'So far as cost of production regulates the values of commodities, wages must enter into the calculation on exactly the same footing as rent' (Jevons 1911, p. xvi).

The neoclassical approach is represented diagrammatically in Figure 2.2. The given supply of land is again indicated along the horizontal axis as OS and rent on the vertical axis. Instead of all the land being used for growing one product, called corn, there are now assumed to be two uses for land, growing potatoes and growing corn. The demand curve for potatoes is represented conventionally by a downward sloping demand curve PP', so that the amount of land used for growing potatoes is indicated along the horizontal axis from left to right, starting from O. The remaining land, the land that is not used for growing potatoes, can be used for growing corn. The amount of land used for growing corn, since the total amount of land available is given, can therefore be indicated in the reverse direction along the horizontal axis, from right to left, starting at S. The demand curve for land for corn can also therefore be drawn from right to left, as the line CC', sloping downwards from the right, since the smaller the amount of land used for growing corn, the smaller the amount of corn for sale, and the higher its price, and so the higher the rent paid for land on which to grow corn.

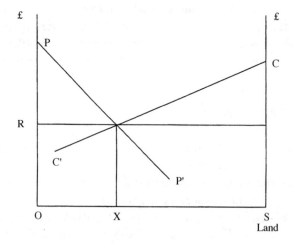

**Figure 2.2**

Equilibrium in the land market is determined, in Figure 2.2, by the inter-section of the two demand curves. At that point the rent payable in each use will be the same and competition between land owners will ensure that this is so. And only at that rent will the total quantity of land demanded for the two uses equal the supply. In the figure the rent is therefore OR, OX is used for growing potatoes and XS for growing corn.

It can easily be demonstrated using this diagrammatic analysis that, con-trary to the conclusions of Ricardian theory, an increase in the rent of land can cause an increase in the price of a good. Suppose that there is, for some reason, an increase in the demand for potatoes, with no change in the demand for corn. The increase in the derived demand for land for potatoes is represented in Figure 2.3 by a shift to the right of the demand curve from PP' to $P_1P_1'$. The increased demand for land for potatoes means that some land which was used for growing corn is now bid for to be used for growing potatoes. The result is a reduction in the amount of land used for growing corn, from SX to $SX_1$, and a commensurate increase in the land used for growing potatoes. There is also, of course, an increase in the rent paid for all land from OR to $OR_1$. But less corn is being supplied to the market since less land is being used to grow it, and at a higher cost, since rents have increased. The price of corn will therefore also rise. Now it is quite clear that the increase in the rent of land is not caused by the increase in the price of corn. Exactly the reverse is true. The price of corn has risen because the rent of land has risen. Thus the price of corn is high because the rent of land is high, and not vice versa.

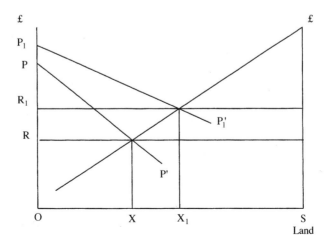

**Figure 2.3**

So the Ricardian analysis can be incorrect, and in most circumstances, where land has alternative uses and can be shifted from one use to another, it is incorrect. The rent of land for a particular use is not solely determined by the demand for the product. Moreover, the second conclusion from the Ricardian analysis can also be incorrect, in that land taxes can affect the use of land. It can easily be seen from Figure 2.2 that an equal tax on both types of land use would certainly be neutral in its effect. But it can also be seen that any form of land tax which differentiated between land uses would not be neutral in its effect, but would result in a shift in the use of land from the higher to the lower taxed use with the tax being passed on in the form of a higher price for the product of the land taxed at the higher rate.

## Ricardian theory remembered

I said in the introduction to this chapter that many people have seemed sometimes only to remember the Ricardian analysis of land values. This was particularly evident during the 1980s in arguments over the effects of planning restrictions, particularly those restricting the development of housing in southern England. At that time Ricardian theory was called on to justify the view that an increase in the amount of land made available for housing would not affect the price of land or of housing.

An example is the evidence given by David Eversley (formerly Chief Strategic Planner at the Greater London Council, Professor of Regional Planning at the University of Sussex, and Professor of Social History at Birmingham) at a planning inquiry into the appeal of Consortium Developments Ltd against refusal of planning permission for a new development at Tillingham Hall in Essex. He said that:

> the price of land is determined by the price the developer (builder) expects to be able to get for the dwelling he puts on the land. This statement is, essentially, only a special case of one of the few economic theories to have stood the test of time: the theory of rent. First propounded in its modern form by David Ricardo, more than 150 years ago, it was adopted by Marx, by the liberal classical economists, and by the neo-classical school, and it has never been seriously challenged. (Eversley 1986, p. 22.)

Eversley's view is extreme in that he states that the Ricardian analysis was accepted by the neoclassical economists, and, as we have shown, this is certainly not true. More usually neoclassical economics was ignored entirely. An example of the neoclassical view being airbrushed from history is a paper by W.S. Grigson for SERPLAN (London and South East Regional

Planning Conference – the regional planning organisation of the local authorities in South East England). He stated that:

> House prices determine land prices not the reverse, because the builder's estimate of the selling price of the building will largely determine his bid for the piece of land. This view is shared by economists and practitioners alike. (Grigson 1986, p. 6, quotation marks in original omitted.)

Of course these writers were not professional economists. But examples can be found in the economics literature. Michael Ball, a housing economist then at Birkbeck College, London, wrote that:

> It is frequently suggested that high land prices cause high house prices. A common argument for such causality confirms an 'implicit adding up' theory of price determination. In it house prices are the sum of adding up land costs, construction costs and builder's profit. Ricardian rent theory and its modern variants would dispute that conclusion by arguing for a residual view of land prices. Residential land prices, it argues, depend on the profitability of housing development. (Ball 1983, pp. 112ff.)

Those economists who go into print on the subject of land economics are usually more careful, but this quotation certainly represented the views at that time of many, if not most, economists who do not work in the field. That this was so was borne out by an informal survey which I carried out among the non-spatial economists working at the University of Reading in the late 1980s. About two-thirds subscribed to the Ricardian views set out above and were unaware of any alternative, neoclassical, view.

## Planning controls and rent theory

There may, of course, be some justification for the Ricardian view being so thoroughly embedded in English thought in that it could be argued that the system of planning controls in modern Britain has caused a situation in which Ricardian rent theory is more applicable and relevant than neo-classical rent theory. These planning controls are fairly rigid and ensure the separation of the markets for different uses. Housing land is land on which residential development is permitted, offices are not allowed to be built in certain areas, green belt land cannot be developed at all, and so on. As a result adjacent and otherwise apparently identical pieces of land may sell at entirely different prices depending on the uses to which the planning system will allow them to be put. For example, according to the Property Market Report for Autumn 2002 (Valuation Office 2002) the price of agricultural land in South East England was about £9000 per hectare, while the price of land for residential development, outside London, was likely to be at least £2 million and possibly substantially more.

Thus each piece of land can be regarded as having a single use, the use currently allowed by the planning system. In these circumstances Ricardian theory certainly appears to be more relevant than neoclassical theory. The situation can be represented as shown in Figure 2.4. Once again there is a given supply of land in the area or region, and this is shown as OS along the horizontal axis. Of this, OX is allowed to be used for housing and XS is land for which agriculture is the only permitted use. The derived demand curve for land for housing HH' slopes downwards from the left. The demand curve for agriculture is shown, however, as a line sloping downwards from the right (as did the demand curve for the alternative agricultural use, potatoes, in Figures 2.2 and 2.3). Although all the land in the area could be used for either housing or agriculture, the planning system separates the markets and different rents are charged in each market. $R_H$ is the rent for land allocated for housing and $R_A$ is the rent for land where only agriculture is permitted. So when the supply of land for each use is fixed within the planning system then the price of land is determined by demand.

Thus the conclusion may rightly be drawn that the price of housing land is high because the price of housing is high and not vice versa. That is indeed true. But we cannot go on to conclude that the level of demand is the only determinant of the price of land and the price of housing. And so go on to draw the illegitimate conclusion that the supply of land, or the 'planned'

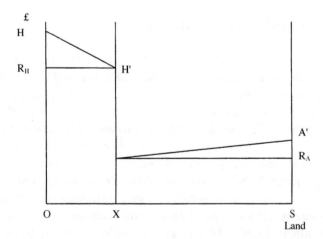

**Figure 2.4**

allocation of land to different uses, does not matter and has no effect on the price of land and the price of housing.

Eversley and Grigson, in the pieces quoted above, did precisely that. They used the conclusions of Ricardian rent theory to argue that the high price of housing land was not caused in any way by restrictions on the availability of land, but was solely the result of a high level of demand. They concluded that, in consequence, there was no need to release agricultural land for housing development because this would have no effect on either the price of housing or the price of housing land. Moreover, for a period of time at the end of the 1980s and the beginning of the 1990s, this conclusion was accepted at the highest levels of government. So, at the end of the Tillingham Hall inquiry referred to above, the Secretary of State's Inspector refused permission for the proposed development, and stated in his findings that:

12.19  Whether or not these latest trends indicate a crisis, I am persuaded that they are not caused by a shortage of building land. Shorter term fluctuations in house prices appear to be caused primarily by financial factors with house prices determining land prices. Expert opinion is agreed that the reverse does not apply.

What has been forgotten in this use of Ricardian analysis is that the supply of land does actually matter, even within the Ricardian framework. Moreover, most economists who write textbooks attempt to make this clear. For example, Richard Lipsey, in a passage which seems to have remained unaltered through all the editions of his book, writes that Ricardo's argument:

was elaborated by considering land to have only one use, the growing of corn. The supply of land was given and virtually unchangeable, i.e. land was in perfectly inelastic supply and landowners would prefer to rent out their land for some return rather than leave it idle. Nothing had to be paid to prevent land from transferring to uses other than growing corn, because it had none. Therefore, so went the argument, all the payment to land, i.e. rent, is a surplus over and above what is necessary to keep it in its present use. *Given the supply of land*, the price will depend on the demand for land which is itself a function of the price of corn. (Lipsey 1975, p. 366, stress in original.)

The argument that the supply of land, if it can be changed, does affect the price of land can easily be demonstrated diagrammatically. In Figure 2.5 the rent or price of housing land is determined initially, as in Figure 2.4, by

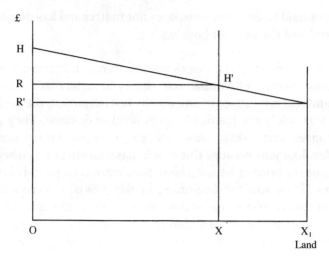

**Figure 2.5**

equality between demand and supply when the supply is fixed at OX, and the demand curve for housing land, derived from the demand for housing, is HH'. The price of housing land is therefore fixed as OR. It is obvious that if the demand for housing shifts, then an increase in demand will cause the price of land to rise and a decrease in demand will cause the price of housing land to fall. To that degree the price or rent of land is demand determined. But now suppose that the supply of housing land is increased as planning authorities give permission for a number of new housing developments. In Figure 2.5 this is indicated by $XX_1$ on the horizontal axis. The supply of land for housing shifts from the vertical line at X to the vertical line at $X_1$. A new equilibrium will be reached with equality between demand and supply at a new lower rent OR'.

This new price has been reached by increasing the supply, given the demand curve. One could therefore argue that the price is supply determined, given the demand curve, with as much justification as one could argue that the price is demand determined, given the supply curve. In truth, of course, as the argument based on Figure 2.5 should make clear, the price is determined by both demand and supply. It may be noted that, for the sake of simplicity and realism we have assumed that the price of agricultural land can be taken as fixed within the area we are considering, as would be true, say, in southern England.

Of course, also for the sake of realism, one should also say that shifts in demand will affect house prices and land prices much more quickly than shifts in supply. A fall in interest rates is likely to result in house prices being higher than they otherwise would be within a few months, possibly a few weeks, since it takes a very little time for buyers to reconsider their mortgage position. On the other hand an increase in the supply of land for housing may take years to affect prices. First, in Britain, planning permission has to be obtained and any associated legal agreements drawn up and agreed. Together these may take a year or more. Then the houses have to be built. This also will take a year or so. Only when they are being sold will prices be affected. Further, if the development is a large development, as Tillingham Hall was intended to be, development of the site will be phased over many years as the land becomes part of the developers' land banks. The reduction in prices which results from an increase in supply is therefore likely to be difficult to disentangle from all the other influences on prices while development is planned and carried out. Of course, if the land and property market were a completely efficient market then the announcement of an increased land supply would result in house buyers and builders immediately lowering prices in anticipation. But the property market is not an efficient market, as we shall seek to show in Chapter 4, so although there may be some anticipatory price reductions these are likely to be few and small.

## Hierarchical planning systems

There remains one situation where both the Ricardian and the neoclassical models may be relevant, rather than one or the other. Some planning systems operate what may be called hierarchical zoning policies. So, for example, only one part of an area may be used for industry but all of it may be used for residential purposes. The policy may be explicit, as it is in some US cities, or it may be implicit, in that, say, in some parts of southern England it may be very much easier to obtain planning permission for the redevelopment of industrial land for housing, but almost impossible to reverse the process.

The situation is illustrated in Figure 2.6. As before, an area of land is represented on the horizontal axis as OS. Rents or prices are indicated on the vertical axis. Sloping downward from the left is a demand curve for land for industry, DD'. The amount of land which is currently allowed to be used for industry is marked as OI on the horizontal axis. The intersection of the vertical supply curve II' with the demand curve DD' fixes the initial price of land for industry $OP_1$. On the right-hand side of the figure the demand for housing is assumed to be initially relatively low, and to be indicated by the demand curve HH' sloping downwards from the right-hand axis. The amount of land available for housing given initially as IS and the intersec-

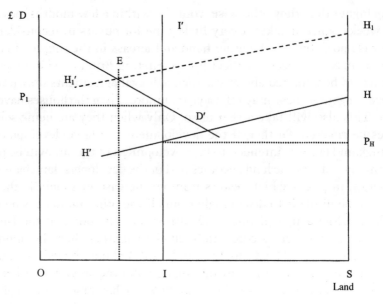

**Figure 2.6**

tion of the vertical supply curve at I with the demand curve HH' sloping downwards from the right-hand axis determines the price of housing land, marked as SP$_H$ on the right-hand axis. Thus the planning constraint is operative and the situation in both markets appears to be best represented by the Ricardian model.

Suppose that the demand for housing and housing land increases so that the housing land demand curve shifts upward to H$_1$H$_1$'. The price of housing land will increase relative to the price of industrial land. Instead of being lower, the price of housing land is now higher than the price of industrial land. It now becomes profitable to develop industrial land for residential use, and this will tend to happen. Some land will be lost to industry, and the price of land for housing will tend to fall and the price of industrial land will tend to rise. The new long-run equilibrium would be indicated in the figure by the intersection of the two demand curves DD' and H$_1$H$_1$' at E.

Thus the situation will change to one which is best represented by the neoclassical model. The change might also have occurred because of a fall in the demand for land for industry. In each case the precise situation and how best to apply the economic analysis has to be reconsidered. The problems in the late 1980s which arose in discussions of the economics of the planning system came about because people remembered only one approach and quoted its conclusions without thinking through the situation, and considering, given the situation, whether these conclusions followed.

## Urban rent theory

As we have tried to show, an understanding of Ricardian and neoclassical rent theory is essential to any understanding of the determination of rents and land values. Both approaches suffer from one major deficiency, however. Both of these basic analyses consider areas of land within which rents and land values do not vary. But as we said in Chapter 1 the economic analysis of rents and land values which has been developed since the 1950s has been based primarily on Von Thunen's model of the variation of agricultural rents and land values with distance from a major market centre. Of course, with the falls in the cost of transporting goods over the last 150 years, since Von Thunen's research, agricultural rents do not, in fact, vary very much because of distance. Nevertheless the cost of daily transporting people to work remains relatively high, and the Von Thunen analysis is the basis of the economic analysis of urban areas.

In the urban version the price of land declines at a decreasing rate with distance from the city centre, as shown Figure 2.7. Distance from the city centre or central business district (the CBD) is represented along the horizontal axis, and rents (or land values) on the vertical axis. The rent of land at the city centre is shown on the vertical axis as OC. The rent of the agricultural land surrounding the city is OA. The rent of land at the centre falls

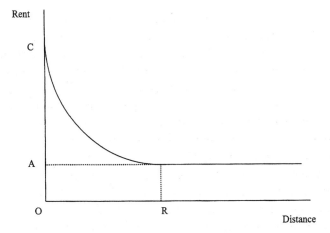

**Figure 2.7**

with increasing distance from the CBD until it becomes equal to OA at the edge of the city, defining the radius of the urban area, in the absence of topographical variation, as OR. The location of the various activities within the urban area, in the absence of planning constraints, will be determined by a 'trade off' between the cost of transport to the centre and the cost of land. So, in terms of residential location, in England or North America households with high incomes and large families and therefore wanting large houses with gardens, may choose to locate far from the centre of the city, even though commuting costs are high, because the savings on the cost of space are even higher. Poorer households may live near their workplaces, which may be at the centre. Being unable to afford to buy much space anyway, the savings from living further out are small, so travel costs become more important. The theory and the evidence are set out elsewhere (see Evans 1973). For our purposes at this point it is sufficient to note the smooth rent or land value gradient which is implied by the theoretical analysis with rents in each use being equal at the (spatial) margin, with a similarly smooth progression of uses, through, say, commercial uses at or near the centre, and industrial and various kinds of residential use to reach the edge.

That these smooth transitions do not occur is evident. With respect to the land market alone there are three reasons why they won't occur. In the first place the land market is imperfect and inefficient, as we shall show in Chapter 4. In the second place, the use of land will be affected by the preferences and behaviour of land owners, about which we shall have much more to say later. And, in the third place, land use is affected by planning controls which consequently affect land values, and that is what concerns us here.

If planning controls limit the availability, that is, the supply, of land for some uses, but demand increases and remains high, then the value of land in those uses will increase. In the absence of planning controls, land in other, relatively less profitable, uses would be converted, either through redevelopment or in some other way, so that it could be used in one of the more profitable uses. The smooth land value gradient would be retained. With inflexible planning constraints such conversions in the use of land are not possible. Therefore some land values may increase as demand shifts, but the land market cannot adjust. The result is a land value or rent gradient of the kind shown in Figure 2.8. Here a green belt at the edge of the built-up area results in a substantial difference between the value of developed and agricultural land, and constraints on the availability of land for commercial and industrial uses result in the value of land in these uses being higher than the value of land in residential use. Instead of a smooth land value gradient we have one with ups and downs like the teeth on a saw.

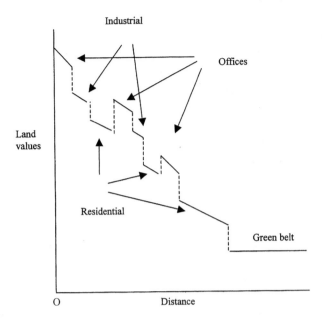

**Figure 2.8**

The Von Thunen/Alonso land value gradient, modified by the effects of planning controls, is a better representation of the situation in urban areas than the simple Ricardian and neoclassical versions set out earlier. Nevertheless, in terms of our understanding of the land market, rather than our understanding of urban areas, little is in fact gained by the additional refinement. In the absence of planning controls the situation, on the demand side, approximates to the neoclassical. In the presence of planning controls limiting the use of land the situation approximates to the Ricardian. But, of course, as we showed in the previous section, if the planning controls are more flexible in one direction than in another the situation may be sometimes Ricardian and sometimes neoclassical. And finally, if the situation is best represented as Ricardian, because of planning constraints, it is at least now understood that the restricted availability of land through the planning system will result in higher land prices.

## Rents, economic and commercial

Before we leave the subject of demand theories of land values there is a question which I raised earlier and to which I would like to return. Why do people misremember the theory? The position with respect to the applicability of the Ricardian and neoclassical theories is, I believe, perfectly clear, and all that has been done in this chapter is to restate it. For the sake of clarity we summarise it here. First, even if the total supply of land is fixed, if the land has two or more uses then it is perfectly possible for an increase in the rent or price of land to cause an increase in the price of one or more of the goods or services produced on that land. Second, even if, because of planning restrictions say, some land has only one use, varying the supply of land for that use, for example by varying the planning restrictions, will cause the rent or price of that land to vary and the price of the good or service produced on it to vary – in particular an increase in the supply of land for a use will cause the rent of that land and the price of the good or service produced to fall.

These two conclusions would seem almost universally applicable. Certainly it is difficult to conceive of a situation where the area of land is fixed and immutable and it only has one use. Any piece of land is either going to have two or more possible uses or the single use for the land has been decreed by a man-made restriction which can be modified.

This being so, why should people, even those with a training in economics, persist in a belief that an almost inapplicable theory is universally applicable? Put another way, why should they forget, indeed erase from their minds, neoclassical theory and remember only Ricardian theory, forgetting even then its qualification – 'given the supply of land'?

There seem to me to be two reasons, the one a matter of practice, the other a matter of theory. As regards the question of practice, in deciding how much to pay for a piece of land a developer will calculate what could be built on it, estimate what these buildings could be sold for, estimate the cost of construction, and deduct these estimated costs from the estimated sales proceeds. The balance is the maximum amount which could be paid for the land to yield a profit. With an allowance for a normal profit this is the 'residual valuation method' of estimating the value of a piece of land.

It is evident that this method of valuation implies that the value of the land is dependent on the sale price of the buildings. Thus this accords with Ricardian theory. From the point of view of the practical man of affairs the Ricardian argument is obviously correct. Ignored, of course, is the fact that the residual valuation method is essentially short run.

The second reason is dependent on the development of economic theory and its terminology. There is a confusion created in the minds of students (and economists) by the two meanings of the term 'rent' when it is used in economics. There is the actual rent paid for the use of land and buildings – commercial rent, the ordinary, everyday usage, and there is the payment to a factor in a particular use over and above the transfer earnings necessary to remain in that use – economic rent, a piece of economists' technical jargon. The problem is that the technical term is actually a legacy of the original Ricardian analysis. One conclusion resulting from this analysis was that (since the supply of land was fixed and only had one use) rent, that is commercial rent, did not need to be paid for land since land would provide its services (to produce the single product) no matter how great or small the reward paid for it. From this it seemed logical to coin the term 'economic rent' to describe the reward which a factor might receive for the use of its services over and above the reward necessary for it to be transferred from the best alternative use, i.e. over and above transfer earnings.

While it may have seemed logical to coin the term by analogy with commercial rent, it was actually very misleading. Students were led to believe that since economic rent is a term coined by analogy with the commercial rent paid for land, it follows that the commercial rent of land is an economic rent. But the only theory of rent which is consonant with this view is the original Ricardian analysis. Trying to sort out the complications of first-year economics it would seem obvious to many that this then is the theory which must be remembered. Psychologically this is called the reduction of cognitive dissonance (Festinger 1957).

Leaving psychology aside, it is actually quite logical that students should remember only the Ricardian analysis. After all, if commercial rents are not economic rents, but mainly transfer earnings, as neoclassical analysis suggests, why do lecturers and teachers of economics say that economic rents are like commercial rents. And if teachers and lecturers say that economic rents are conceptually like commercial rents, students can be forgiven if they then remember that commercial rents are (like) economic rents, and then remember only the theory of rent which justifies this conclusion.

The trouble is that this not some piece of arcane theory of interest only to professional economists. It has some practical importance. There must be few areas of economics as expensively argued over as the theory of land rent during full scale planning appeals featuring Queen's Counsel, junior barristers, and the cross-examination of expert witnesses, as at the Tillingham Hall Inquiry. And which even then led the Inspector to the wrong conclusion! Of course, the situation was clarified over time. Other planning inquiries also discussed the problem, with other witnesses, including the author. And after some years the Department of the Environment employed consultants to produce a report to try to settle what had by then become known as the Evans–Grigson dispute (Department of the Environment 1992).

All of this is useful in generating fees for experts and consultants, but it would have been better if the confusion had not arisen in the first place. In this respect the most useful step which could be taken would be to abandon the term 'economic rent'. For if, in almost all conceivable circumstances, commercial rents are not economic rents, what is the point of the analogy?

Of course, the concept is useful, but it would be best if its name included the word surplus: after all, in explaining the term 'economic rent' lecturers have to explain that it is a surplus, so why not use this term? The best replacement would appear to be 'surplus earnings'. Then it would be clear that surplus earnings and transfer earnings are a division of total earnings, and that the two terms go together. Moreover, one could then at least talk of the rent of land being divided into surplus earnings and transfer earnings without engendering the confusion which can result from talking of rent being partly economic rent.

## Summary and conclusion

In this chapter we have set out the basic Ricardian and neoclassical theories of the rent and value of land. We went on to show that the existence of planning controls may make the Ricardian theory of greater relevance than it would first appear. Because a planning constraint fixes the supply of land for a use, it creates a situation which accords with Ricardian theory which assumes that land is fixed in supply and only has one use. But we also show that this does not mean that the price of this land is wholly demand determined, since the supply can actually be changed, and we have shown that changes in supply through the planning system will affect the price.

We showed that there may be circumstances, with what might be called a hierarchical planning system, where the Ricardian model may sometimes apply, and the neoclassical model may also sometimes apply, depending on the economic circumstances. We also set out the basic analysis of the urban land value gradient, and indicated how it too may be modified by the existence of planning controls.

Finally, we discussed the confusion created by economists' use of the term 'economic rent' to indicate surplus earnings to a factor over and above transfer earnings, since the unwary are led to assume, wrongly, that commercial rents paid for the use of land are economic rents, and are led to remember only Ricardian theory as the theory for which this is true. It would be best, I suggest, and would avoid much confusion, if the term 'economic rent' were replaced by a term such as 'surplus earnings'.

Unfortunately I have little hope that this suggestion will be adopted by the economics profession. First, because changing the names of concepts after they have been in use for a century or more is difficult to achieve. Second, the economics of the land market and of land rent is regarded as of little importance by general economists so that the fact that the general usage creates more confusion than clarification in land economics will not be regarded as any reason for change. And, since this is so, it is advisable for those involved in studying and teaching land economics to be very aware of the possibility of confusion and misunderstanding. This is particularly possible since general economists may sometimes use the term 'rent' when they mean 'economic rent', as in the term 'rent seeking activities'. The use of this term in the study of the economics of land use planning can create total confusion in the minds of students of land and property, who can easily fail to realise that the rents being sought are not commercial rents but economic rents.

In the next chapter we turn from considering the demand for land to considering the supply of space, the way in which the land market adjusts to increases in the value of land, either by bringing more land into use, or by changing its use, or by increasing the capital investment at the site in order to increase the amount of space by building more.

# 3

## Coping with Changes in Demand

### *'The continuing story of Bungalow Bill'*

---

### Introduction

The basic theory set out in the previous chapter stresses, as we have shown, the demand side. Land values and rents are determined by the demand for land and space. But when demands change then the supply of space must change in response to the shifts in demand. In the previous chapter we touched on this in discussing the neoclassical approach when we showed that an increase in the demand for one product will lead to a reduction in the supply of land for the production of another.

Buchanan (1929) calls such changes 'changes at the margin', and indicates that the change may be at the extensive margin or at the intensive margin. In the first case an increase in the demand for space for some purpose results in the amount of land used for that purpose being extended. In the second case, however, the same amount of land may be used but it will be used more intensively.

The extensive and the intensive margins are applicable to both agricultural and urban uses, and the classical economists spent some time discussing the more intensive use of agricultural land. Marx, indeed, constructed a whole theory based on the concept of there being two kinds of differential rent (Marx 1894/1962; Ball 1977; Evans 1992). But both the extension of the area of some agricultural land, and the possibility of its more intensive use, are less important for our purposes than the extension of urban uses or the more intensive use of urban land. Therefore it is the process of adjustment in the latter case, the intensification of the use of urban land, with which we shall mainly be concerned in this chapter. For the sake of comprehensiveness, however, we start with a discussion of the extensive margins.

## The extensive margins

There are only two ways in which a land use may be increased by extension. Either land may be brought into use which had not been before, or land may be taken over from some other use.

The first case is best illustrated using Von Thunen's model, as in Figure 3.1. Rent is indicated on the vertical axis, and distance from the urban area, the market for the agricultural produce, is indicated along the horizontal axis. The initial rent gradient is shown by the downward sloping curve AR. Land within a distance OR from the city is cultivated, land further out is not. Any increase (or decrease) in the demand for agricultural produce of the region will lead to a shift in the margin of cultivation. Most obviously any increase in the population living in the urban area will lead to an overall increase in the demand for agricultural products. This can be represented in the figure by an upward shift in the rent gradient to the dotted line BS. To provide the increased product some additional land is brought into cultivation at the edge of the area already being farmed – the margin of cultivation is extended. The radius of the area under cultivation increases from OR to OS so that a ring of width RS is brought into use. Of course in addition, and necessarily associated with the extension of the area, rents over the area which is already being cultivated will increase and that land will be used more intensively.

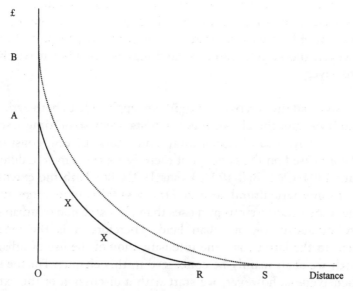

**Figure 3.1**

The model can be varied. We have demonstrated the concept using the Von Thunen model applied to agricultural land. Alternatively the modern, Alonso, version of the model can be applied to urban land alone in which case extension at the margin becomes an increase in the size of the built up area as employment at the centre increases.

Even as regards agricultural land most of the classical economists thought in terms of differences in fertility rather than distance from the market. Figure 3.1 can be thought of as representing this if fertility were measured along the horizontal axis, instead of distance, with the degree of fertility highest at the left and lowest at the right. The least fertile land is not cultivated, whilst the most fertile is. An increase in the demand for the agricultural product, because of increased population or increased incomes, will lead to increased rents and a shift in the rent gradient from AR to BS. In the figure RS therefore indicates the previously uncultivated, less fertile, 'marginal' land which is now brought into cultivation.

We have already analysed the neoclassical extensive margin in the previous chapter and need not repeat that analysis here in detail. What was shown there, in Figure 2.3, is that an increase in the demand for one product, in that case potatoes, will lead to land being bid away from other uses, in that figure corn was the alternative use. As the increased demand for potatoes leads to the price of potatoes being higher, the increased price means that, initially, higher rents can be paid in that use than in any alternative. As land is bid away from the alternative, less profitable, uses, the price of land in those other uses increases since they have to pay competitive rents. Less land is now available for those other uses, in Figure 2.3 for growing corn, and the reduced land area produces less. The reduced supply of corn leads to an increased price for the product which in turn allows the higher rents to be paid on the now reduced land area used for corn. Thus the extension of the area used for one use necessarily occurs alongside a reduction in the area used for other purposes. It also occurs alongside consequential changes in land values and rents for those other land uses as well as changes in the prices of the products.

Similar arguments apply if we envisage an increased demand for some land use within an urban area. Suppose that the existing rent gradient can be represented by AR in Figure 3.1, and that we are considering the land use occupying the ring of which the inner and outer boundaries are marked by the points XX, say industrial land use. An increase in the demand for industrial land, because, say, of technical change, would lead initially to an increased demand for land in the industrial area, i.e. in that ring, and hence to higher rents and land values there. But this would quickly affect the adjacent areas as higher prices were also paid for land just outside this ring to bid land on the fringe of the industrial areas away from other uses. The reduction in the amount of land available for other uses would lead to higher rents in these adjacent areas. In turn the consequences would spread throughout the urban area, as rents rose everywhere else and the increased demand for urban land as a whole would lead finally to an extension of the urban area bringing agricultural land at the urban margin into urban use.

The interconnectedness of the parts of the land market is evident. Though we should note two things. First, as we shall show in the next chapter, the market for land and property is imperfect and not economically efficient. The changes described above are unlikely to occur so smoothly, but to work their way through the market in fits and starts with many a hiccup along the way. Second, in some circumstances, as the price of land rises in urban areas it becomes worthwhile creating land. This is particularly likely to be so when there is shallow water within the urban area where land values are high. In the last century much of Hong Kong's business district was created by filling in parts of the harbour. Another even more extreme example is the former Portuguese colony of Macao where a third of the area was land recovered from the sea (Glaser *et al.* 1991). And to choose a less obvious example, in the nineteenth century the Thames in London which was at one time twice as wide as it is now, was narrowed and constrained by the construction of embankments (Hibbert 1969/1980). This kind of extensive margin is less rare than it might be imagined to be. What is necessary is that the value of the land when it has been recovered is high enough to give a return on the capital invested in creating it. In this respect this kind of extensive margin is closely related to the intensive margin, in urban areas at least, where it is not land that is being created by new investment but new buildings and new space.

## The intensive margin

An understanding of the intensive margin is of particular importance to an understanding of the land and property market. The analysis of the extensive margin tends to ignore all the problems in land supply which we shall discuss later. On the other hand the intensity of use of urban land, even when affected by supply side problems, can be seen to be particularly relevant in situations, as in England over the past 50 years, where the price of land has been rising strongly. Urban land is primarily merely a location for buildings, and these buildings can have different configurations and different heights. Various types of increased intensity are therefore possible. The land itself may be used more intensively as less and less is left un-built on, and where the land is built on the buildings may become higher. The effects can be seen in the centre of any major city, particularly compared to its suburbs.

In terms of the factors of production it is evident that capital is substituted for land in the production of space, as land becomes more expensive. We can represent this in two ways diagrammatically. For the first approach which is more basic, but slightly more complicated, we use Figure 3.2. In this figure quantity of land is measured along the vertical axis and quantity of capital along the horizontal axis. The product obtained from capital and land is built space, and increased amounts of each factor will allow more space to be built. A quantity of built space, say Q, can be obtained using varying amounts of each factor and the technical possibilities are represented in the figure by the downward sloping curve QQ, called an isoquant. The slope of the curve indicates that if the amount of one factor were gradually reduced then increasing amounts of the other factor would be needed to produce the same amount of space. The combination of factors used in any situation is determined by their relative prices. A possible price ratio is represented in the figure by the downward sloping straight line BA, called an isocost line. At current prices OB of land could be bought at the same total cost as OA of capital, and any combination of capital and land represented by points on AB would have the same cost.

It can easily be seen that the maximum amount of space which can be obtained at this total cost is indicated by the tangency of BA with the iso-quant QQ, with OL of land being used and OC of capital. If, however, the

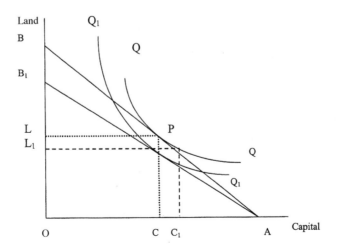

**Figure 3.2**

price of land were to rise so that only a maximum area $OB_1$ could be bought at this total cost, then a new isocost line would have a different, lower, slope, and would be tangent to a different, lower isoquant $Q_1Q_1$. Because of the increase in the price of land less space can now be constructed for the given amount of money. Further, it can also be seen that an isocost line with the new lower slope reflecting the new price ratio would be tangent to the original isoquant QQ at point P, lower down the curve than the tangency with the original price ratio. What this illustrates is that the same amount of space, Q, can still be constructed, but the cost will be higher than it was, and that the most economically efficient method of construction would now use less land ($OL_1$ on the vertical axis) and more capital ($OC_1$ on the horizontal axis).

An increase in the ratio of capital to land results in an increase in the density of development which in turn usually results in an increase in the height of the buildings constructed. Simplifying therefore, by assuming that all land is used and only building height matters, the impact of price changes on the density of development can be represented in a slightly simpler way, as in Figure 3.3. In this figure density of development or building height is represented along the horizontal axis and the price at which space is rented out is indicated on the vertical axis. In the case of commercial space this may be a rent per square metre. In the case of residential space it may be regarded as the rent for a standard apartment. Also indicated on the vertical axis is the cost of construction per unit of space. The average cost of construction is a function of development density or building height and is represented by the upward sloping curve marked as AC. This slopes upward at a diminishing rate because this is the empirically

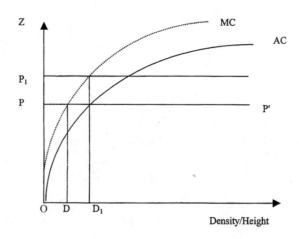

**Figure 3.3**

established relationship (though empirically the relationship is less smooth because at certain heights there are jumps in the costs when, for example, lifts have to be installed).

Given the average cost curve AC a marginal cost curve, marked as MC, can be derived showing the additional cost of each additional unit of space at each density. This curve lies above the average cost curve simply because average costs increase with density. The reasons for this are fairly clear. Each additional floor of a building costs more than the average cost of the lower floors, because the floor itself has not only to be constructed, but all the floors below it have to be reinforced to take the additional weight.

Suppose the market rent per unit of space is given as OP on the vertical axis. It is assumed here (the assumption is varied in Chapter 15) that the price will not vary with density so the given price is represented by the horizontal line PP'. The developer wishes to maximise profits. The density or height, OD, at which this is achieved is indicated in the figure by the intersection of the marginal cost curve and the price line or 'demand curve' PP'. At higher densities the additional cost of an additional floor would be greater than the additional rent received so no increase in building height would be profitable. At lower densities the additional cost of an extra floor would be more than covered by the additional rent so an increase in density would be profitable. Since price lies above average construction cost at the most profitable density there is a difference between the average rent received and the average cost incurred, and therefore between total rental income and total construction cost. From this the value of the land can be derived, by the residual valuation method, in that the difference between the total income from the development and its total cost of development indicates the value of the site to the developer. Competition between developers for sites will tend to ensure that this is generally so.

Obviously if the price at which the space can be rented increases, say to $OP_1$ in Figure 3.3, then the optimal, profit maximising, density or building height also increases, from OD to $OD_1$, as of course does the value of the land, determined as above by the residual valuation method.

The two approaches, that using Figure 3.2 and that using Figure 3.3, look at the problem in different ways. In the first it is seen primarily from the supply side. If the price of land increases then the cost of space increases and the land is used more intensively as capital is substituted for land. In the second the problem is seen primarily from the demand side. If the rent of space increases then land will be used more intensively and the price of land will rise. In fact, as has been shown, we hope, by the discussion in this and the previous chapter, the two approaches are complementary. Sometimes demand may cause the price of space and of land to rise in one use but the increases in the price of land will impact on the rents charged for other uses.

## Capital longevity and the asymmetry of change

The analyses set out above assume that it is easy to construct buildings. If rents or land costs rise the existing buildings can be replaced by new, higher density, construction. But this is the economics of Legoland, as I have described it in another context (Evans 1975). In fact, in the housing and property market the use of capital cannot be varied at will. The capital cost of construction is so high that in investment calculations it will usually be assumed that the expected life of the building is at least 25 years, usually 30, in order that the capital costs involved in its construction can be recouped. This means that an increase in rents or land values will not necessarily have any immediate effect. When we said in the discussion of Figure 3.3 that an increase in the rent of space will result in an increase in the density of development, this does not mean, in practice, outside Legoland, that redevelopment will immediately occur. Whether, and when, redevelopment does occur, depends on the age of the existing building and the increase in rent which has occurred (and, of course, on planning controls). A large increase in rent is more likely than a small increase to result in the demolition of an existing building.

It also needs to be recognised that change is asymmetric. A large increase in rents may cause an existing building to be demolished and the site redeveloped. A fall in rents, no matter how large, does not have the same stimulus. If market rents fall so that the optimal density is now lower that of the existing development, it is obvious that it would not normally be profitable to demolish the existing high density development and replace it with a lower density development. This can be demonstrated using Figure 3.3. Suppose that the rent of space is initially $OP_1$ and falls to $OP$. The optimal density then falls from $OD_1$ to $OD$. It follows that the total revenue in the first case can be represented by the rectangle $OP_1.OD_1$, and in the second case by $OP.OD$. If the old building is left standing, however, so that the density remains at $OD_1$, then the total revenue after the rent decrease if the site is not redeveloped would be $OP.OD_1$. Since this is clearly larger than $OP.OD$, it is obvious that redevelopment would not be profitable. Only, therefore, if the original building is very old and obsolescent and costly to maintain will redevelopment be likely to occur through the market. The fact that the continuing existence of obsolescent buildings in an area will help to drive rents further down, thus further delaying development, provides part of an explanation for the existence of run down areas and their associated buildings. Thus old buildings, in some circumstances, may live long past their expected life, while in other cases in towns and areas where the economy is booming they may quickly be torn down and replaced. Sometimes this lack of redevelopment may be regarded by later generations as a boon. Some of the best preserved towns from a previous age are those which went into a long economic decline. A classic example is Stamford, in Lincolnshire, which was a major town on the Great North Road from London to Edinburgh, and which boomed during the stage coach era at the beginning of the nineteenth century. Because of the opposition of the local major land owner, The Marquess of Exeter, the railway from London to Edinburgh did not have a station at or near Stamford (Hoskins 1955). The result is that central Stamford remained much as it did in 1840 for the next 150 years, becoming the ideal location at which to film *Middlemarch* in the 1990s. On the other hand, because south-east England has boomed economically for most of the last two centuries, you can find almost no 'untouched' town centres, even in part, because the process of redevelopment has been virtually continuous.

## The process of change in the housing market

The analysis set out above based on Figure 3.3 simplifies, as we pointed out, since it assumes that the only response to variations in price is, in effect, variations in building height. The analysis set out first and based on Figure 3.2 is more realistic, if more complex since it assumes only that the response to higher rents and land prices is an increase in the ratio of capital to land in the production of space. This increase in the capital:labour ratio can occur in many ways and not only through an increase in building height. The variety of possible responses when the price of space and the price of land increase can be seen most obviously in the housing market in suburban areas. There, land may be used either as a base for a building or left as open space for gardens or as a driveway. Further, as can be seen in virtually any city in England or America or elsewhere where market forces dominate, as we move towards the city centre and the price of land rises, so the proportion of the total land area which is not built on decreases, gardens become smaller, private parking space becomes less – in short the land is used more intensively.

From our point of view the interest is in the question of how this increase in intensity occurs if the price of land rises. Because of the asymmetry mentioned above, if the price of land falls the amount of change is likely to be minimal. From the point of view of this chapter falling land prices are therefore of less interest than rising land prices.

What can and does happen can be illustrated by looking at the housing market in England, in particular in south-east England, over the last 30 or 40 years. During the 30-year period up to about 1990 house prices rose more or less continuously, in money terms, though land prices fell substantially after 1974 and 1979, even in money terms. Overall, however, land and house prices rose substantially more than both incomes and prices. On the demand side this was caused by rising incomes, which more than doubled over the period, and on the supply side by the constraints imposed through the planning system on the availability of land for housing or other development. Figure 3.4 shows the changes in land prices, house prices, and incomes, over the period for the south-east of England outside London (the 'Rest of the South East' or ROSE), and changes in retail prices for the country as a whole.

One kind of response is shown in Figure 3.5. This shows, for England and Wales, the proportion of the total dwellings of each type of dwelling – bungalow, detached, semi-detached, terrace or town house, and apartment, built by the private sector in each year over the period of continuously rising house prices between 1969 and 1990. The process of change is exemplified at each end of the 'land intensity' spectrum. At the beginning of the period only 3% of new private sector dwellings were apartments. By 1990 the proportion had risen to 15%. Of course, this may have been due, in part at least, to the decline in public sector housing construction, after 1979, when the Thatcher government came into power. This would not explain, however, the decline in the proportion of private sector housing built as bungalows, from 26% in 1969 to 12% in 1990. The change in the type of construction, from land using to land saving, is a supply side response to the increasing cost of land.

Of course, it might be argued that the shift was the result of changes on the demand side. That with more single-person households and smaller households there would be a greater demand for apartments and a lower demand for larger houses. In fact, this is not borne out by evidence on the changes in the prices of different types of houses over the period. Figure 3.6 shows the price indices for each type of dwelling where the index for 1969 equals 100 in each case. The figure clearly shows that over time the more land-using dwellings – bungalows and detached houses, have risen in price faster than the others with apartments, which use land most intensively, rising in price over most of the period at the slowest rate. If the change in the pattern of construction were a response to changes in demand, with demand

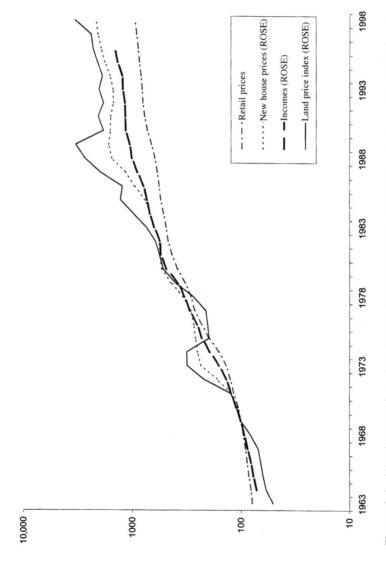

**Figure 3.4** New house prices, housing land prices and incomes in the south east (outside Greater London) and retail prices (national). Source: *Housing & Construction Statistics, Family Expenditure, Economic Trends.*

Legend:
- – · – Retail prices
- · · · · · New house prices (ROSE)
- — Incomes (ROSE)
- ──── Land price index (ROSE)

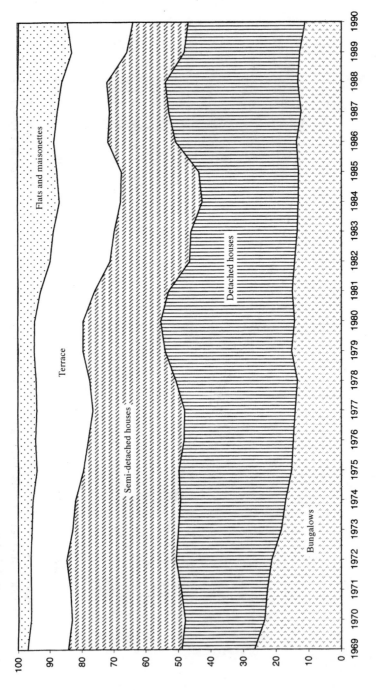

**Figure 3.5**  Distribution of different types of dwelling mortgaged. Source: *Housing & Construction Statistics.*

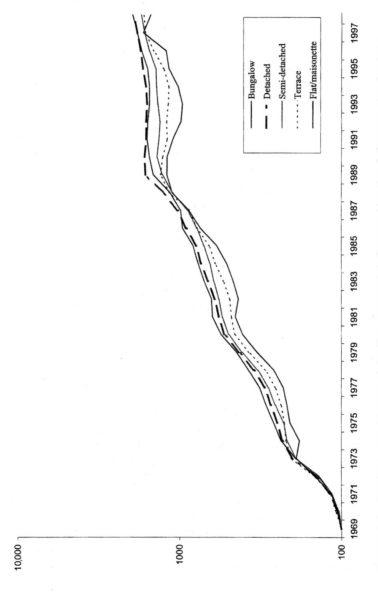

**Figure 3.6**  Dwelling price by type of dwelling mortgaged. Source: *Housing & Construction Statistics.*

increasing for apartments we should have expected to see apartments rising in price faster than the other types of dwelling.

Other forms of change are also possible in the housing market, and could be observed over the period, particularly in the suburbs of London. Detached houses with large gardens might be sold, demolished, and replaced either by apartment blocks, or by the development of terrace or town houses.

Sometimes, if access to the garden was possible without demolishing the house, the house itself might remain standing, but a part of the garden would be sold and additional housing constructed on the site. However, the most frequent way in which the capital:land ratio was increased as the price of land and housing rose was through the construction of extensions to existing houses. Both of these types of response became financially feasible because the price that people were willing to pay for land as garden space fell behind the price which builders would be willing to pay for land for development. This could be seen in the way that new houses were constructed. These new houses had gardens which were considerably smaller than older houses of similar internal area.

In the first case, the financial calculation would be that, say, the back half of the garden might be sold for development for £80,000, but the price of the property might only fall from £250,000 with the larger garden to £200,000 without it. In the second case the financial calculations are slightly more complicated. One possible scenario is that a family may own a house which they bought some years ago. It might have, say, three bedrooms and one bathroom, but a largish garden, and as such it could be sold for £200,000. Because of increases in income and/or increases in the size of the household, they may start to look around for a larger house, one, for example, with four bedrooms and two bathrooms. It will become apparent during the search that newer, more affordable, houses of this kind have much smaller gardens than the one they have become accustomed to. They will do some calculations and realise that it would be possible to extend the existing house for, say, £60,000, and that it would then be worth more than its total opportunity cost of £260,000 (its value unextended of £200,000 plus the cost of the extension). If this is so, that is its estimated value when extended is £270,000 or more, then the process is feasible. Extension will allow them to attain the larger house that they want, with only slightly less garden space than they are accustomed to, and gain an increase in value which will make the trouble and inconvenience involved in the construction worthwhile.

An alternative scenario is that a household, having made the same discovery that larger modern houses have very small gardens, will set out to buy a smaller house with the intention of extending it. With the British planning system this carries slightly more risk, since there is a chance that the necessary planning permission may not be obtained, but outside conservation areas this risk is not high. If I can add an unwonted personal note to this discussion, this is what my wife and I did some years ago. And, of the eleven houses on our street in an outer London suburb, six have been substantially extended, by a third or more, in the last 30 years or so, sometimes in two or more stages, three have been extended but by very little, and two, both occupied by single persons for more than 30 years, have not been extended at all.

This anecdotal evidence shows the way in which the process of adjustment is necessarily dependent on social factors so that there is a strong random element as to whether a house will be extended or not. A house occupied by someone with no wish to move, and no need for extra space, an elderly couple, for example, will remain untouched while surrounding houses are changed substantially. If the property market were a perfectly competitive market the increase in the value of the property might induce the owners to sell and in some cases it does. There is some, mainly anecdotal, evidence that when people living in the London area retire, they may sometimes cash in their highly valued property and move to where housing is cheaper. At this point the property may be extended or redeveloped. More often no reason will be seen for a move. The possible advantages of moving may not be easily calculable. The owners are under no pressure to sell since the capital remains invested in the house even if it is not sold now. The capital can be realised later if it becomes necessary. And the possible financial advantages of moving may not seem so very great in comparison with the advantages of remaining in a known environment.

Nevertheless, while the process of change may be affected by social factors, economic factors play their part. The increases in land values, we have argued, stimulate the idea of extension. There is also evidence that the process of extension is greater on the upswing of prices in the housing market than it is on the downswing. This is as one would expect (Gosling *et al.* 1993).

## Summary and conclusions

In this chapter we have set out the way in which the urban property market adjusts to cope with changes in factor prices and in demand. We have shown how the basic classical and neoclassical analyses primarily concerned, originally with the agricultural land market, indicate the way in which land uses are extended at the margin, and the way in which shifts in demand lead to shifts in land use.

Of most interest to us has been the analysis of the way in which the use of land changes 'at the intensive margin', that is, the way in which land is used more intensively if its price increases. Changes in the intensity of use of urban land require the addition (or the alteration) of the capital invested in the land in the form of bricks and mortar. The way in which this occurs will depend upon existing land uses, social factors, the age and past history of the buildings, etc. These changes will not be smooth, will not be universal, and will often be only partial. Thus the land market will appear to be what it is, an imperfect market. In the next chapter we will look more closely at its measurable imperfection and inefficiency.

# 4

# How Efficient is the Property Market?

## *'The fool on the hill'*

## Introduction

In the first three chapters we have discussed the way in which the land and property market works, the way in which land is supplied, and the way in which its use changes as demands for different uses change and as, in consequence, its price changes. In particular, in the previous chapter, we have looked at the way in which land will be used more intensively as its price increases. Not only is there a possible change in the use of the land, but there is also likely to be an increase in the capital:land ratio, and an increase in the labour:land ratio.

These adjustments are predicated on the assumption that the owners of land are aware of changes in market conditions and respond to them. This in turn presumes that they are aware of the price, i.e. the opportunity cost, of the property that they own so that they can respond to such changes. But land and property owners may be only incompletely aware of changes in the value of their properties. Most usually they will be aware that prices are rising, or that prices are falling, the direction of change, but not the extent of any change, and their responses may be slow. If they were fully aware, and responded quickly, then the market could be described as economically efficient. But if they are not fully aware, and do not respond quickly, then the market is, in economic terms, not efficient.

In this chapter and the next we discuss this question of efficiency, beginning with the conditions which would be necessary for the market to be efficient, and to be regarded as such. We argue that the conditions are difficult to fulfil, first, and that, second, the evidence suggests that the land and property market is not completely efficient. I have argued in the past (Evans 1995), that it could in fact be described as 90% efficient. This degree of 'inefficiency' is fundamentally a consequence of the heterogeneity of properties, and the other causes and consequences of this inefficiency for the way the market itself works are discussed in the next chapter. For if the characteristics of the market affect its efficiency, so, reciprocally, does the lack of efficiency of the market affect its characteristics.

## The economic concept of efficiency

What do we mean by the concept of market efficiency? An enormous amount of research has been carried out over the past 30 years or so in analysing and exploring the efficiency of stock markets. Inevitably, therefore, we have to start from, and with, the concept of efficiency which has been used as the basis for that research.

The basic assumption is that in an efficient market all the information currently available is reflected in, that is capitalised into, the price of the object being traded, in the case of the stock market the ordinary shares of companies. In turn, the price is determined in and by the market through the activities of buyers and sellers some or all of whom are in possession of this information and act on it. This definition is 'static' since it refers to the determination of the price of the object at a point in time. It also has implications for changes over time, however, since the implication is that new information is discounted into the price as it becomes available. Thus, as we shall see, research into the efficiency of the stock market has largely concentrated on movements in prices over time. The fundamental question has been perceived to be the extent to which price changes respond to new information. Do prices appear to anticipate or respond immediately to the arrival of new information or do they react with a significant time lag, over a period of time?

We start, however, with the prior concept, the conditions necessary for all information currently available to be reflected in, or fully capitalised in, the price of a piece of land or property.

## Efficient markets

How are efficient markets supposed to work? The most primitive model is the basic model of supply and demand used in introductory economics. In this 'perfect' market there are many buyers and many sellers, there is a homogeneous good being sold, usually thought of as some agricultural product like wheat of a specific grade, and the participants in the market have full information as to the prices of alternative products, etc. In this model the demand schedule for the good can be represented in a diagram by a downward sloping line, the demand curve, and the quantity of the good supplied at different prices, the supply schedule, can be represented by an upward sloping line, the supply curve. Equilibrium in the market occurs at the price at which the quantity demanded equals the quantity supplied, and both price and quantity are determined in the market. In effect the participants in the market, both buyers and sellers, have no control over the price which is perceived as given to them. That price reflects the information which is available to the participants, and which is itself reflected in their demand and supply schedules, so that the market is efficient.

In economic terms this is a model of an explicit market. The market is described as 'explicit' because the good itself is explicitly being traded. The model is not usually completely applicable to the market for real estate, however. This is because, with land and property, because they are fixed in location, it is almost invariably true that what is apparently being traded is one thing, land, but that what is actually being traded is some characteristic of that piece of land. This is certainly true in the two basic models of the determination of the price of land that we discussed in Chapter 2. In the Ricardian model it is the fertility of land which determines the price paid for it, the more fertile the land the higher the rent paid. In the Von Thunen model it is location which causes the rent to vary, the closer to the market centre that the land lies, the higher the rent that is paid. So the price paid for the land may be stated as a rent per hectare, but the price varies with the characteristics of the land, with its fertility or with its location, so that the land market is, in fact, an implicit market for this characteristic.

Even in this simplest possible case the problem that the land market has to solve is rather more complex than the problem which has to be solved in the explicit market modelled by the demand and supply schedules. The latter has merely to determine a price at which all the goods will be traded. The land market has to determine, not a single price, but a schedule of prices for the land and for its characteristic. Moreover, this price schedule will often be non-linear. For example, Alonso (1964) showed that the rent or land value gradient, the rate at which rents fall with distance from a market centre, will be curvilinear. The rent payable will fall with distance, but at a decreasing rate as distance increases. Knowing the rent at a certain distance from the centre does not allow us to say what it will be at twice the distance. With an explicit market, however, setting aside the possibility of quantity discounts, knowing the price of a certain quantity of a good allows one to say what the cost of twice that quantity will be.

Moreover, even the cases analysed by Ricardo, Von Thunen, and Alonso are over-simplified since in their models land has only one characteristic, either location relative to a point or fertility. But in practice, even in the case of agricultural land, a piece of land has several characteristics, its fertility with respect to different kinds of product and its location relative to several different other locations. The market then has to solve the problem of determining the price for the land which takes into account all of these characteristics and, in effect, implicitly prices each of them. Additionally, in the case of most pieces of land capital has been spent constructing buildings on the land. Since these have to be paid for as part of the price paid for the land, the characteristics of these buildings are also implicitly priced in the price paid for the whole property.

It is evident that the problem which the market has to solve is much more difficult than that of settling the price for a good which is being traded in an explicit market, but that does not mean that the task is impossible. Certainly it is theoretically possible that the market could solve the problem specified and could determine the price schedule for each individual characteristic and so for each piece of real estate. In the definitive article on implicit markets by Rosen (1974) the problem was analysed diagrammatically as in Figure 4.1. The quantity of a characteristic is represented along the horizontal axis, for example some measure of the quantity

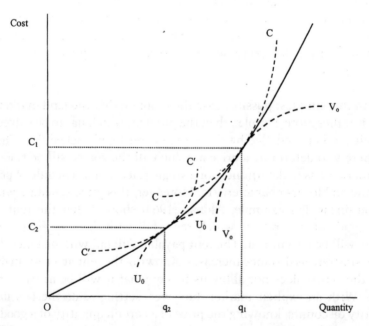

**Figure 4.1**

of central heating available in a house. The financial cost is represented on the vertical axis.

It is evident, to continue with the example of a central heating system, that a house can be heated in a number of different ways, and that the system which is the most economical in a smaller property may not be the most economical in one which is larger. Whatever the systems used we would expect, however, that the cost will increase with the size of the property, and hence of the system. So, in the diagram, the upward sloping curve marked CC represents the cost of a large scale system, while the curve C'C' represents the cost of a smaller scale system. It is evident that the property will be heated using the cheapest system, at any level of service. Therefore a curve can be constructed, an envelope, which connects the points representing the lowest possible cost of heating the property over the whole size range. Thus this curve, sloping upwards from the origin O in the figure, represents the expected relationship between the cost of the service and the size of the system.

These prices or costs will only be observed in the market as a response to a demand by consumers of the good expressed through their purchases of properties of different sizes. These preferences can be represented diagrammatically by sets of indifference curves, though they are not drawn in the conventional way, sloping downwards from left to right. It is evident that any household will prefer more of the service, but they will prefer to have it at a lower cost. The indifference curves of a household can therefore be represented by curves which slope upwards at a decreasing rate, and more preferred states will be represented by curves which are lower and to the right. Households will attempt to choose their optimal level of consumption, given the cost, and their choices will be represented by tangencies between the cost envelope and the highest attainable indifference curves of households with different tastes and different incomes. These are represented in the figure by the curves $U_oU_o$ and $V_oV_o$.

It follows that in the market the costs of each level of service are revealed by the choices of the participants in the market for different levels of service, and so the price schedule implicit in the market transactions, the line sloping upwards from O, can be identified. In principle, therefore, the implicit price, and the implicit price schedule, can be identified for every characteristic of any property, and the total price paid for the property is made up from these. There is, in turn, an implication that each of the participants in the market will be aware of the price being paid for each characteristic, a set of prices which is implicit in the price for the whole property. And this implies that the buyers will determine the price they offer and the sellers will determine the price they ask from this knowledge.

So, in principle, the prices of every characteristic can be determined by the market because they are implicit in the prices at which properties are sold. Moreover, if the market is efficient they will be determined by the market. One has to ask, however, when the nature of the problem which the market has to solve is set out in this way, whether it is in fact too difficult.

## The evidence

Nevertheless, difficult or not, the theoretical argument is that the price schedule for each characteristic can be determined in the market. And this implies that participants in the market are, consciously or subconsciously, aware of these prices, and therefore of the true market price for the property being traded, which is determined in the market. And, if this is so, then it should be possible to identify, statistically, the prices of the characteristics from the prices paid for the properties, and from information as to the characteristics of the properties being sold. Formally the prices of the characteristics are unknown but they can be identified.

It is as though one wished to know the prices paid for goods in a particular supermarket, but, for some reason, was not allowed through the door. One could, however, stand outside the store and ask customers as they came out how much they had spent in total, and what goods they had bought. With enough answers it would become possible to identify the prices paid for each item. Mathematically it is a question of solving a set of simultaneous equations where the prices of the goods are the unknowns.

If property prices were wholly determined in the market so that the relationships were exact, and known, then the price schedules of the characteristics could also be found in this way, as the solution to a set of simultaneous equations. The relationships are not exact, however, and not usually known, so that statistical methods have to be used to find the best estimates for the prices and to indicate the margin of error. One difficulty, for example, is that the price schedules will not, in many cases, be linear but curvilinear, as, for example, in the way that rents fall with increased distance from a market centre. It follows that this curvilinear relationship has to be found, or at least the closest approximation to it. Yet a further difficulty is that there may be interactions between characteristics which affect prices. Thus the cost of the central heating system will depend, not only on the floor area, but also on the height of the ceilings, and hence the volume which has to be heated, and whether the house is one, two, or three storeys high. These various interactions should theoretically all be taken into account, but to try to do so fully may make the econometric analysis extremely complicated, and possibly overly complicated for any possible gain in accuracy.

If econometric methods are used to identify the price schedules of the characteristics of properties, and then used to predict the expected prices at which properties will be sold, what is the degree of accuracy which can be obtained? Most statistical analyses of the determinants of house prices can 'explain' some 90% of the variation in market prices as being due to, and determined by, variations in the characteristics of the properties. Looking at the problem in a slightly different way, if the price schedules for the characteristics can be identified from previous property sales, then the prices which properties put up for sale should fetch can be calculated and predicted from a knowledge of their characteristics. The evidence is that the average difference between the predicted price and the price at which a property is actually sold is about 10% (Wilcox 1979; Meacham 1988).

Is this margin of error due to the fact that the statistical methods used are faulty? Might the margin of error be improved with more advanced statistical methods or with a more complete knowledge of the characteristics of properties? The answer would appear to be 'no'. For when assessors or valuers are asked to use their professional expertise and experience to estimate the prices at which properties will be sold, in their case too, there is an average difference of about 10% between the estimated or predicted prices and the prices at which the properties are actually sold. Thus it is not as though the statistical analysis is failing to identify features of the market which are evident, even if intuitively or heuristically, to participants in the market, even to experts like professional valuers and assessors.

The point is this. There is no evidence to suggest that improvements in the statistical methods used would achieve significant gains in accuracy. There is no evidence to suggest that experts in the valuation of properties can achieve greater accuracy. We are left with the finding that any predicted price is likely to be, on average, about ten per cent different from the price actually obtained. Note that even this degree of accuracy is less than it sounds. A property may be sold for £100,000 and the estimates made beforehand may be lower or higher than this. Estimated prices of £90,000 and £110,000 both represent errors of 10%. Thus estimated prices for properties sold for £100,000 will range from significantly less than £90,000 to significantly greater than £110,000. So in one study McAllister (1995) found that about 60% of the valuations of 57 commercial properties in Milton Keynes were within the range 10% plus to 10% minus actual sale prices. But this meant that the 'error' exceeded 10% in 40% of the cases, and was actually greater than 30% in 10% of the cases.

If prices cannot be predicted beforehand more accurately than this, then it does not appear that the property market is efficient in the sense required, that is, there seems no reason to suppose that all the information available is reflected in the price of a property. Nor does it seem as though the prices at which properties are sold are determined in and by the market. At best statistical methods and professional valuers can predict a price range within which the price at which a property is actually sold will lie. In fact, it seems correct to say that there is no true market price, and to conclude that the property market is, to a significant degree, inefficient.

## Tests of market efficiency

We noted earlier that a great deal of research has been carried out into the efficiency of stock markets. Some of the same kind of research has been carried out into the efficiency of property markets. The primary concern of this research has been with the dynamics of these markets, with price changes over time. It is argued that if a market in an asset is efficient then the market will ensure that all the relevant information available at any one time will be capitalised into the value of the asset, and that evidence of this should be perceived in price changes over time. Whether this is correct is open to question, and it is a question to which we will return later in this section.

In the most elementary form of these tests, the so-called 'weak test' it is argued that good and bad information arrives randomly over time (Fama 1970). Further, if a market is efficient then the new information will be capitalised into the price of the asset immediately and without any lag. The price will find its new level at the time that the new information becomes available. It will not adjust to the new level over a number of days, weeks, or months. Therefore, it is argued, since information arrives randomly so prices will move up and down randomly. Further, since the market must respond instantly to new information if it is efficient, there will be no significant correlation between price movements in one period and price movements in a preceding period. This 'weak test' of market efficiency has been applied to stock markets throughout the world and in a number of different ways. In general it is true to say that stock markets pass this test of efficiency with flying colours, and without exception.

Two other tests of the efficiency of stock markets have been suggested. The first, the 'semi-strong test' checks the influence of particular identifiable events on the price of a company's shares. For example, a company may announce a 'bonus issue' or 'stock split', that, say, for every share held by a share holder, that share holder will receive a further free share, the total number of shares issued therefore being doubled. It would be expected that, in the absence of any further information, the price of the shares will halve. But a stock split of this kind will only be carried out by a company if it anticipates that future profits will increase, and the announcement is itself a signal of the directors' confidence in their company's future. The question at issue, the test, is whether the price of the share responds after the announcement, at the time of the announcement, or, having taken account of other information, whether it has responded beforehand, so that the announcement is not a surprise.

In general stock markets pass this 'semi-strong' test. In the case of bonus issues or stock splits, for example, the finding has been that, on average, share prices adjust before the announcement to the perception that the company's position has improved. The actual announcement therefore has no effect, again, on average, on the share price. The announcement is not a surprise and the information conveyed by it has already been capitalised into the market price of the company's shares.

The third form of test, the 'strong test', is not, however, one that even stock markets can pass. The 'strong test' requires the market to be so efficient in processing information that even those with inside information have no advantage, on the grounds that the scattered signals available to non-insiders, and their acting upon them, erode any possible advantage to the insider. The evidence is, in fact, that insiders do have an advantage, and so that professionals trading on the basis of their professional knowledge can make an 'abnormal' profit. It might actually be questioned whether any market would be able to pass this test, which was proposed by Fama in 1970, along with the other two types of test, but Grossman & Stiglitz (1980) showed that any market could only be completely efficient if information was free. Since information is not free, and cannot be free, so that no market can be 100% efficient, the question is rather to what degree it is efficient.

The evidence with respect to the property market, surveyed recently by Gatzlaff & Tirtiroglu (1995), is that although some property markets will pass the 'weak test' of market efficiency, many others will not even pass this 'weak test'. That is to say in many cases there will be some correlation between price movements in the current period and price movements in a previous period. Moreover, even where a property market passes this test, it is passing what is in effect a much weaker form of the weak test than is applied to stock markets. In tests of the efficiency of stock markets the time periods over which price changes are recorded are short, usually a day. On the other hand in tests of the efficiency of property markets the periods are long, usually a year, because those are the only periods over which time changes are recorded. Thus the requirement with respect to the property market that, for it to be weak form efficient, there should be no correlation between price movements in consecutive years, is a very weakened form of the weak test. Which, in many studies, property markets fail. And the possible response, that price changes are not identifiable in the property market on a day-to-day basis is not a counter argument but evidence, in fact, of its inefficiency relative to stock markets.

It is argued that there is some possibility of retrieving the situation, however. If it is recognised that no market is 100% efficient, since the acquisition of information in itself takes time and money, then an alternative definition of efficiency, which takes this into account, is therefore that there should be no rule which would allow a trader following it to make a profit, that is, a rule which would allow the observation of past price movements to predict future price movements, and to cover the costs of the necessary sales and purchases. On this kind of test, one which is easier to pass than the simple 'weak test' of efficiency, property markets might be described as efficient. In some cases it has been observed that rules can be defined which would allow traders to make profits, but these profits would be largely wiped out, in most cases, by the costs of carrying out the transactions (Rayburn *et al.* 1987; Case & Schiller 1989).

There is, however, a yet further qualification to the conclusion that, even on this test, property markets could be described as efficient. Almost all of these tests have been carried out with respect to North American property markets where the commission charged by real estate agents is of the order of 5% or 6%. In some other countries, in particular in the United Kingdom, the rates charged may be much lower, say between $1\frac{1}{2}$ and $2\frac{1}{2}$ per cent. The question has to be asked as to whether, if transaction costs were that much lower, similar tests would show that property markets could still be described, even on this test, as efficient. Probably not, but we cannot be sure since such tests have not been carried out in markets where transaction costs are low.

Finally, the fact that rules can be found which would allow profits to be made in the absence of transaction costs carries the implication that real estate professionals, who do not have to pay themselves commission, but can trade on their own account, would be able to make profits by following such rules. But then this means merely that property markets would be likely to fail the strong test of market efficiency. But stock markets fail this test, so that there seems no reason at all to suppose that property markets, which have difficulty passing the weak test, would pass the strong test.

But are these tests of market efficiency themselves good tests? When we have been discussing market efficiency earlier in this chapter we considered it in terms of the accuracy of the market in determining prices, both at a point in time, and by implication, over time. But tests of the efficiency of stock markets have, as we have shown, been concerned with price movements over time, and have inferred that if these movements take certain forms this is evidence of market efficiency. Even if they do, market prices may still be inaccurate. This alternative view has come to the fore over the past 10 years or so as research has accumulated evidence as to the inaccuracy of market prices. Some of this is well known. For example, it has frequently been observed that price of shares in investment trusts (or closed end mutual funds), companies whose only assets are shareholdings in other companies, trade, for most of the time, at a discount to the market value of the underlying assets. The same is generally true of property companies – the price of shares in companies whose only assets are properties trade, usually, at a discount to their estimated net asset value. Anomalies of this kind have been known about for years but have been regarded as just that, anomalies. But these anomalies have now been put together with other evidence which is difficult to explain away if one wishes to believe that the stock market is efficient. Perhaps the clearest example is the relationship between the value of shares in Royal Dutch and Shell Transport and Trading. The background is set out by Froot & Dabora (1999).

> Royal Dutch and Shell are independently incorporated in the Netherlands and England, respectively. The structure has grown out of a 1907 alliance between Royal Dutch and Shell Transport by which the two companies agree to merge their interests on a 60:40 basis while remaining separate and distinct entities. All sets of cash flows, adjusting for corporate tax considerations and control rights, are effectively split in these proportions. Information clarifying the linkages between the two companies is widely available. Royal Dutch and Shell trade on nine exchanges in Europe and the U.S., but Royal Dutch trades primarily in the U.S. and the Netherlands (it is in the S&P 500 and virtually every index of Dutch shares), and Shell trades predominantly in the UK (it is in the Financial Times Allshare Index, or FTSE).

It follows that since everything is divided between the two companies in this 60:40 ratio, the market value of the shares in the two companies should also have this 60:40 relationship, that is the total market value of Royal Dutch should be 1.5 times the market value of Shell. Moreover, it also follows that if there were any significant deviation from this it should rapidly disappear as arbitrageurs sold the dearer and bought the cheaper, and as, in the longer term, investors bought the relatively cheaper share whenever they wished to invest in the Royal Dutch/Shell business.

This has not been the case, however. Deviations from the 60:40 ratio have often been significant and very long lasting. The evidence is shown in Figure 4.2. From the figure it can be seen that it would be true to say that the ratio has been more often significantly different from 60:40 than close to it. The implication of this kind of evidence is that, whatever might be the indirect evidence of efficiency derived from the study of price changes over time, stock markets are nevertheless inefficient and imperfect. If they cannot accurately value shares such as Royal Dutch and Shell, shares which are widely held and widely traded, then there seems no reason to suppose that they can accurately value other shares where similar tests of consistency cannot be made. Thus one has to conclude that all the information available is not necessarily capitalised into the value of companies' ordinary shares.

Why this lack of consistency, or lack of accuracy, should occur is still a matter of research. Shleifer (2000) argues that the market is imperfect largely because much, if not most, trading of stocks and shares is carried out,

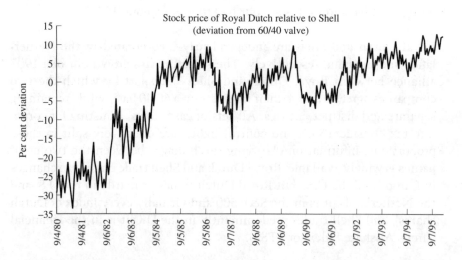

**Figure 4.2**  Log deviations from Royal Dutch/Shell parity. Source: Froot & Dabora (1998).

not by professionals, but by private investors. In his view these tend to be 'noise traders'. That is they respond to fluctuations ('noise') rather than information. They seek to invest in stocks and shares which tend to be rising and to disinvest from shares which are falling. Psychologically, he argues, they tend to undervalue and not react to new information which is contrary to their general preconceptions. Thus if four pieces of information regarding a stock are positive, but one is negative, then the latter will be ignored. Similarly if one piece of new information is positive but four other pieces are negative, the positive news will be ignored. Thus noise trading tends to push the price of stocks higher or lower than they should rationally be.

He also argues that the pressures created by the noise traders are difficult to resist even if the professionals know that prices are distorted. Arbitrageurs cannot themselves correct market fluctuations, and they do not have the financial resources to resist and outlast the pressures exerted by the noise traders. To return to Royal Dutch and Shell, from Figure 4.2 it looks as though buying Royal Dutch and selling Shell in 1980 would have been a good idea, since the one was underpriced by ten per cent relative to the other, but, seen as an arbitrage, the figure shows that it would have taken four years before a profit could have been shown, and in the intervening years the arbitrageur could have been carrying substantial losses.

A recent example of the importance of 'noise trading' was the 'dot com' boom which peaked in the spring of 2000. In late 1999 and early 2000 it was obvious to most professional investors that the dot com companies, few if any of which had ever reported a profit, were, to say the least, overvalued. The shares continued to increase in value, however. Whatever fundamental analysis might demonstrate, however, acting on the evidence that the shares were overvalued and selling them short was a way of losing money, not making it. And this was true at all stages of the boom up to the peak in March 2000. Profits were only to be made by investing in shares which were increasing in value in the expectation of selling them later, before the market peaked.

The property market is also subject to similar booms and slumps of course. Property prices too can become overvalued when the market booms and negative information can be ignored. The property booms such as the British house price boom and the Japanese price bubble, both of which peaked at the end of the 1980s, are obvious examples.

## Conclusions

There is no reason to suppose that the property market is more efficient than the stock market, and recent research suggests that the stock market is not as efficient as it used to be thought. Certainly, with respect to the analysis of changes in prices over time, the property market appears to be less efficient than the stock market, and in a number of cases individual property markets have failed to pass the weakest tests of market efficiency.

With respect to the static statistical evidence on the accurate prediction of sale prices the property market fails a test which is not one which the stock market has to meet, namely the accurate estimation of the price at which a property will sell. In the case of shares the price is set by the market, the broker merely has to look at a screen and make a judgement. But the estimation of the sale price of a property is more nearly approximated by the estimation of the price of the shares of a company at which the company can be 'floated' when the shares are first made available to the general public. And the evidence here is that the stockbrokers and merchant bankers involved in these flotations do find great difficulty in estimating the correct price. In the case of the numerous flotations of privatised utilities which occurred in Britain in the 1980s, the shares changed hands at prices considerably above the issue prices on the first day they were traded.

But this difficult problem is one that valuers and assessors have to try to solve all the time, and the question arises as to why it should be so difficult. Leaving aside, therefore, the assessment of efficiency in terms of price movements over time, in the next chapter we return to the question of the determination of the price of a property by the market. Or rather its lack of determination as valuers, assessors, statistical packages and computers achieve only 90% accuracy in estimating the price at which a property will sell. The causes of this inefficiency, and its consequences, we discuss in the next chapter.

# 5

# Market Inefficiency: Causes and Consequences

## *'Help!'*

---

## Introduction

In the preceding chapter we looked at the way in which the property market would have to operate for it to be regarded as efficient. We concluded that the problem for it to solve, namely, first, to determine prices for the characteristics of properties and then, through this process, to determine the prices of properties was, to say the least, extremely difficult. We then looked at the evidence and showed that the property market fails many of the tests of efficiency which have been used. In particular, it has proved difficult for property agents to estimate accurately the price at which properties may be sold. With respect to the stock market, whether or not the prices at which stocks are sold are an accurate reflection of their expected earnings (and the evidence suggests they may not be) the prices of the shares are determined in the market, and are, in the very short term, predictable. In the property market prices do not appear to be determined in the market and cannot be accurately predicted, even in the very short run.

In this chapter we look at the reasons why this is so, the factors which make the property market imperfect and inefficient, in particular the heterogeneity of the properties being sold. We then look at the consequences of this inefficiency, the way in which the agent has a role in determining prices and the way in which the behaviour and psychology of buyers and sellers can affect prices.

## Why the property market is imperfect and inefficient

The conditions which economists assume to be necessary for a perfect market are that there should be many buyers, many sellers, a homogeneous product, and full information. Now, there certainly seem to be many people selling properties, and many people buying them. And the amount of information available as to what properties are available at any time and what their characteristics are does not seem to be inadequate. It cannot be denied, however, that properties are not homogeneous.

The primary reason for the inefficiency of the property market is then the heterogeneity of the properties being sold. To refer back to the problem of valuing a company for flotation mentioned at the end of the previous chapter, just as each company is different, so to a greater or lesser extent, is each property. Just as the merchant bank finds it difficult to estimate a share price, so the real estate agent finds it just as difficult to estimate a sale price for a property.

What are the reasons for this heterogeneity? The primary reason is the fundamental characteristic of real estate, that it is fixed in location. In other markets goods can often be brought together and traded in a single market. But similar, even identical, properties cannot be physically brought together and traded in a single market place. Moreover, while the price of identical goods in other markets will tend to be identical, the prices of otherwise identical properties will differ because their locations are different, and, of course, cannot be changed. It follows that there is always some adjustment for differences in location which have to be made when comparing properties and their prices.

But is not location merely another characteristic which can be taken into account? Yes, to a limited extent, but a second reason for the high degree of heterogeneity is that the problem of location is compounded by the fact that the price of the characteristics of properties may vary with location. For example, the view of a lake or a park in residential area will apparently be valued more highly if the houses are occupied by the rich than if they are occupied by the poor, since the latter will be less willing to pay for a 'luxury' such as a view than the former. Conversely a disamenity such as aircraft noise will reduce the value of the houses of the better off more than it will reduce the value of the houses occupied by the poor. To give an example, some time ago researchers looking into the possible economic effects of a proposed Third London Airport found that high levels of noise might reduce the price of expensive houses by over 20%, and the price of cheaper houses less than 10% (GB Commission on the Third London Airport 1970, Table 20.3, p. 375).

The economic theory outlined in the previous chapter suggests that, in order to accurately determine the prices of properties the market must, in the process, accurately determine the prices of the characteristics of the properties. But if the prices of these characteristics can vary from area to area and from location to location the problem that the market has to solve is made substantially more difficult. This is because of a third problem, namely that all properties differ in some way, consisting of differing bundles of characteristics.

But if all properties are different and if the prices of their characteristics may differ from one to another, the pricing problem can become insoluble. Why this is so can be put in several ways. From a professional valuer's point of view the number of comparable prices and properties may be too few. From a statistical point of view the amount of data available may be insufficient to determine estimates with any degree of reliability. And for the same reasons the size of the market may not be sufficient for the participants to know what they should ask or pay for a property and to set the prices of properties through their trading.

The problem, which is already difficult, is compounded by a fourth problem, the fact that most of those trading in the market do so infrequently. So people buy houses and remain in them for many years before they move on to another house. In Britain the average period of occupancy is said to be about seven years, although it may be shorter in some countries such as the US and longer in others such as Italy. In the commercial property sector firms buying or selling offices or warehouses or plants do so infrequently whether they occupy the premises themselves or invest in the property to let it out. In this the property market is totally different from most other markets, including the stock market, where identical goods may be traded on a daily basis by most market participants, both buyers or sellers. Given they trade infrequently, most of these participants do not acquire information over time, but only have to do so when they wish to buy or sell property. It follows that the cost of acquiring information is high relative to the cost of the transaction. Participants will therefore not have full information as to, say, the cost of alternatives, when they trade since this will not normally be worth obtaining. Thus there is no reason to suppose that market participants will themselves ensure that the pricing of properties is efficient.

This problem of trading infrequency is exacerbated by the fact that prices change over time so that the information gathered the last time a market participant traded is rendered obsolete. Prices change both because of general price changes, that is price inflation, and because relative prices change. The prices in one area will rise, or fall, relative to prices in another.

Both of these kinds of price change mean that the information which an infrequent trader may have obtained at the time of the last transaction is almost useless at the time of the next. It may be estimated that a property which sold for £100,000 in 1980 might be bought for £250,000 in 1990. This looks to be a significant increase, but what has been the increase in the general price level in the period? And what has been the average increase in property prices nationally, in the area, in the neighbourhood? This information would certainly be useful, but few, if any, market participants would be able to find out all of it and do the necessary calculations.

Finally, some part of any change in relative prices results from economic change. This is continuous so that relative prices are changing all the time as the urban economy adjusts to economic changes which have occurred or are occurring. It has been suggested, for example, by Mills (1970) that it takes five years for an urban economy to move half way towards any new 'equilibrium'. Since economic and technical change is constant this 'equilibrium' is itself always changing, and the urban economy is always in the process of trying to approach an equilibrium which it actually never reaches.

Even when changes in relative prices because of economic change can be identified afterwards by academic research, participants in the market may nevertheless be unaware of the changes which are occurring around them. Evans & Beed (1986), for example, found that prices in the Melbourne suburbs were rising relative to those in the city centre up to 1978, but following an increase in petrol prices in that year fell relative to those in the city centre in the following few years. Yet there appeared to be no perception at the time, in the Melbourne area, that these substantial relative price changes were occurring.

## Price determination and the theory of the core

From the above discussion we draw the conclusion that properties are heterogeneous, that participants trade infrequently, and that, as a result, each transaction is to some extent independent of other transactions. The implications of this for the determination of property prices can be drawn from a piece of economic analysis which is called the theory of the core of an economy. A full analysis would be mathematical, but the principles and implications can be drawn from a simplified diagrammatic analysis of the kind set out in Figure 5.1.

The figure represents a simple two-person, two-good economy. The two

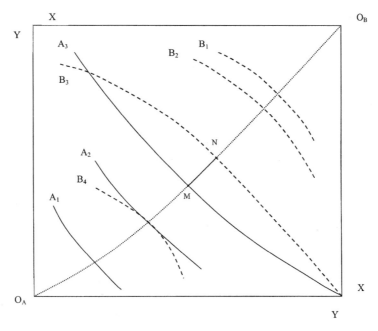

**Figure 5.1**

goods, X and Y, are represented along the horizontal and vertical axes respectively. The consumption of the two goods by the first individual, A, is represented by distance from the bottom left-hand corner of the box, at $O_A$. The preferences of this individual can be represented by conventional indifference curves, convex towards this point $O_A$. Similarly consumption by the second individual, B, is represented by distance from the top right-hand corner of the box, at $O_B$, and the preferences of B are represented by indifference curves which are convex to $O_B$.

To simplify the argument we assume that the total stock of the good X is held initially by A and indicated by the point X on the horizontal axis, and that it is measured by the distance $O_A X$ on the horizontal axis. Similarly we assume that the total stock of the good Y is held initially by B, and it is measured by the vertical distance downward on the right-hand axis, that is by $O_B Y$ on this axis. The point in the bottom right-hand corner of the box therefore indicates the initial stocks of X and Y held by the two individuals. Starting with these holdings they can, however, freely trade and the question is, firstly, whether they will trade, and, secondly, what will be the final allocation of the goods between them which results from this trading.

The first question can be answered more definitely than the second. Given the initial allocation indicated by the point in the bottom right-hand corner of the figure, it is clear that they will trade if they can. The indifference curves of A and B which pass through this point have been drawn and form an ellipse. It is evident that any trade which results in an allocation represented by a point in the interior of the ellipse would make both parties better off. They can therefore be expected to trade.

Will they trade further after this initial trade? The answer is that they can only be expected *not* to trade if the allocation between them is represented by a point on the diagonal line connecting $O_A$ and $O_B$. This connects or runs through all the points of tangency between the two sets of indifference curves. This line is called the contract curve. They will trade if an allocation is off the contract curve because trading can improve the position of both of them. The indifference curves drawn passing through this point will result in an ellipse and moves to the interior of this ellipse would make both parties better off. This is not so if the allocation lies on the contract curve. Trade from any such point would make one or both parties worse off.

It follows that, if trade starts from an initial allocation represented by the point in the bottom right-hand corner of the figure, trading will lead to a final allocation represented by a point on the section of the contract curve lying between the two indifference curves passing through this point. It will not lie on any other sections of the contract curve because that would mean that one of the two parties would have been made worse off. This section of the contract curve, in this diagram, represents what is called the 'core' of this simple economy. It is the set of allocations which will result from trading between the two parties.

Now it can be shown mathematically that if the number of individuals in the economy increases, the size of the core becomes smaller. People have greater opportunities for bargaining and forming coalitions. As the size of the economy becomes larger and larger the core tends towards being a single point. That is, if the number of people trading is large the allocation is determined by the market. But if the number of traders is small the size of the core may be large. The final allocation is not then wholly determined by the market but depends on the bargaining positions, and negotiating skills, of the parties. In the simple economy represented by Figure 5.1, if A is a very good bargainer and B very bad, the final allocation is likely to be to the north-east end of the section of the contract curve which represents the core. Similarly if B is good at negotiation, and A weak, the resulting allocation is likely to be at the south-west end of the 'core'. But as the number of participants increases so the size of the core diminishes.

But in the case of the property market we have argued that there are few participants in any trading situation because of the heterogeneity of properties and the infrequency of trading. So, if few people are interested in a property it becomes difficult for a seller to try to play one off against another, and the size of the core is large. The implication is that in the case of any trade, the allocation, that is the price, is only determinate within a range. It is not wholly determined by the market. Other factors have a role to play in helping to determine the price at which a property changes hands.

The theory of the core provides a theoretical explanation for the inability of valuers and assessors to estimate accurately the prices at which properties will sell, and why the margin for error is large. The property market is inherently imperfect, so the market only determines a range within which the actual sale price will lie. The prices of properties are not wholly determined by the market.

## The consequences

But if prices are not wholly determined by the market, are only determinate within a range, it follows that other factors have a role to play in determining the final price. This final price has to be reached by the seller and the buyer. This affects their behaviour, and in turn their behaviour can affect the price. Each buyer and each seller is manoeuvring to obtain the best deal that they can, given the other properties on the market, the costs of the strategies pursued, and their bargaining abilities and positions. There are a number of consequences.

### Buyers and sellers search the market

The first is that neither the buyer nor the seller knows what the price is, or ought to be, at which a property will sell. As a result each must search the market, in some way, in order to acquire information which will help them in deciding on the price which they will ask or accept, in the case of the seller, or the price they will offer, and, if necessary, pay, in the case of a buyer. We will fully review this problem of lack of information, or uncertainty, in Chapter 12, and the strategies pursued by buyers and sellers are only outlined here.

The seller, for example, will usually employ an agent who is expected to provide, from experience and because of professional expertise, guidance as to the price which the property might sell for. Since, as we have shown, this estimate is unlikely to be accurate, the seller then has to decide on a strategy to try to obtain the best possible price in the light of this guidance. The strategies adopted will vary with the character of the property and will also usually conform with the strategy normally adopted in that section of the market. In the English housing market, for example, the usual procedure is that the property is offered for sale at an 'asking price' which is slightly higher than the expected price and then to 'wait and see' what offers are made. In some parts of England, however, the property is advertised for sale at a price which is known to be lower than the expected sale price. It is then expected that the offers made will be higher than the asking price, rather than, as more usual, lower. In parts of Scotland it is not unknown for properties to be advertised for sale with no price being indicated. In each case, of course, the first offer is not necessarily the one which is accepted. The aim of the strategy adopted is to elicit a number of bids so that the highest can be accepted.

In some cases, when the property is unusual in some way, it may be sold by auction. The seller then indicates no guide price, though the auctioneer may suggest a figure, and the seller may give a 'reserve', a price below which the property will not be sold. An auction elicits a price by bringing together the potential bidders and making them bid against each other. The English auction, used in the English speaking countries, starts with a low bid and the property is sold to the highest bidder, the one left after all the other bidders have dropped out because they do not want to bid as much. The price at which the property is sold is then the bid which is the lowest necessary to outbid the second highest bidder, or underbidder. A Dutch auction is also possible. Here the auctioneer offers the property for sale at a high price and steadily reduces this 'asking price' until someone makes a bid. It is the method used in the Dutch wholesale flower market. In theory this method could result in a higher price than with an English auction because the buyer is forced to reveal his or her reserve price, and this may be higher than the price necessary to outbid the underbidder. In an English auction, however, the bidders may become excited as they bid against each other and so bid more, in the heat of the moment, than they intended to do when they came to the auction.

Buyers too have to search the market. They are less likely to be assisted by an agent. In the residential market at least, they must look at alternative properties to acquire information as to the characteristics and quality of the properties which are on the market, and as to the price at which they have sold or may sell. Having done this they have to decide whether to bid for the property they prefer, and how much they should bid (and how much more they might wish to offer in any negotiations). The fact that buyers search for information is more obvious than that sellers do, since buyers do literally, physically, search. To do the job properly they will need to tour the area they are interested in, either on foot or in a car, visit real estate agents, look at newspaper advertisements, consult relevant websites, etc.

## The psychology of buyers and sellers

The second consequence of the imperfection or inefficiency of the property market is that the psychology and bargaining positions of the market participants will affect the price at which the property is sold. This follows from the analysis of the theory of the core in the preceding section. Given that the final allocation is in the core, the price is only determined within a range. The final position on the contract curve will, as we showed, be affected by the bargaining abilities of the traders.

Sometimes it may indeed be merely a question of psychology. I have known one person who declared that she hated the whole process so much that she and her husband offered to pay the asking price for the first house that they looked at. At the other extreme I have known someone who simultaneously carried on negotiations with five separate potential sellers, each of whom believed that he was going to buy their house, before entering into a binding written agreement to buy the house which he thought offered the best deal. In this he was taking advantage of the English legal position with respect to buying and selling real estate, whereby verbal agreements are not legally binding. And it may be worth noting that his job as a company lawyer involved negotiation so that it is not surprising that in buying a house for his own use he used the skills which he used professionally.

These two examples are drawn from each end of some kind of psychological spectrum. Most people lie closer to the centre of this spectrum. In their case their negotiating position is likely to be determined more by their circumstances than their psychology or their profession. For example, the person who is moving from one part of the country to another, possibly to take up a new job, who has a family to move, and who may have to rent accommodation or stay in a hotel until a house is bought, is in a much weaker bargaining position that someone who simply wants to move to a different house in the area in which they already live. The latter may search the market for years before finally moving. The former has to settle the move within a few weeks.

Again, on the seller's side, the person wishing to move to a larger house in the same area, which may not yet have been found, is in a strong position to hold out for a good offer. On the other hand, the executor of the estate of someone who has died is in a far weaker position. The house has to be sold, and, while it is for sale, its running costs have to be paid and the capital invested in it is not earning any return for the estate or its beneficiaries. Indeed the most anxious to sell, at any price, is likely to be an institution such as a bank acting as the executor for someone with no relatives whose estate is left to a charity. The executor has no incentive to hold out for any length of time for a high price, and every incentive to accept the first reasonable offer.

Personal relationships will also affect the way in which people negotiate. One is less likely to drive a hard bargain with a friend than with a stranger whom one may never see again. In one of the rare studies of social relationships in this context Perry & Robison (2001) studied the sales of farm land in Linn County, Oregon. They found that, as against an estimated price derived from the characteristics of the property, some bought land at a discount, notably relatives, but also neighbours, while others paid a significant premium. This latter group included tenants buying from their landlord but also people coming from outside the area and buying in response to advertisements or through real estate agents.

Finally, the contractual position will affect people's behaviour. Under the Scottish system a verbal agreement for the sale of real estate is binding. Surveys are therefore carried out before an offer is made, and deals can be made quickly. As a personal example, when I bought a house in Glasgow some years ago, I saw it advertised in *The Glasgow Herald* on a Tuesday morning, visited it on the Tuesday afternoon, had a building surveyor inspect it on the Wednesday morning, and reached a binding verbal agreement on the Wednesday afternoon. I moved in a month later.

Under the English system, on the other hand, as noted earlier, people may enter into verbal agreements but these are 'subject to contract' and are not binding so that either party may back out before contracts are exchanged. Since it takes time for lawyers to prepare the contracts this means that if prices are rising the seller may back out and ask for a higher price and if prices are falling the buyer may reduce the price offered. And either may back out if they wish to for any reason whatever. Some, of course, may feel that their word is their bond, and that they are bound in honour to the agreement. Others may not. To give another personal example, when I wished to move from Scotland to England to take up a job one October, I started looking on a visit to London in March and agreed to buy a house. In May, the English house owner withdrew because he had changed his mind about selling. Visiting again in May a new agreement was reached to buy another house. In August the seller said that because prices were rising he wanted 20% more for the house. After some negotiation a price 10% higher was agreed, and the seller agreed to vacate the house in December, two months later than had been originally agreed.

These examples are just that, examples, and they are drawn from personal experience relating to the housing market. But they are sufficient to demonstrate that the price at which a property is sold will depend not only on its own characteristics but also on the position of the buyer and the seller and the circumstances surrounding the sale. Since these circumstances cannot be taken into account in putting a value on a property the fact they help to determine the price helps to explain why assessors and valuers cannot accurately predict the price which a property will fetch on the open market, but can only suggest a range.

## Time on the market

Another feature of the property market which can be explained once it is realised that the market is inefficient and that a price has to be 'found' is the way that properties can be 'on the market' for a short or a long time. One would expect that properties which were 'underpriced' by the seller would sell quickly, while those which were 'overpriced' would stick. Certainly when prices are generally rising there is a tendency for properties to be sold quickly as the initial asking price begins to look cheap. And when prices are generally falling, there is a tendency for properties to be on the market for longer as sellers are reluctant to reduce their asking prices.

The position is not simple, however, since time on the market may itself be a factor in determining the price at which a property finally sells. To introduce a further personal example, I recently acted as executor for an estate. The house belonging to the estate was sold four times to people who changed their minds for one reason or another. On each occasion lawyers were instructed and other possible buyers were told that a sale had been agreed. Although none of the would-be purchasers withdrew because they found anything significantly wrong with the house on a survey, the impression was given that they had. Potential buyers therefore tended to assume that there were structural problems which they would only find out about if they spent money on a survey. They therefore became reluctant even to look at the house and the price had to be substantially reduced. Houses which, for some reason, are a long time on the market may, in the end, be cheaper than those which are accidentally sold quickly.

There is some empirical evidence to suggest, however, that time on the

market may be affected systematically, to some degree, by the characteristics of the property. Properties which are of a standard type, and which can
therefore easily be compared with other similar properties would appear to
sell more quickly than properties which not standard, but different and
individual (Haurin 1988). This finding does seem plausible. With a standard
property both buyers and sellers can find out from other comparable sales
what the likely price range is, and they are therefore likely to reach agreement relatively quickly. On the other hand, with a non-standard property
there are, by definition, fewer comparable properties and both sellers and
buyers are more in the dark as to what an acceptable price might be.

It is also possible that there will be fewer possible buyers for non-standard
properties. As a result in any given period the number of offers made is
likely to be smaller than for a 'standard' property. A non-standard property
would therefore have to be on the market for a longer time than a standard
property for a would-be seller to receive the same number of offers and to
gain the same amount of information as the seller of a standard property.

## The Role of the agent

It is customary for the seller of a property to employ an agent, and we
referred to this earlier in discussing the search process. The agent fulfils two
functions. The first arises because the seller is usually only infrequently
involved in the property market. The agent is therefore expected to advise
on the price which might be obtained for the property, and on the best
strategy to achieve it – what the asking price should be, how the property
should be advertised, etc. Second, the agent's office or premises may act as,
in part, a marketplace, at least with respect to residential property. Information on properties for sale is made available, indeed displayed there,
prospective buyers will come there seeking information on what is available and to arrange to inspect properties. Of course, the sellers of a house
can choose to do without an agent, for example by advertising the house in a
local newspaper, but this requires them to select their own asking price and
they must deal with inquiries themselves. In the commercial sector it is less
likely that a would-be seller will act without an agent, and the market is
somewhat different. For example, in Britain anyone selling land for development would be likely to employ one of a limited number of large firms as
the agent, and the property would almost inevitably be advertised in the
weekly magazine, *The Estates Gazette*.

Is it worthwhile employing an agent? With respect to the residential market
there is some evidence from an American study (Jud & Frew 1986) that

sellers who employ agents get a higher price for their property. The difference is not great, however, only about 2%. Since American realtors charge 5% or 6% for their services it could be concluded that the seller is better off not employing an agent. This ignores the opportunity costs of the process of dealing with inquiries and so on, and the actual costs of advertising. The fact that the former may be time consuming is certainly one reason why commercial firms use agents. They cannot divert management time to selling the property, and put a high cost on that time. The seller of a house may have time on their hands and put a low cost on it.

The evidence is therefore not conclusive. In particular, we do not know whether the same difference of 2% would hold in, say, the British market where agents do charge only 2% or so, but, on the other hand, do far less for their money than the US realtor in terms of selling the property and assisting prospective buyers. So although we may conclude that employing an agent results in a property being sold for a higher price, we cannot conclude that the seller is better off as a result. Again, buyers appear not to benefit because the price they pay is higher, though they may actually benefit, on average, from the greater efficiency of an agent rather than an (amateur) seller, and from the more centralised availability of information on the properties available through the agents.

Nevertheless, whether or not sellers or buyers are better off, the study does provide some evidence that agents can affect prices, and this in itself is a confirmation of the view that the property market is inefficient and that prices are not wholly determined by the market. If this had been so the activities of agents would not affect prices.

The fact that prices are not determined in and by the market so that an agent's activities can affect the price has a downside, however. If the price is not determinate, so that neither the buyer nor the seller can know what it should be, an unethical agent can manipulate the market to their benefit but at the cost of their client, the seller of the property.

For example, a study by the British Consumers' Association, published in their monthly magazine *Which?* found evidence of several illegal or unethical practices, which, though not prevalent, they could prove to have occurred.

The first derives from the fact that the agent's reward is a commission which is almost invariably a simple percentage of the sale price. It follows that the agent does have an incentive to maximise the sale price, but only if the cost, to the agent, of doing so does not exceed the increase in the commission. So a property might be easily saleable for £90,000, and might with difficulty be sold for £100,000. The commission at 2% from the first would be £1,800. The commission from the second would be £2,000. But the first £1,800 could be easily earned while the extra £200 might be very hard to earn in terms of the effort and cost involved in advertising, showing people around, and so on. So from the agent's point of view a quick sale at a lower price is better than a sale at a higher price, but later, and with much cost and effort. This means that the agent may advise the principal to accept a lower figure for a quick sale when a higher figure could still be obtained.

The second problem arises because agents may find themselves providing services to a prospective buyer as well as to the seller. Faced with two buyers, the first of whom offers to pay cash and a higher price the agent may prefer to recommend the second, who offers a lower price but says that he or she will need a mortgage loan and who asks the agent to facilitate this. The agent's total commission would therefore be greater if the property were sold at the lower price. The Consumers' Association found that some agents then recommended the lower offer to the seller, either concealing the existence of the higher offer or finding reasons why the higher offer should be rejected.

The third tactic used by some agents was to share out prospective buyers. If two people are interested in buying a property, the seller's interests may be best served by allowing them to bid against each other so that the property is sold at the highest possible price. But if this occurs it takes time and one of the prospective buyers will, in the end, drop out dissatisfied. The agent's interests are better served if one of the parties is allowed to buy the property at a lower price than might have been achieved, while the other is encouraged to take an interest in other properties on the agent's books. In this way two commissions may be obtained instead of one.

The research carried out by the Consumers' Association showed that the (unethical) behaviour of selling agents could affect the price of properties which would be sold at a lower price than could be achieved, though yielding a higher return to the agent. From our point of view this shows that the inefficiency of the market and the possibility of unethical behaviour go together. Because the price is not determined by the market, but only determined within a range, an unethical agent can get away with behaviour which affects the price, since the seller is unaware of what the price should be.

This inefficiency, or indeterminacy of the price, is the characteristic of the market which allows an agent to do this and so results in real estate agents getting a bad name (e.g. 'Estate agents are people who aren't up to selling used cars' or 'On popularity scale ranging from 0 to 10 estate agents would score minus 5'). And this may even be accepted within the profession. As one agent said to me when I commented on what I perceived to be the unethical behaviour of someone in another firm, 'Agents will be agents'. Thus while this cannot be defended, the situation can be explained. In other, more efficient markets, the participants might be just as unethical but are prevented from being so because the price is determined by the market and is not manipulable, in the same way at least.

The same problem of lack of regard which affects residential estate agents can also affect the firms of chartered surveyors operating in the market for office, commercial, and industrial buildings. Here there is no suggestion of unethical behaviour, but there is certainly a sense that they are not regarded as highly as others working in the field of finance and investment because of their inability to provide an absolutely accurate valuation of a commercial property. If the stockbroker can provide an accurate valuation of a share portfolio, why, it is asked, cannot a chartered surveyor value a property with similar accuracy (Hager & Lord 1985).

As we pointed out earlier, however, this criticism ignores the fact that the surveyor is valuing an asset which is in some sense unique. The true comparison, as we argued in the previous chapter, is with the merchant banker setting an issue price for the shares of a company which is to be floated. The evidence is that when this comparison is made the financial expert does no better, and possibly does worse, than the property expert. The latter has a difficult task, and the task is made difficult by the character of the property market, its inefficiency and imperfection (Evans 1995).

## Conclusions

In the previous chapter we argued that the property market was 'inefficient' in the sense that the market could not determine the prices of properties. We argued that the problem set for the market to solve was too difficult and quoted evidence to suggest that the property market was less efficient than the stock market. As we also showed, recent evidence suggests that the prices determined by the stock market may not accurately reflect and discount all the information available. In that sense the stock market too is not necessarily efficient. Nevertheless it cannot be denied that, whether or not the price of a stock represents its true value, the market does set the price. But, whether or not the price of a property represents its true value, the price of a property is only determined within some range.

As we have showed in this chapter the economic theory of the core can be used to demonstrate why this should be so. In effect properties are too heterogeneous and the buyers and sellers trade too infrequently. The market is therefore imperfect and other factors help to determine the price at which a property will sell. Most importantly, the price will be affected by the negotiating abilities of buyers and sellers, and by the strength or weakness of their bargaining positions. The imperfection of the market has other effects. In particular it gives the agent a role to play. Real estate agents provide information to their principals, the sellers of property, and help the market to function by publicising the properties which are for sale. We note, however, that because the prices of properties are not fully determined, first, unscrupulous agents may increase their income by acting unethically and, sometimes, illegally, and, second, the inability of agents to predict prices accurately may be taken as a reflection on their abilities. They may be regarded as inefficient rather than the market itself.

But the inefficiency of the market may be seen by some as having advantages. Its inefficiency means that information is valuable and individuals willing to take a risk may see, and take advantage of, opportunities which would not exist in a more efficient market where information is rapidly capitalised. It is no accident that many large fortunes have been built up through operations in the property market, probably more than any other industry. Actual histories are infrequent, but the interested reader might look at Oliver Marriott's *The Property Boom* (1967) which details the operations of a number of property tycoons in Britain in the 1950s and 1960s.

# 6

## The Supply of Land for a Particular Use: Speculation and Uncertainty

### *'Tomorrow never knows'*

---

### Introduction

The assumption has often been made by economists, and by others, that land owners will always try to ensure that their property is used to obtain the greatest possible current income. In a phrase which is derived from its use in the surveying profession, land is expected to be used for its 'highest and best use'. But to expect this is to fail to recognise the differences between the land market and the market for other kinds of goods. The farmer who did not seek to sell his product at the best price currently available would be thought eccentric. But land does not have to be sold now, and if it is sold now, then, to state the obvious, it cannot be sold later. In practice, as we shall show in this and succeeding chapters, a land owner may have very good reasons for not selling now, for not obtaining the highest possible current income from a piece of land. So a piece of land may continue to be used for some purpose which yields a lower current income than might be obtained in some other use. And this can occur with the full knowledge and by the conscious decision of the owner.

We leave aside, therefore, for the moment, the view that we have tried to establish in the preceding chapter, that the land market is an imperfect and inefficient market and that land owners may not actually know what alternatives are available for their piece of land. Also, that this lack of knowledge may be true not only of the present owner but also of those who might have bought it and used it. In the next six chapters, however, we assume that owners do have full knowledge of the possibilities available for their land. We can thus show more convincingly that, even with this knowledge, they may explicitly choose to derive a lower current income than they might have done. Having shown that land ownership does affect the supply of land we then return to the subject of uncertainty and lack of information in Chapter 12.

The phrase 'the supply of land for a particular use' was coined by Max Neutze (1987), and it relates to the topic of this and the next chapter. We seek to explore reasons why land owners may hold land off the market, as we have indicated above, and therefore why they may need to be encouraged by higher prices to release their land. Thus, with respect to the supply of land for a particular use, usually for urban development, there is an upward sloping supply curve.

In the current chapter we discuss, first, speculation, where the anticipation of higher future prices may lead the owner of a piece of land to delay its sale, and, second, uncertainty about the future which may lead the owner to delay development until this uncertainty is resolved.

## Speculation

Speculation is the most well known, possibly the most notorious, reason why an owner of land may deliberately choose to accept a lower income from the site than might be available. In the original and primary meaning of the term 'speculation' meant 'thinking' or 'guessing'. This use is now rather old fashioned, but one may still speculate as to the chances of the next American president being a Republican, or the chances of the Conservative Party forming a government after the next general election in Britain. In the latter case, and possibly in the former, one may even speculate, in a slightly different way, by placing a bet in a betting shop.

In this sense, of course, speculation involves an assessment of a degree of uncertainty, the characteristic of the market which, at this point, we are trying to ignore. For we want to show here that, even if we set aside the problems of uncertainty and assume that the future is known, with complete certainty, then thinking about the future, in fact planning for the future, can involve accepting a lower current income in the short term.

The approach used is derived from Max Neutze (1973, 1987). Using his diagrammatic analysis we can show how planning for, or speculating about, the future, will result in property being left in lower income uses for some time until it becomes optimal for it to be developed or redeveloped.

Two linked diagrams are used, Figures 6.1(a) and 6.1(b). Time is represented

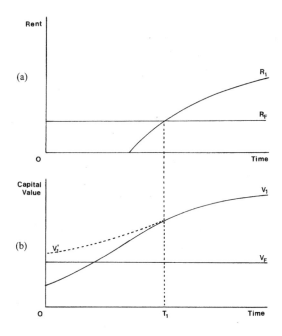

**Figure 6.1**

along the horizontal axis of each. The annual rent of a piece of land, or the income from its use if it is owner occupied, is indicated on the vertical axis of 6.1(a). Since these are the rents expected over time, given the discount rate, the capitalised value of the expected future rents indicated in this figure can be calculated for any point in time, i.e. the present value of all the rents to be obtained at that date and in the future. The capital value of the piece of land calculated in this way is indicated on the vertical axis of Figure 6.1(b). Thus the upper figure shows rent or income as a function of time, while the lower figure shows capital values as a function of time. The information in the lower figure is derived from that in the upper figure.

To simplify the analysis we assume that the land has initially not been developed and is being farmed. The income (or rent) from farming the land is shown in the upper diagram by the horizontal line marked $R_F$. The line is horizontal since it is assumed that the income from farming the land will remain the same over time. Associated with this is the horizontal line in the lower figure marked $V_F$ which indicates the capital value of the land if it is currently farmed and is expected always to be farmed in the foreseeable future.

The piece of land is, however, assumed to be in an area in which urbanisation is anticipated, but not until some time in the future. The income from the development of the land for, say, housing is shown in the upper figure by the line $R_1$. This slopes upward being initially below $R_F$, but at the date indicated as $T_1$ on the horizontal axis it rises above $R_F$. So, until $T_1$ the income from farming is greater than any income which could be obtained from development. After that date the income from development would be greater than the income from farming. Therefore development should take place at time $T_1$.

While the optimal date for the development of the land is obvious in the upper diagram, it is not obvious in the lower diagram showing the trends in capital values. Just as there is a line representing the capital values associated with the perpetual use of the land in farming, so there is a curve, marked $V_1$, which shows the capital value of the land if it is never farmed and is left unused until an income can be obtained from the urban development, housing, at which point it is developed.

For most of the time period shown in the figure, the curve $V_1$ lies substantially above the line $V_F$, and this is so at the time of development. This is because the expected future income from housing at this date is substantially greater than the expected future income from agriculture. Moreover, this is true even before the date of development. So the line $V_1$ lies above $V_F$ then as well.

In practice, of course, one would expect the owner of the land to allow it to be used for its most profitable use at all times. Then it would be farmed up to date $T_1$ and used for housing after that. The capitalised value of the land if it is always used for this 'highest and best use' is shown in the lower figure by the dashed line $V_1'$, in the period before development. This always lies above $V_F$, because future urban development is always anticipated, but it converges and meets with $V_1$ at time $T_1$ when urban development occurs and farming actually ceases.

The difference in the trends in rents and the trends in capital values is important, and it is not that obvious. The price of farmland increases well before it becomes economic to develop the land, and becomes too expensive for a would-be farmer who merely wishes to farm it. As we shall show in Chapter 8 the American evidence is that in a free market at this point 'investors', speculators in the sense used in this chapter, step in to buy up the land, anticipating being able to sell it for development later, and who may, or may not, rent it out as farmland in the meantime.

Moreover, the price of the land at the date of development, even if this takes place as soon as it is financially feasible, will be substantially greater than the price of simple farmland. It is easy to fail to realise this. Since development should occur when the rent from the urban use equals and begins to exceed the rent from agricultural use, it is easy to assume, mistakenly, that at the time of development the capital value of the land if developed will also equal and begin to exceed the value of the land in agricultural use. It is an easy mistake to make. I have seen it made, though not in published form, by at least one highly respected professional land economist.

Of course, an economic explanation for the existence of this price difference may not make it more acceptable. It is quite possible that in the areas where these price differences exist because of anticipated urban development they will be ascribed to the activities of speculators, nasty men and women from the city driving out and breaking up the farming community and driving them off their land. The anticipation of economic events will have social repercussions, although here we are concerned with the economics. Our concern here is that the analysis provides an explanation of the price differences.

In the analysis above, the land is always used to yield its highest current income, for its 'highest and best use'. Of more interest in the analysis of speculative activity is the situation shown in the two integrated Figures, 6.2(a) and 6.2(b). As with Figure 6.1, the elapse of time is shown on the horizontal axis in both the upper and lower figures, while the upper diagram shows annual rents on the vertical axis and the lower diagram shows capital values, the capitalised present value of future rents, on its vertical axis.

As before the income from the land in agricultural use is shown in the upper diagram by the line marked $R_F$, and the associated capital value is shown in the lower diagram by the line marked $V_F$. In this instance, however, it is assumed that there are two urban uses. One of these urban uses is the same as before, we shall call it housing. The possible income from this is shown in the upper diagram by the curve $R_1$. As before development for housing would be profitable at time $T_1$, since after that date the income from housing would be greater than the income from agriculture. A second urban use is possible, however. For example, the site could be used for the construction of a shopping centre, but this would be profitable only after the surrounding area has been substantially developed so that there is a population to sell to. Therefore only at a date much later than $T_1$ will the income from using the site for commerce be positive, and at a still later date, $T_2$, greater than the income from agriculture, and at an even later date, $T_3$, greater than the income from housing.

One possible sequence would be that the land would be developed for

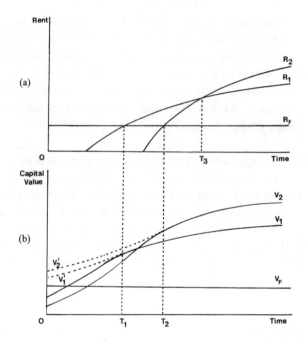

**Figure 6.2**

housing at time $T_1$ and then redeveloped for commerce at time $T_3$. This might not be the most economic or the most profitable sequence, however, since an alternative would be to leave the land being farmed after $T_1$ and to develop it at time $T_2$, and this would certainly be the best option if the cost of housing development is high and the time interval between $T_1$ and $T_3$ is not long. It is not a good idea, either from a public or a private point of view, for buildings to be put up and demolished shortly afterwards. Thus speculating about the future, or even planning for the future, would suggest that the land might be left in agricultural use, or even left vacant, until time $T_2$ when it can be developed for the commercial activity.

It is here that the second diagram showing capital values, Figure 6.2(b), becomes useful. The horizontal line $V_F$ once again shows the capital value of the land used solely as farmland for the foreseeable future. The line $V_1$ shows its value if used solely for housing, as in Figure 6.1(b), with the dashed line $V'_1$ indicating its value if it is used for agriculture up to the date of development $T_1$. Similarly the line marked $V_2$ shows the site's value if it is used solely for the second urban use, retailing, with the dashed line $V'_2$ indicating its anticipated value if it is farmed up to the date of development $T_2$. The lines $V'_2$ and then $V_2$ lie everywhere above the lines $V'_1$ and $V_1$, showing that the capital value of the site will always be greater if it is anticipated that it will be developed for commercial activities at time $T_2$. And this is so even if the land yields a lower income than it might between $T_1$ and $T_2$.

Two factors taken together suggest why speculation has a bad name, even though it may be clear that it is in the general interest that land is left underused. The first we have already mentioned. The original users and occupiers, the farmers, are gradually unable to afford to buy the farmland because the anticipated future development means that its price is substantially higher than farmland elsewhere. Thus, 'the activities of land speculators are driving poor farmers away'. (I once asked on a visit to Taipeh County, Taiwan, whether peasants did not sometimes speculate by holding on to their land in anticipation of being able to sell at a higher price later. The question was treated as irrelevant. It was thought, it was obvious, absolutely impossible that a peasant, 'good' by definition, could be a speculator, 'bad' by definition. It is a linguistic view which is widely shared.)

Second, land may be left undeveloped even though it might seem to the nonspeculative mind that it ought to be developed since land around it already has been. And third, since the income from land awaiting development may be very low relative to its capital value, the land may not only be left undeveloped by the 'speculator' but may actually be left unused and empty. Leaving it empty may also avoid difficulties when the tenants have to be told to move on. Tenants, as we shall show in Chapter 8, are in a different position to owner occupiers, they gain nothing from the sale of the land and lose because they have to move. And on some occasions they have won the political battle.

The behaviour described above may be sound economics. It may also be regarded as entirely right when the land owner and investor, the 'speculator', is in the public sector. So when Cumbernauld new town was being built in central Scotland in the 1960s a small shopping area was built at the centre of the town in the initial stages. The land surrounding this commercial core was left vacant, however, a belt of open land terminated on its further side by housing. The intention, of course, was that as the population of the town increased, this belt of land would be developed and the commercial centre increased in area to cope with the increased population. This planned development had the same result as speculative activity would cause to occur through the market. In both cases, for a period, land was not being used for its current 'highest and best use'.

Of course, there is a difference between the planned and the market situations. The planning authority of a British New Town is in its own area virtually omniscient. It knows what land will be used for commercial use because it has itself planned that this should be so. In a free market context, however, the owners of land in the path of urban development are not omniscient, they are, in the original meaning of the term, speculating about the pattern of future urban development. Different land owners will make different assumptions, and some of them will certainly make the wrong guess, leading to a waste of resources. In this way at least, the public, non-market activity of planning does differ from the activities in the market of different land owners and developers.

But it is still possible for a planning authority to make mistakes. It may over-provide or under-provide space for different activities. These mistakes will not be obvious, however. Under-provision may result in higher rents and a more intensive use of the space that is provided. The results of over-provision may be obvious if it results in vacant unlet space, but it may simply result in lower rents and a less intensive use of space than would be justified in market terms.

## Uncertainty

In analysing the way in which 'speculation' or planning the future can result in land being used, at least temporarily, for less than its highest and best use, we have followed Neutze in assuming that the speculator can accurately predict the future. One reason for following this course is to make clear that this can happen even if the future were correctly predictable, and that the effects of uncertainty about the future can therefore be analysed separately. But, of course, the future is uncertain and cannot be predicted with certainty. The same piece of land may have many possible uses and which will be the best one to choose, or to have chosen, will depend upon how things turn out.

The land owner's problem is what to do now – should the site be developed in one way, or in another way, or should it be left undeveloped until it becomes clear what the most profitable development is likely to be? The problem was analysed by Titman (1985). His stated motivation for concerning himself with the problem was that on his way through downtown Los Angeles he saw vacant sites which were not being developed but which were used as car parks on what appeared to be a long-term basis. How, he wondered, could this seemingly inefficient use of extremely expensive land be explained? In a British context the most probable explanation would be that the owners were engaged in complicated negotiations with the local authority to try to obtain the most profitable kind of planning permission.

Even in America it might be that the land had been sold and the new owners were waiting on the production of plans by their architects, engineers, and other specialist consultants. For major buildings these cannot be produced overnight.

While these are possible explanations the view that Titman put forward, and his background is in finance not real estate, was that the ownership of an undeveloped site was like holding an option on a share. The site could be developed in one way or in another, and it could be developed now or later. And what would be the most profitable development and when it should take place will depend on future, unknown, economic conditions. But in the final analysis one thing is certain and that is that development of the site closes off the alternatives. It is equivalent to exercising the option. Because of this similarity, he argued, we could use similar methods of analysis, in particular we could use the methods developed by Black & Scholes (1973) for the valuation of stock options for the analysis of the valuation of vacant land and the effects of uncertainty.

The formal analysis is mathematical, but an outline of the argument can be presented relatively easily. Let $p$ be the price of some unit of development, for example one of a number of housing units to be constructed on a site. The price of land, $L$, will depend on the price at which the housing units can be sold, so $L$ is a function of $p$. If the current price of the units is $p_o$ then the value of the land if it were developed now would be $L(p_o)$. To simplify the analysis it is assumed that it is otherwise intended to develop the site at some future date, and that it is expected that at that time the price of the units may be either high, $p_H$, or low, $p_L$. For example, the housing market may currently be in recession, but the higher price will be obtained if the recession has ended by then, the lower if it has not. The value of the land at this future date will therefore either be $L(p_H)$, if the housing market has recovered and the price of housing is high, or $L(p_L)$ if it has not and the price of housing is low.

Of course, what is not known is what the price of housing will be at this future time, but an assessment of the probabilities can be made. We assume that it has been estimated that the probability of a high price is $x_H$ and the probability of a low price is $x_L$. Since it is also assumed that the economy must be in one state or the other then it follows that $x_H + x_L = 1$.

The risk-free rate of interest for the period is $R$ – that is if the period were a year, $R$ is the rate of interest for a year, if the period were two years $R$ would be the rate of interest for two years. The present value of the land if the future rent were to be high would therefore be $L(p_H)/(1+R)$, and the present value if the future rent were to be low would be $L(p_L)/(1+R)$. If we take into account the probabilities of their occurring, and that one of the states must eventuate, then the present value of these future possibilities is given by

$$V = \{x_H.L(p_H) + x_L.L(p_L)\}/(1+R) \tag{6.1}$$

The terms $x_H/(1+R)$ and $x_L/(1+R)$ are called by Titman 'state prices' and can be designated as $s_H$ and $s_L$. The equation (6.1) can then be written as

$$V = s_H.L(p_H) + s_L.L(p_L) \tag{6.2}$$

The decision to be made depends on a comparison of the value of the site if it is developed now, when the price of the housing units is $p_o$, and the implied value $L(p_o)$, with its value now, $V$, as given in (6.1) or (6.2), if its development is delayed. Obviously if $p_H$ and $p_L$ are both substantially higher than $p_o$ then delay will be preferable. But delay may also be profitable even if $p_L$ is lower than $p_o$. Then the decision will depend on the relative prices, the probabilities, and the cost of waiting, indicated by $R$.

Suppose that $V$ is greater than $L(p_o)$, so that the value would be greater if development were delayed. There is still the risk that the worst will occur. The future price will then be $p_L$, this will be lower than the current price $p_o$, and so the future value of the land will actually be lower. Delay therefore can impose a cost even though, on the balance of probabilities, delay looked to be profitable. In fact, if markets for futures exist then this risk can be avoided. Titman shows that if units can be bought and sold forward, that is sold before construction for delivery later, and then bought back if they are not built, then it would be possible by forward trading to be certain of making a profit by delaying, even if future conditions are bad and the eventual price is $p_L$. This is because the price of the units, now, for delivery at the end of the period is also dependent on the state prices, that is the price of a unit now for delivery later is equal to $s_H.p_H + s_L.p_L$. The developer can sell now, at this price, for delivery later, but may buy some of them back at the lower price $p_L$, if conditions are poor, but deliver if the price is higher.

While this kind of trading is feasible in the stock market, forward trading of this kind is very rare indeed in the property market, though it is not unknown. As we sought to show in Chapter 4, the property market is not particularly efficient, and it would need to be as efficient as the stock market for this to occur on a wide scale. Indeed, in the stock market itself, option trading rarely occurs except with regard to widely quoted stocks in large companies. There is no equivalent of this in the property market where properties are traded infrequently, less frequently than the smallest of firms in which shares are traded on a stock exchange.

Leaving aside these finer points, Titman's analysis demonstrates several things about the market for land and property which are not intuitively obvious. In the first place uncertainty about future conditions may in itself lead to sites being left vacant for considerable periods of time. It follows that, in the second place, uncertainty in and of itself is likely to result in an absence of development, and so increased uncertainty is likely to lead to less development. So that, in the third place, while it is always assumed that rising demand for sites and rising land values will lead to increased pressure to develop, if the rising demand and rising land values are accompanied by increased uncertainty about the future, then the rate of development may actually decrease. So, even if all the alternatives would result in profitable developments, rising land values will *not* necessarily lead to increased development or redevelopment. And, in the fourth place, the converse of this, if future economic conditions become more certain then this increased certainty will, in itself, lead to increased development.

Finally, of course, with respect to the general argument in this chapter, the analysis demonstrates that pieces of land may knowingly be used for an activity which yields a current income lower than could be obtained in some alternative use.

## Summary and conclusions

In this chapter we have looked at two ways in which the possibilities for future development will affect what is done with a site now. In both cases it can be demonstrated that for perfectly valid economic reasons a site may be used currently for some activity which yields a lower income than might be obtained in some other use, that is the site is not used for its 'highest and best' use.

In the first case, in an analysis of speculative activity, the owner is aware of the fact that, in the not too distant future, some other use will be more profitable than any which might currently be profitable. Because of the cost of construction and demolition which would be incurred in the development and use of a site for a short period in one of the currently profitable uses, it will be seen by the owner to be better to leave the site undeveloped or in its existing use.

In the second case uncertainty about what is likely to be the most profitable use of the site in the future can lead the owner to delay development until the uncertainty is resolved and the most profitable use is clear. In the interim it will be economically rational to leave the site undeveloped or, what may be the same thing, to leave it in its existing use, accepting a lower income in the interim in the expectation of a more profitable development later.

# 7

## The Supply of Land for a Particular Use: Occupier Preferences and Residential Attachment

### *'Can't buy me love'*

### Introduction

Speculation and uncertainty about the future can help to explain why land owners' views about the future can cause them to hold their land off the market and leave it being used for some activity which yields a lower current income than they could get in some other use. The anticipated increase in profit in the long term is expected to outweigh any shortfall in income in the longer term. In this chapter we look at a different kind of reason why land and property, especially residential property, may be held off the market and continue to be used in its existing use despite the fact that a higher income could be obtained if it were sold. If the land is occupied by the owner, particularly if it is where the owner lives, then he or she is likely to have some attachment to the site. This attachment can and does lead to owners not wanting to sell, and if they do sell, wanting a price for their property which compensates them for having to sell. Indeed some owners may be unwilling to sell at any price which would be regarded as reasonable! This 'residential attachment', as it was called by Dynarski (1986), was first put forward as explaining various features of the market for land and property by the author in 1983, and developed in a series of papers by myself and others (Evans 1983,1986; Wiltshaw 1985,1988; Neutze 1987).

### Owner occupier attachment

Let us start with some evidence, which we shall return to and discuss more fully later. In the course of research for the Roskill Commission's inquiry into the location of a projected third London airport in the early 1970s a sample of owner occupiers was asked at what price they would be willing to sell their homes and move elsewhere. In effect they were being asked what compensation they would require for having to move, for example to make way for a new airport, though this was not mentioned in the survey. It was recognised that most would not have wanted to move at that time, and so might require some compensation. The results of the survey showed that while some 10% of the householders would be willing to accept the current market price, most would need to be paid a substantial amount over and above the market price in order for them to regard themselves as fully compensated for having to move.

That this should be so can be easily understood. The house which they bought has become a home. It has been furnished and decorated and the garden, if it has one, will have had substantial amounts of labour invested in it. Once the house has been lived in for some time it may also acquire a sentimental value, and this will be particularly true for the elderly, as, say, the house is the house in which their family grew up. The occupiers will have built up social relationships with others in the neighbourhood, and will also have built up economic relationships.

When the land is used for agriculture and occupied by the farmer, these economic relationships may assume more importance in ensuring some 'attachment value', as may the accumulated knowledge of the potential and the problems of the land, knowledge which will have been built up over the years and which would have to be built up anew on a different piece of land, if the farmer were to sell up and move elsewhere. The argument can apply even to businesses. In a study of the effects of compulsory purchase on small businesses in Cardiff, Imrie & Thomas (1997) found that they all felt it would be difficult and disruptive to find and move to equivalent property.

The fact that the value of a good to a user may in some sense be different to its price was something which was discussed at length by the classical economists, from Smith (1776/1910) to Marx (1894/1962). Why, it was wondered, should water which was necessary to life itself have a low price, while diamonds, which were merely decorative, have a high price? In their terminology there was a difference between what they called a good's 'use value' and its 'exchange value', a terminology which was reintroduced into discussions of the land market in the 1970s, particularly by the geographer David Harvey (1973). The neoclassical answer to the diamond/water para- dox was that each good's value to the consumer as a ratio of its price was equalised 'at the margin'. Nevertheless, in the case of inframarginal goods there was a difference between the value to the consumer and the price that was paid for it. This difference was called by Marshall (1890) the 'consumer surplus'.

To use the terminology of neoclassical economics, therefore, what we are trying to say is that the owner and occupier of a property, its consumer, will usually not sell unless some compensation is received for the loss of this consumer surplus. In the terminology of classical economics it will not be sold so long as use value exceeds exchange value. So long as this consumer surplus exists the property would not normally be put on the market, in effect it would be 'inframarginal'. Of course, some owners would be willing to sell at the market price. For whatever reason, retirement, change of job or location, family reasons, increasing income, they wish to sell and would be willing to sell at the market price. For them use value equals exchange value, there is no consumer surplus. The rest would require compensation which might be large or small depending on the circumstances.

To formalise the analysis let us assume that we are dealing with an area of agricultural land just beyond the edge of the built up area of a city, and with the market for this land within a particular period. As usual we assume that there are no planning controls, and initially we also assume that there is no immediate prospect of urban development. The given area of land is represented in Figure 7.1 along the horizontal axis by the length OB. Prices or rents are represented on the vertical axis, and the price of the land for agricultural use is indicated by OP on the left-hand axis. This market price is set by the ruling price for agricultural land elsewhere in the region. We would expect that any land bought and sold in this area would be traded at

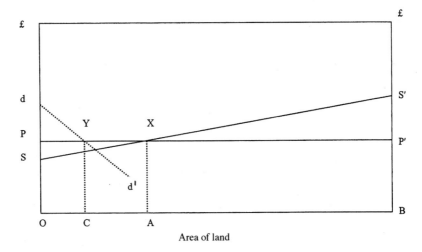

**Figure 7.1**

the price OP, and so the demand for land for agricultural use can be represented by the horizontal line PP'. No buyer of land for agriculture would pay more than this since similar land is available at this price elsewhere.

The supply of land to this market in the given period is represented by the upward sloping line SXS' and its position and slope are those suggested by the discussion above. As we have said, some land would be put on the market in any period and willingly sold at, or even possibly below, the ruling market price because the owner wishes to get out of farming, or to retire completely, or the owner has died and the executors wish to sell. These sellers are represented by the section of the curve SX indicating the supply of land at prices at or below the market price. Other owners of land would be willing to sell at widely differing prices, but all above the current price for agricultural land. Some would require little persuasion and would accept a small premium, others would require prices substantially higher than the market price to persuade them to sell. The schedule of acceptable prices for this group is indicated by the section of the curve XS'.

In this simple situation represented in Figure 7.1, simple because there is no pressure for urban development, the area of land which will come onto the market and be sold at the price OP is indicated by the intersection of the supply and demand curves at X and is represented by OA on the horizontal axis. The rest of the land in the area, AB, will not come on to the market in this period. Of course, in a later period the social and economic circumstances of those who did not wish to sell in the current period will have changed and a new, but similar, supply curve can be drawn.

Suppose now that there is an increased demand for the goods and services produced in the nearby city. In consequence there is an increased demand for labour there, people migrate to the city and consequently there is an increased demand for housing. We first assume that the increased demand is fairly small, and this can be represented, still, in Figure 7.1. The area of land we are considering is therefore only slightly affected by this increased demand for housing, and in the figure the demand for land for development for housing is represented by the downward sloping demand curve dd'. It slopes downward because if the price is high in this area then developers will consider land slightly further from the city, which may be available at a lower price. The higher the price that has to be paid in this area, the lower will be the demand for land from the developers, since they will look for land in other, but possibly less competitive locations.

Since the demand for land for urban development is assumed to be small the demand curve dd' is drawn close to the left-hand vertical axis, and it cuts the line PP′ at Y which is, by assumption, to the left of X. In this situation of low demand the intersection of dd′ with PP′ at Y fixes an area of land represented by OC on the horizontal axis. In effect developers will be able to buy this amount of land for development at the ruling agricultural price or very slightly above it, since they will be able to just outbid those seeking to buy agricultural land. However, since as we have shown OA comes onto the market in the period at this agricultural price, some of this land, CA, will still be sold for agriculture.

Note that the land which is sold for development in this period is sold because of the preferences and priorities of the owners. It is not necessarily contiguous, nor is it necessarily the land in the area closest to the city. The result will therefore almost inevitably be some degree of urban sprawl with scattered non-contiguous urban development. In the standard Alonso/Von Thunen model a small increase in demand would merely result in a small contiguous expansion of the area of the city. Every land owner would be willing to sell their land at the best price available and the price paid by developers for land adjacent to the city would be higher than the going rate for agricultural land, the price which would be available everywhere else outside the urban area.

Suppose that the population of the city now increases still more so that the demand for land for development at the edge of the built up area becomes greater. The situation is represented in Figure 7.2. This figure is the same as Figure 7.1 except that the demand curve has shifted to the right to the

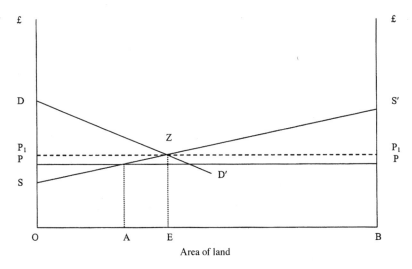

**Figure 7.2**

position shown by DD′. Obviously the demand for urban land is now so great that all the agricultural land that would come onto the market any-way, for sale at the ruling price as agricultural land, will be sold for urban development. This is the area of land indicated by OA on the horizontal axis in the figure. The demand for land is so great, however, that developers will bid the price up to well above the market price for agricultural land, and the higher price will induce some owners to sell their land who would not otherwise have done so.

In the figure, equilibrium in the land market for this area in this period is indicated by the intersection of the demand curve DD′ with the supply curve SS′ at Z. The price of land in the area is then indicated as $OP_1$ on the vertical axis so that a premium, $PP_1$, is paid over and above the current agricultural price. Some land, OA, would be sold anyway but the owners of an additional amount of land, AE, are induced to sell by the premium being paid. Despite the higher price, however, not all the land is sold for devel-opment, so that in the figure EB represents the land which remains in agricultural use.

As in the analysis of the previous figure where we showed that if demand is low there is still likely to be some urban sprawl, this figure indicates that even when demand is high the land which will be developed in the area beyond the existing built-up area will not necessarily be contiguous with it. Further, because a higher price is now being paid for land in this area close to the built-up area it becomes worthwhile for developers to look for land further from the city. Therefore some development will now occur further from the city. Thus with a higher demand for development land urban sprawl will spread over a greater area.

Of course, over time the space between developments will gradually be filled in. Figure 7.2 represents the position in a particular period. In the next period the position will have changed. The family circumstances of those who have retained agricultural land will have changed in one way or another, and some will certainly be more willing to sell, for life cycle reasons, than they were in the preceding period. Moreover, the intrusion of urban development into the area is likely to reduce the profitability and attractions of continuing to farm there. In the next period, therefore, the demand and supply curves will have changed, and anyway some of the land available in the previous period will have been transferred, permanently, into urban use. A premium will continue to be paid for development land, however, and over time land will gradually be trans-ferred out of agricultural use and developed for housing or some other urban uses.

What may also happen, as Wiltshaw (1985) pointed out, is that the owners of relatively larger areas of land may make partial sales, choosing both to remain in farming *and* to sell their land. The income and capital derived from these sales may be great enough to reduce their need or wish to sell the rest, particularly if farming is the only occupation that they know, and if little land is sold in the region at the agricultural price so that it would be difficult to transfer their farming skills and knowledge by buying land elsewhere in the region. And, in any case, the land that they continue to own can be expected to be still saleable at a premium price in the future. Because land is a capital asset a higher price does not necessarily increase the immediate pressure to sell, particularly if the owner also believes ('speculates') that the price obtainable will be higher in the future.

This analysis provides a possible explanation for the continuing urban and rural sprawl around a rapidly growing large city such as Tokyo. The owners may sell some of their land, say when a daughter is getting married, but can continue to farm the rest of the land that they own very intensively (Hebbert & Nakai 1986). The continuing high demand for land for urban development means that any land which does come on to the market is sold for development. None is therefore available in the whole region for any peasant who might want to sell up and move somewhat further from the city. We discuss other aspects of this problem when we talk about land reallocation in Chapter 16.

## Some empirical evidence

At the beginning of this chapter we referred to a survey carried out on behalf of the GB Commission on the Third London Airport (1970), the Roskill Commission. The results of this survey are shown in Table 7.1. It should, perhaps, be borne in mind in looking at the prices in sterling in the table that the survey was carried out in the late 1960s. Shortly afterwards inflation accelerated and continued at a high rate for nearly 20 years. The prices stated are therefore substantially lower than they would be today, and it is necessary to accept the survey's view of what are high or low house prices.

Each row of the table refers to differing levels of house price, low – an average of £3,000, medium – an average of £6,000, and high – an average of £10,000. The columns then indicate with respect to each price level, the percentage of the house owners who would be willing to sell at the market price, or at prices £1,000, £2,000, etc., above the market price. The maximum premium given in the table is £5,000, since, possibly unfortunately, for our purposes, this maximum figure was imposed by the researchers. If

**Table 7.1**   Survey for the Roskill Commission of householders' willingness to sell at the market price. (Percentage distribution of compensation (consumer surplus) required for each price range.)

| House price Range (ave.) | Compensation required | | | | | | |
|---|---|---|---|---|---|---|---|
| | 0 | £1k | £2k | £3k | £4k | £5k | Total |
| Low (3k) | 11 | 55 | 11 | 10 | 5 | 8 | 100 |
| Medium (£6k) | 11 | 34 | 21 | 11 | 5 | 18 | 100 |
| High (£10k) | 11 | 15 | 19 | 12 | 9 | 34 | 100 |

Source: GB Commission (1970, p. 373).

any owner indicated that they would need to be paid more than £5,000, then the figure of £5,000 was imposed.

Some 11% of the owners were willing to sell at the market price, and this figure of 11% holds for each of the three price ranges. It presumably indicates the group which, we argued earlier, would be willing to sell anyway for demographic, job change, or family reasons. From these arguments it might be expected that the proportion 'in the market' in each price range would be similar, but their complete coincidence is somewhat unexpected.

The table also shows that for those not willing to sell at the market price the premium required tends to be higher, the higher is the market price of the house. The situation is clearer if the figures in Table 7.1 are interpreted graphically as in Figure 7.3. The arbitrariness of the cut-off imposed on the premium which could be asked for then becomes apparent. In the figure, as in Figures 7.1 and 7.2, the premium payable above the market price is shown on the vertical axis, though the market price for each group is shown by the same point. Along the horizontal axis, instead of land area, the percentage of the total households in each group is shown. The stepped functions which represent the data given in the table are clearly similar to the kind of supply curve shown with respect to the land market in Figures 7.1 and 7.2. A proportion of the households would be in the market anyway, and the others would require a premium to persuade them to sell. The stepped functions are steeper the higher is the price of the property, indicating, as one might expect, that the premium required would generally be larger the higher is the value of the house. While few of those with houses valued at about £3,000 would require a premium of £5,000, a premium which would be equal to 167% of the market value of their house, at least a half of those owning houses worth £10,000 would require this sort of premium, and this seems reasonable since it is only equivalent to 50% of the value of their houses.

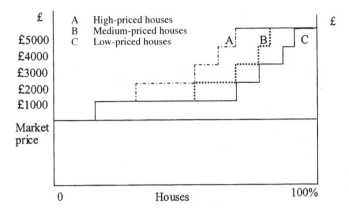

**Figure 7.3** Consumer surplus.

Empirical evidence of a different kind is reported in research by Dynarski (1986). In a study using cross-sectional data for the United States he found that he could identify what he called 'attachment' value. The value of their home to the house owners could be identified in his econometric study as giving a value over and above the market value of the house, the 'attachment value'.

## Summary and conclusions

The attachment of owners to their land and, in particular, to their homes, can explain various features of the property market. First, the price of land for urban development will be higher than its agricultural use price, even were this 'urban' price not affected by the anticipation of price increases in the future, of the kind we discussed in the previous chapter. Second, even in the absence of speculation, the varying degrees of attachment to their land of the owners will mean that some land will be sold, because the premium is high enough to induce a sale, while some will not be sold because, for those owners, the premium will not be high enough. The result will be scattered urban development and urban sprawl such as has occurred around, for example, American and Japanese cities, and which occurred in British cities in the first 40 years of the twentieth century before planning controls were imposed to prevent it.

Third, the faster the rate of urban expansion, the higher the price paid by developers for land is likely to be, even, once again, in the absence of speculation. Fourth, urban sprawl can coexist with partial sales of their holdings by owners of land as they trade in parts of their holdings and continue to hold the rest.

This and the previous chapter have put forward three reasons why land owners may continue to hold on to their land rather than sell it for development, or develop it themselves, even when a higher current income could be obtained from doing so. But it is evident that, in practice, it would be difficult to identify the particular motivation for any specified land owner's behaviour. They may be motivated by their attachment to their holdings, by speculation about the future, and by uncertainty about the future, or by all three together. Together, however, the three kinds of motivation do explain why land may not be used for its current 'highest and best' use.

# 8

## The Ownership of Land and Change in its Use

### *'Let it be'*

---

### Introduction

In the discussion in the previous chapter it was assumed that a property was used and occupied by its owner. But this is not necessarily the case. Most other types of capital asset are owned by their users, but land and buildings are frequently let to tenants so that a piece of real estate may be occupied and used by a person or firm which is not its owner. Indeed, at some times, in some uses, and in some countries or regions, this may be the general rule.

In the economic analysis of real estate in the past the economic implications of this have been generally ignored. The widespread neoclassical assumption would be that the forms of ownership should make no difference to the use to which land is put. It is assumed that the owner of the property will ensure that the highest possible current return is obtained from its ownership, whether this is in the form of a rent received from a tenant or an income derived from its use, an income which is implicit in the case of householders. But in the previous chapter it was argued that owner occupiers had an attachment to their land. They would frequently be willing to carry on occupying it and using it in the way they were accustomed to, even though they could obtain a higher current income from changing its use and, if necessary, selling it. What we shall show in this chapter is that the owners of land are likely to be more willing to allow a change in its use, to sell it if necessary, if they are landlords letting their property to tenants. This means that the supply of land for development is likely to be more elastic if land in the area is let to tenants by landlords than if it is owner occupied.

But the way in which land is owned may be important in other ways. We shall show that in the transition from the use of land for agriculture to its use for urban development, the character of the owners of the land may change in stages, from users to investors or speculators to developers. We referred to this transition when we discussed speculation in Chapter 6. The analysis there and in Chapter 7 are brought together to show how the motivations and characteristics of owners are important factors in causing this changing pattern of ownership.

## Tenants, owner occupiers and the supply of land

In the previous chapter we argued that owner occupiers would generally require some compensation if they were to be induced to sell their properties and move somewhere else rather earlier than they would otherwise have wished. Using this argument, supported by the available empirical evidence, we showed that the supply of land for a particular use could be represented by an upward sloping supply curve, SXS' in Figures 7.1 and 7.2. In this chapter we argue that the supply of land will be affected by the ownership of the land. In general the elasticity of supply will be lower if the land is occupied by its owners than it would be if it were occupied by tenants and owned by landlords. However, the position will be significantly affected by the details of the legal relationship between tenants and landlords, in particular, the extent to which tenants have security of tenure.

The difference between the economic position of an owner occupier and that of a tenant with respect to their continued occupation of a property can be illustrated and explained in terms which have come into prominent use in the evaluation of environmental attributes using survey, or 'contingent valuation' methods. For example, people may be asked to state the value to them of something such as the existence of a Green Belt around a conurbation (Willis & Whitby 1985), or the existence of archaeological remains (Riganti 1997), or a visit to a cathedral (Willis *et al.* 1993). But in practice the question is not simple. Of the various problems the one that is relevant to us is that it can be asked in two different ways. Using one approach it can be put in terms of willingness to pay (WTP) – how much would you be willing to pay to ensure the continued existence of, say, a Green Belt? The second approach asks the question in terms of willingness to accept compensation (WTA) – how much would you be willing to accept in payment in order to feel that you would have been compensated for the loss of the Green Belt if it were to cease to exist?

It is evident that both questions relate to the valuation of the same environmental attribute, but it is also evident that different answers may be obtained from the two forms of the question. People are likely to give a lower figure if they are being asked to part with the money, than they would give in respect of money they might expect to receive. The answers are likely to be close if the amounts involved are small, a few pounds per year, indeed they might be expected to be virtually identical if the amounts involved are very small indeed. The divergence between the answers is likely to be greater the larger the sums involved.

In the context of the land market it is the continued occupation of a piece of land which is the equivalent of the environmental attribute in these surveys. In the previous chapter, the owner occupiers were in effect being asked how much they would be willing to accept to give up their property. When the property is occupied by tenants and owned by a landlord the position is, however, completely different. Assume that the circumstances are as set out in Chapter 7 but that the land is occupied by tenants. The owner of a piece of land may receive offers from developers who wish to purchase it. If the demand for urban land is high enough the developers will be willing to pay more than the value of the land in its current agricultural use. The owner of the land does not live on it and presumably therefore is likely to regard the land as merely a capital asset. If the owner considers only his or her own interests there is therefore no reason why the higher offer should not be accepted and the property sold. No reason, that is, unless the existing tenants can be persuaded to pay a higher rent so that the land yields an income equivalent to what could be obtained from the proceeds of sale.

But this higher rent will be higher than the current market rent for agricultural land, and therefore higher than the tenants would have to pay if they moved elsewhere. The tenants can only continue at the same location by paying a premium. The arguments used in the previous chapter suggest reasons why they might be willing to do so. They will have built up social and economic relationships in the area and will have accumulated specific knowledge of the land that they farm. They will have a 'sentimental' attachment to their home. All of these advantages of the current location will be lost to them if they have to move. But they are not being asked how much they would accept to give these things up. The hypothetical question is how much would they be willing to pay to continue at their present location and keep them. Given that the sums involved are substantial in relation to incomes it follows that the Willingness To Pay by tenants will almost certainly be considerably less than the Willingness To Accept of owner occupiers.

The difference between the two situations is illustrated in Figure 8.1 which shows the two possible supply curves. As in the figures used in Chapter 7 an area of land just outside an existing urban area is shown measured along the horizontal axis as OB. In those figures it did not much matter whether the vertical axis represented rents or capital values. In this case it does and the vertical axis indicates the annual income from the property or the annualised income from its sale. This may be the rent paid if the property is let to a tenant, or the annual equivalent income derived from the property, where it is owner occupied, or the income derived from the sale proceeds, if it is sold. On the vertical axis OP is the market rent payable for agricultural land of this type so that the horizontal line PP′ indicates the demand curve for this land for agricultural use.

The demand curve for land for urban development is, as before, DD′. The supply curve of tenanted land to the market is shown as SXT. As before we assume that some land will come onto the market anyway at the current agricultural price as tenants die, wish to retire, move elsewhere, or give up farming for some other occupation, and this is represented by the section of the curve SX lying below the line PP′. If landlords force up rents then it is probable that the remaining tenants would be willing to pay slightly higher rents to remain at their current location. The premiums they would be willing to pay would not be high, however, since there is always the possibility of moving elsewhere and paying the going market (agricultural) rent. Their position is represented by the section of the curve XT.

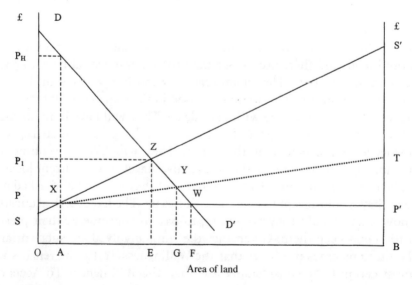

**Figure 8.1**

The supply curve if the land were owner occupied, as analysed in Chapter 6, is shown as SXS', as before. Because of the difference outlined above between Willingness to Pay and Willingness to Accept, the line XS' lies substantially above XT. Because of this the demand curve for land for urban development intersects XS' at Z above and to the left of its intersection with XT at Y. The implication is that the transition from one use to another is likely to differ, if the land is tenanted, from what it would have been if the land were owner occupied. First, it is evident that the price at which the land is sold to developers will be lower when it is let to tenants by landlords than it would be if the land were owner occupied. Second, more land will be sold in a given period if it is owned by landlords and let to tenants than if it is owner occupied, so that the rate at which land is transferred from one use or another will be much faster in the former case than in the latter. In effect landlords will be far more willing to eject their tenants in order to derive a marginally higher income than owner occupiers would be to move off their own land. This means that if land is tenanted the rate of change could be very rapid. The position could indeed be close to that implied by the neo-classical assumption that if the price for the land in another use marginally exceeds its price in its current use then it will immediately be transferred into the higher paying use.

The rate of change will, however, be significantly affected by the legal situation, in particular the contractual agreements between tenants and landlords with respect to their period of tenure and the rent payable, and also any legislation affecting the legal position of tenants. At issue are the rights that tenants have to the land they currently occupy. If they do not have any right to security of tenure but can be evicted at the will or whim of the landlord then the position is as described above, and this will be so whether or not there is any control or regulation, contractual or otherwise, over the rent that has to be paid.

If rents are controlled and tenants have complete security of tenure then the rate of change and the price that developers would have to pay will depend upon whether 'side payments' can be made to tenants, or whether these are regarded as bribes and morally or legally reprehensible. If no such compensatory payments are allowed then tenants have no incentive to move at all and cannot be forced to do so. The only land which will come on to the market is the land which tenants would vacate anyway for demographic reasons – death, retirement, etc. In Figure 8.1 this is OA on the horizontal axis and the supply curve becomes the vertical line through A and X. The supply of land and property is unaffected by economic factors and the price, indicated in the figure by the intersection of this vertical line with the demand curve DD', is, as a result, very high, $OP_H$ on the vertical axis. If, on the other hand, land owners, or developers, can negotiate with tenants and make compensatory 'side payments', the supply of land to the market and its price are going to be similar to what they would be if the land were owner occupied. Price and quantity sold will be indicated by the intersection of the demand curve with SXS'. This is because the tenant can claim compensation for being forced to move from the land owner (or the developer) and this is measured by Willingness to Accept not Willingness To Pay. The price the developer has to pay is higher because the tenant has to receive full compensation and the land owner has to receive, at least, the agricultural market price.

Of course, there are a large number of variations on the possibilities outlined above. The most likely in practice is that tenants have limited security of tenure and can be forced to move only after a certain period. The rate of change will be determined by the length of the period of notice. If it is short, a few months, the rate of change will be faster and the price of land to developers lower than if the land were owner occupied. On the other hand if the period of notice is long, a number of years, the rate of change will initially be slower and the price higher. When the period of notice ends, however, the amount of land coming on to the market is likely to be high and the price is likely to fall.

It is also worth remembering that the social, or extra-legal, situation may also be important. If a tenant has security of tenure at a controlled rent then both the landlord and the developer have an incentive to try to get the tenant to move 'voluntarily'. In the late 1950s in Britain tenants of residential property had complete security of tenure and rents were controlled at far below market levels. In these circumstances some landlords certainly used illegal or quasi-legal methods to induce tenants to move. For example, repairs could be carried out to the house, but very slowly, so that it was in a permanent state of disrepair. Noisy and disruptive tenants could be moved in to other parts of the house, in effect employed by the landlord to make life as difficult as possible for the sitting tenant. The practice became known as Rachmanism after the most notorious of these landlords, Peter Rachman.

Going still further back in time the plight of tenants without security of tenure is demonstrated by the Highland Clearances in Scotland in the early nineteenth century. Finding that grazing sheep on their land yielded a higher income than renting it to crofters, many of the land owners, the lairds, drove the crofters off the land, pulling down the villages and leaving them to decay. Having nowhere else to go the crofters moved to newly industrialising cities such as Glasgow, or emigrated, large numbers settling in Canada. This historical example has its ironies. The lairds and their tenants were usually all members of the same clan, and the lairds, as leaders of the clan, were meant to have a social responsibility for their clansmen. Because of this the lairds' actions seemed the more immoral – driving their own clan members to leave their land and their country, and replacing them by sheep, called, sarcastically, the laird's 'four footed clansmen'. The full story is told by John Prebble (1963). From an economic point of view, of course, the emigration was inevitable in the long run. But it would have occurred more slowly and with less sense of loss if the crofters had greater security of tenure or had been land owning peasants.

## Ownership and change

The discussion above uses the previous chapter's analysis of the attachment of occupiers to their land to show that the way in which land is owned and occupied will affect the process of development and change – ownership affects development. The discussion in this section looks at the process in a different way. Here we use the analysis of speculation in Chapter 6, as well as the analysis of ownership and occupation in the previous chapter, to show how the anticipation of development will tend to alter the characteristics of the land's owners – development (or its anticipation) affects ownership.

The motivation for the argument derives from empirical evidence of the ownership of land in the United States gathered by Brown *et al.* (1985). They studied the characteristics and motivations of the owners of (rural) land in two types of situation. In the first case development pressures could be described as weak. In the second case they were strong.

When development pressures were weak the researchers found that the land tended to be owned by those they described as 'users'. These people either farmed the land or lived there, that is the land was in residential or agricultural use and occupied and used by its owners. The attitude of these users to their land could be described in terms of 'a strong personal commitment', in particular they were 'not interested in selling'. If they were to consider selling this would be for family or life cycle reasons. Brown and his fellow researchers concluded that the supply of land, in this context, was responsive to demographic factors rather than economic factors.

It can be seen that the position of these land owners as described by Brown *et al.* is similar to the way in which we characterised the motivations and characteristics of owner occupiers in Chapter 7 – their primary interest is in the continued occupation and use of 'their' land. The US researchers did not go on to ask their respondents whether there was some price at which they would be willing to sell, and what it might be. While this might have been useful to the analysis presented here the question was not asked, it was not part of their research interest at the time and would probably have been seen as irrelevant since they were considering a situation when development pressures were weak so that no such higher prices were likely to be offered.

What Brown *et al.* do show is that when development pressures are strong the characteristics and motivations of the owners of land are likely to be different. They found that when development pressures were strong more land was likely to be owned by those whom they called 'investors'. These 'investors' were people or firms who had bought the land when it came on to the market but had no intention of occupying or using it themselves. They held it solely as an investment. 'Investors' were often uninterested in any current income from letting the land and might leave it vacant and unused waiting for the right, higher, price to sell it. Brown *et al.* found that when development pressures were strong most land which came on to the market was bought by investors not users. It can be seen that gradually, over a period of time, as development pressures strengthened, an increasing proportion of the stock of land in the area would be owned by investors and a decreasing proportion by users. The pattern of ownership would pass through a transition. Finally, as one might expect, it was found that these 'investors' would be willing to sell if they were made a good enough offer, obviously enough since their interest in the land was financially motivated.

An economic explanation for this transition in the pattern of ownership can be set out using the analysis set out in Chapter 6 in the discussion of speculation. In Figure 8.2 time is represented along the horizontal axis. Rent is indicated on the vertical axis in the upper figure (a) and, as in Figures 6.1 and 6.2, capital values are represented on the vertical axis in the lower figure (b). As before the horizontal line $R_F$ in the upper figure indicates the annual income obtained from the continuing use of the land for agriculture. Again, as before, $R_1$ in the upper figure indicates the income which could be derived from the land when and if it is developed for some urban use such as housing. In the earlier part of the period this will be low, and then will increase until at some date it becomes greater than the income which could be obtained from the continuing use of the land in agriculture. At this date, $T_1$ on the horizontal axis, the land will be developed.

From this analysis based on the current income or rental obtainable from the land there seems no obvious reason why the land should not be owned

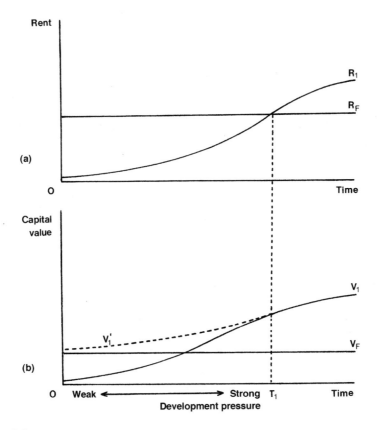

**Figure 8.2**

by users up to the date of development and developers afterward. To see why 'investors' come into the picture we have to look at the capital value of the land basing the analysis on Figure 8.2(b). In this figure the horizontal line $V_F$ shows the capital value of the land if it is used for agriculture now and is expected to be used for agriculture in the foreseeable future. Since the income from farming remains the same for all time the capital value which is the discounted present value of the future income also remains unchanged. Hence $V_F$ is horizontal.

The capital value of the land if it is left vacant up to the date of development, $T_1$, and then developed is indicated by the line marked as $V_1$. Because the income from the developed land is substantially higher than the possible income from farming after the date of development and $V_1$ indicates the present value of these expected future rents then, as with Figure 6.1, the line $V_1$ lies substantially above $V_F$ both after the date of development and for some time beforehand. Of course, the land need not be left vacant before

development but could be farmed. The capitalised value of the land if it is
always used to obtain an income is shown in the lower figure by the dashed
line $V_1'$ in the period before development. This always lies above $V_F$ because
development is always anticipated, but if development is many years into
the future it will be virtually the same as $V_F$. As the date of expected
development approaches it rises above $V_F$ and converges with and joins $V_1$
at the date of development $T_1$ when urban development occurs and farming
ends.

What this graph makes clear is that the capital value of a piece of land which
may possibly be developed profitably at some time in the future is very little
different from its value as farmland pure and simple if the anticipated
development is far in the future. However, as the prospect of development
draws closer, the value of the land, because of its anticipated value when
developed, becomes substantially greater than its value as farmland. A
would-be 'user', for example someone who wishes to purchase a piece of
land to pursue a career as a farmer, therefore has a decreasing interest in
purchasing the land. In the first place it can only be used, whether as
farmland or as residence, for a period of time which is limited to the period
before development. Second, and possibly more importantly, farmland
which is unaffected by any anticipation of development can be purchased at
some other location at a much lower price.

The value of the land is primarily determined by its anticipated development so that as the date of development nears therefore the land becomes of
decreasing interest to users. On the other hand since it is not yet profitable
to develop the land it is not worth while for any construction or building
firm to buy it. The way is open for some other kind of owner, an 'investor',
to buy the land, hold it, possibly let it, and then sell it on at the appropriate
time to the construction company, the developer. Since most of the value of
the land is determined by anticipation of development and very little by the
income from farming it follows that if any 'user' were to purchase the site
then they would, willy nilly, be transformed into an 'investor' by the huge
premium they would have to pay over and above agricultural use value. For
example, if the land were valued at three times its agricultural use value
then only one-third of the total investment would be related to agriculture
and farming but two-thirds would depend on the anticipation of future
urban development.

In the terminology used by Brown *et al.*, when 'development pressures are
weak', the impact of any future urban development on the value of the land
is also weak, and land continues to be bought by 'users'. In the figures these
are dates close to the vertical axis or even to its left. As development

pressures become stronger, however, as we have shown above, it becomes feasible and necessary for 'investors' to buy land as it comes on to the market, treating it as a capital asset which can be held until it is optimal to sell it on to a 'developer' for urban development.

When 'development pressures are strong', therefore, land tends to be held by 'investors'. The transition in the ownership of land is from 'users' to 'investors' to 'developers'. The role and character of the 'users' and of the 'developers' is obvious and easy to understand. The characteristics of the 'investors' are less obvious even though their role seems clear, that is to invest their capital in an asset whose current value is derived from its anticipated future value. Moreover, given that the future is rarely as anticipated, they bear the risks involved in this investment.

Many of the characteristics of investors might be inferred from the role that they play, and a survey of investors in vacant land carried out by Witte & Bachman (1978) confirms this view. They found that investors will tend to have more capital to risk, and that the land that they own will often be held as part of a portfolio of assets. They also found that investors tended to be less risk averse. Given the riskiness of investing a substantial sum in an asset which can only be realised at some time in the future and whose value cannot be predicted, only estimated, these characteristics seem, to say the least, plausible. Though the investment is risky, this risk can be reduced if the piece of land is held as part of a portfolio – elementary portfolio theory would imply that the 'non-systematic risk' can then be reduced, if not eliminated, because the other investments will have differing and only partially correlated risks. Holding many assets means that any loss or shortfall on the final sale of the land should be balanced by profits or gains on the sale of other assets.

Another characteristic that they identified is a little less obvious, namely that an 'investor' in real estate may have some professional involvement in real estate. But once identified the reasons are clear. The possession of information about the real estate market, whether this is inside information gained from involvement in the market, or the professional information and expertise which is gained from professional involvement, will make the market less risky to the investor than to an outsider. Indeed the information about the market, and the future of the land, is what will have attracted the investor to the investment in the land in the first place. But the possession of knowledge and familiarity with the market will also reduce the extent of the unknown and so the apparent level of risk.

The final characteristic of some investors is not obvious at all. Witte &

Bachman found that 'investors' were not infrequently institutions. The explanation for this would seem to be that these institutions, universities or churches for example, had long time horizons. It may be anticipated many years in advance that development of a piece of land will occur in due course, but the shareholders, and the managers, of a limited liability company tend to have rather short time horizons and to be interested primarily in profits which can be realised within the next few years. Individuals may have longer time horizons but may lack the capital required for an investment which may yield little income for 10 or 20 years or more. The time horizons of institutions such as the church or universities may be longer even than this. The fact that development of the asset and realisation of its value may occur far in the future is not necessarily seen as a disadvantage. The asset can continue to be held and be something for the institution's head to hand on to his or her successors. My own university, Reading, owns large areas of farm land to the south and east of the town of Reading. Some was developed in the early 1980s, some more recently, and some is likely to be developed over the next few years. In an institution which has existed for over a hundred years and has no intention of closing or moving within any foreseeable future, the slow pace of development is a pity, but no reason to sell the asset and invest elsewhere. Other institutions, the Church of England, the Roman Catholic Church, universities such as Oxford or Harvard, have longer histories than any joint stock company, and certainly have longer time horizons.

The surveys of the owners of land by Brown *et al.* (1981) and of investors in land by Witte & Bachman (1978) were carried out in the United States, and some years ago. They therefore relate to a country with a much less regulated land market than elsewhere, and probably one less regulated than it would be today. How then would the situation differ if the level of intervention to limit or control development were greater and the planning controls more stringent?

In part the answer was supplied by other research carried out by Brown *et al.* (1981). They also looked at the pattern of land ownership in Calgary in Canada and found a much less obvious process of a transition in ownership from user to investor to developer. Their explanation for this was that planning controls were stronger in the area they were studying in Calgary than they were in the other areas that they had looked at, four cities in the United States as well as Toronto in Canada. As a result the value of land was less easy to calculate and the change in the value of land over time was less predictable. The role of the investor was therefore less clear, and land was more likely to be transferred directly between users and developers.

The current position in the United Kingdom is at the opposite extreme from the free market of the United States in the 1960s. Development is tightly controlled through the planning system. Because of this the value of land on the edge of an urban area which might be developed in the future is virtually independent of the passage of time. The diagrammatic analysis used earlier in this section is therefore of no use. The value of land does not increase over time as the optimal time for development approaches and the urban area expands. The British urban area may be constrained by a Green Belt or other forms of planning control. The value of the land is then almost wholly dependent on the probability of obtaining planning permission. And, as we noted in Chapter 3, the value of a piece of land may leap a hundredfold or more, in southern England at least, if planning permission is given for the development of agricultural land for residential or other urban uses.

A study by Goodchild & Munton (1985) of land ownership in the 1980s in Britain sheds some light on the situation. They found that just as the value of land depended on the probability of obtaining planning permission so did the ownership. When and where the probability of getting planning permission for development was very low, then the value of the land was near agricultural value and the land was owned by farmers (users). If, on the other hand, the probability of getting planning permission was high, the land was frequently owned by investors. These investors might let the land or it might be left idle since any rent that could be obtained would be minuscule in relation to the capital value of the land, and its expected value if planning permission were to be obtained. In practice they found that if the property were used, then, often, because it was very close to an urban area, it was used for what has come to be called 'horseyculture', grazing, maintaining and exercising horses used for recreation by the urban residents.

Since Munton & Goodchild carried out their research the practice of using options has grown up, indeed was developing at the time that they were writing in the 1980s. The use of options to buy a piece of land virtually eliminates any role for 'investors'. What happens is this. A developer will pay the owner of a piece of land a relatively small sum of money in exchange for an option to buy the land if planning permission can be obtained for development. For example, in the late 1980s an oil company paid the University of Reading £5000 for an option to buy a piece of farmland with frontage onto a main road on which they hoped to be able to build a petrol filling station. The developer then applies for planning permission, and pays all the costs of doing so. If it becomes necessary the developer may appeal to the Secretary of State (i.e. central government) against refusal to grant planning permission by the local authority. Indeed the option agreement sometimes may commit the developer to appealing against a refusal.

If planning permission is not obtained then the land owner receives nothing further. And planning permission was not obtained by the petrol company in the example given above so the University received only the £5000 (but still owns the farmland). If, on the other hand, the developer does get planning permission then the land is sold by the user to the developer. The way in which the price is determined but not the actual price will have been laid down in the original contract. The price cannot be agreed at the time of the contract because the actual sale of the land will take place some time later, possibly years later, and the price will depend on the market at that time. Further, the price will also depend on the terms and conditions of the planning permission which has been finally obtained.

The owner of the land does not receive the full market price of the land at the time of sale, however. The developer has incurred the costs of obtaining planning permission, and the costs of an appeal, with barristers, solicitors, planning consultants, and expert witnesses, can be very high. Moreover, the developer is expected to bear these costs even when the application for planning permission is completely unsuccessful. In effect the developer receives a share of the market price as compensation for the firm's costs in both the successful and the unsuccessful applications. In the mid- to late 1980s the proportion received by the land owner was nearly 90%, but by the early 1990s this proportion had fallen to 60% as developers found that they were having less and less success in appealing decisions, and therefore required a larger share of the proceeds of any successful application to pay the costs of all the unsuccessful ones.

It can be seen that the role of the investor in facilitating the transition from one use to another may be very evident in an uncontrolled land market, but may be very much less evident in a land market as tightly controlled as that in Britain. Nevertheless, even in a controlled market, given that the original 'user' and the final 'developer' have highly specific interests in land and will want to avoid risk, there is still likely to be some role for the investor who can spread the risk of land ownership through a portfolio of holdings, whether in land or other assets. The institution with the very long time horizon is also likely to have a role. The view may be taken that at some time planning permission may be given on some of the land, even if this is in 20 years time or more. With a longer time horizon the institution is prepared to wait longer than the company or the individual.

## Summary and conclusions

The discussion in this chapter has been concerned with the motivations and the characteristics of the owners of land. The motivations of owners will affect their behaviour with respect to their holdings. The simple, and simplistic, assumption that land owners will simply seek to extract the highest possible current income from their land, that it will always be used for its 'highest and best' use, is simply wrong. The owner occupier is likely to behave in a different way to the landlord who lets the land to a tenant. In particular, since the owner occupier has to be compensated for leaving while the tenant may have to pay a higher rent to stay, the rate of change is likely to be faster if the land is let to tenants than if it is owner occupied. The legal position of tenants will affect the rate of change, however. If they have security of tenure the rate of change may be very much slower.

In addition expectations as to the future of the land are likely to affect its ownership. A piece of land which is expected to be developed within the next few years is likely to be purchased by a person or firm, an 'investor' with one kind of motivation and characteristics. A piece of land which is likely to be farmed for the foreseeable future will be purchased by a farmer or 'user' with quite different motivations.

# 9

# Land Ownership, Politics and Society

## *'A little help from my friends'*

### Introduction

In this chapter we discuss the social relationships implicit in the role of the land owner and in the landlord–tenant relationship. These social relationships have been important in the past in determining political, social, and economic changes. They are now of less importance than they have been in the past, but they nevertheless cannot be completely ignored.

We go on to discuss alternative forms of land ownership. At one extreme we analyse the economics of common land ownership and show that rules are frequently agreed and enforced by the users to ensure that the land is used efficiently. At the other extreme we analyse the libertarian view that land should be owned free of all controls, taxation, and regulation by the state, since if controls are necessary the private sector will supply them through the market. We indicate that experience does not suggest that this is necessarily true.

### Society and the ownership of land

In the discussion in the previous chapter we have attempted to show the way in which the motivation and characteristics of the owners of land may affect the process of development and be affected by the expectation of development. Even here, however, we have assumed the motivations of the owners to be relatively simple and primarily economic. But we should not completely ignore the fact that the ownership of land can affect the owner's social and political behaviour. In the past this was more self-evidently true than it may be today for the ownership of land carried social and political obligations and these affected the owners' behaviour since they affected their motivations.

In English society, as in most of the rest of Europe, the reasons go back to the feudal relationships of the Middle Ages. The relationship between the owner and his tenants involved a set of duties on either side, amongst which were the duty of providing armed men, by the tenants, and the duty of defending the tenants, by the lord. In turn, of course, the lords owed similar duties to their feudal lord, the king. Over the years the mediaeval, feudal, relationships were modified, although relics remain. One such is the legal fiction in English law that the monarch is theoretically the owner, in the final analysis, of all land, the actual freeholders holding their land from her (or him). A relic in Scottish law is the payment of a 'feu' to a 'feuholder' by an owner who in all other respects is the owner of a freehold (and the feu-holder now is most probably an insurance company or similar institution).

The relics of the feudal system had continuing effects on English political life well after the feudal system, as such, had vanished. The English aris-tocrats and landed gentry believed in holding their estates together and in passing them on, increased in area if possible, to the eldest son, younger sons being left to shift for themselves in the church or the army. This meant that estates were large and not split up as they might be elsewhere in Europe where primogeniture was not the rule. And in the eighteenth century, when power had passed from the House of Lords to the House of Commons, the owner would expect that his tenants would vote for the candidate whom he supported, possibly his eldest son or his heir if the landlord were in the Lords. Since the ballot was not secret until 1868 this assumption could be well founded, and even after that date could still be assumed and acted upon in some estates. Thus the ownership of land gave political and social power as well as economic power, and the ownership of land had an importance over and above any income which might be derived from it.

The relics of the feudal notions of the tenants owing duties to their landlord while the landlord had a responsibility to them were the reason why the Highland Clearances were, as we have noted in the previous chapter, widely seen as immoral, even if they were legal. The laird had a social contract, as well as a legal contract, with his tenants since they were also his clansmen.

The clearances, the enclosure of common land, the rise of manufacturing and the manufacturing towns hastened the decline of land as an asset which might be thought socially and politically important. The large land owner still had the power to alter the course of development, however. Some, such as the Duke of Bridgewater hastened it, in his case by developing the earliest industrial canal in order to allow coal to be carried from mines on his land to Manchester (Porter 1982/1998, p. 192). Others might slow development. As we mentioned in Chapter 1, the Marquess of Exeter prevented the construction of the railway from London to York and Edinburgh across his land outside Stamford, so that it was diverted to pass through Peterborough and Stamford became and remained a backwater (Hoskins 1955, Chapter 9).

Land is still different, however, and its ownership may still have a political dimension. A modern example is the importance attached to the ownership of property by Margaret Thatcher and the Conservative Party in the 1980s. A policy of allowing the tenants of local authority housing to buy the houses that they lived in was introduced. Since the properties could be purchased at a substantial discount to their true value this was politically popular amongst the tenants. A major reason for the implementing the policy was that it was a widely held view, amongst Labour party activists as well as Conservatives, that owner occupiers were more likely to vote Conservative, while council tenants were more likely to vote Labour. If this view is correct, and I know of no reason to doubt that it is, the decline in the numbers of council tenants and the increase in the number of owner occupiers provides at least a partial explanation for the rightward drift in British politics in the 1990s as the Labour party itself shifted its ground.

## Alternative forms of ownership and tenancy

One feature of land which distinguishes it from most other forms of capital asset is that it can be owned and operated in many different ways. The tenancy of a property may be fixed for a number of years. Frequently the length of a lease will be fixed, but provision will be made in the contract for periodic rent revisions. In agriculture an important type of tenancy in some countries has been one where the rent paid by the tenant is not fixed in money terms but is a share of the crop. The economics of sharecropping have been extensively analysed, most notably by Cheung (1969), a reason for this interest being that it represents a different allocation of the risks inherent in agriculture. In a 'normal' tenancy the rent is fixed in advance and the tenant bears the risk that for one reason or another the crop is worse than expected, as, of course, the tenant gains all the benefit that the crop is better than expected. With a share cropping contract the risks are more equally shared between landlord and tenant. Such a contract is more likely both where the risks are greater than in the more temperate parts of the world, and where the tenants are so poor that they have to minimise the risks that they bear in any way that they can. Thus a 'sharecropper' in the southern United States is likely to be the poorest kind of tenant and the term is used in that way.

One form of ownership which can still have political and social importance in some countries is that of ownership in common. Neoclassical economic analysis with its stress on self-interested behaviour suggests that common ownership of land, indeed of any resource, is inefficient and it provides an explanation, and a justification, for the disappearance of common owner-ship in most developed economies. A well known historical example of the process of disappearance is the enclosure of common land in England in the eighteenth and early nineteenth centuries. Since this occurred at the same time as, indeed is regarded as part of, the agricultural revolution, and during the early stages of the industrial revolution, it was, and is, easy to see this as an inevitable development, as economic progress.

The economic analysis which supports this view can be presented dia-grammatically. Figure 9.1 represents the situation with respect to an area of land which may be owned and used in common by people grazing their cattle on it, or may be owned by a single individual. The individual land owner and each of the common owners seek to maximise the return they get from using the land. Total use or investment in the land is indicated along the horizontal axis. This might be, say, the number of cows grazed on the land. For anyone seeking a relevant present day example of common ownership the resource could be an area of sea and the investment in its use is measured by the number of boats fishing that area.

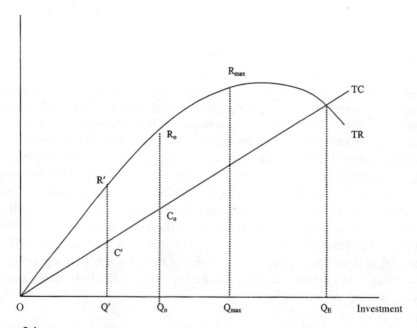

**Figure 9.1**

The vertical axis represents the total revenue from and the total cost of the use of the site, that is the total revenue derived from all the cows grazing the land and the total costs of the cows to the owner or owners. It is assumed that the cost of any cow is the same so that the line indicating total cost, TC, is a straight line sloping upwards from the origin – because the cost of each cow is the same the slope is constant. On the other hand it is to be expected that the revenue derived from grazing a cow on the land will be highest when there is only one, but the revenue derived from each additional cow will tend to fall as the number of cows increases. Grass is scarcer and has to be sought, and what there is becomes more and more likely to be trampled over and turned to mud. This means that the total revenue from increased use of the land tends to increase at a decreasing rate, in economic jargon there are diminishing returns to scale. So the total revenue curve, TR, as drawn in Figure 9.1, slopes upward at a decreasing rate.

Indeed, as it is drawn the curve reaches a maximum at an input of $Q_{max}$ and after this point total revenue derived from the land actually starts to fall with an increased investment. The implication is that, in terms of the example, as an increased number of cows are brought on to the land it becomes so crowded with cattle that each additional cow actually reduces total income because the scarcity of fodder outweighs any increase due to the addition. In the case of the example of the fishing ground it is as though at this point the fishing boats start to over-fish the area, fish don't grow to maturity and fishing stocks and total catches fall. The immediate relevance of this example can be seen in the attempts to control fishing in the oceans and seas by internationally coordinated action.

Suppose that the land is owned in common and each of the owners can choose, consulting only their own interests, how many cows they wish to graze on the land. Each will invest in further cattle so long as the average revenue obtained from each cow is less than its average cost. This will be true so long as the total revenue from the land is greater than the total cost, since average cost and average revenue are simply total revenue and total cost divided by the same figure, the total number of cows.

In terms of Figure 9.1, therefore, additional investments will be made up to the point at which total revenue equals total cost, that is up to the point that TR intersects TC, a total investment indicated by $Q_E$ on the horizontal axis. That this would be over-investment in this case is obvious since $Q_E$ is greater than $Q_{max}$ so that total revenue could be higher with less invest-ment. From the point of view of social efficiency it would clearly be better to obtain a higher total output from a lower total input.

Although the input $Q_{max}$ indicates a level of input which achieves one possible optimum, the maximum total output, this is not in fact the most economically efficient output from a social point of view. The reason why it is a maximum is that at this point any investment in further cattle does not increase total output at all. This means that an investment which costs resources yields a zero return, and from society's point of view this is clearly not optimal. The resource is still being overused, and it would be better if there were fewer cattle being grazed there. The optimal output is that at which an increase in the value of the output resulting from additional investment is just equal to the cost of that investment. In Figure 9.1 the optimal level of investment, the investment which yields the optimal output, is marked on the horizontal axis as $Q_o$. At this point the slope of the curve TR is just equal to the slope of the curve TC, that is marginal revenue equals marginal cost. At lower levels of input the additional revenue would be greater than the additional cost, so further investment would be profitable. At higher levels of input than this the additional revenue would be less than the additional cost so cutting back would increase profits.

It is evident that this level of investment is economically efficient. It is also clear that if the land were under the control of a single person or firm seeking to maximise profits then $Q_o$ would be the profit maximising level of input. So the level of investment and of output would be economically efficient from society's point of view if the land were owned by a self-seeking single owner, but not if the land were owned and used communally by people, also, of course, assumed to be individually pursuing their own interests.

Obviously the conclusions derived from this analysis provide a justification for the view that the enclosure of land and the abolition of common ownership improves efficiency and is an inevitable step to take in the course of economic progress.

Curiously the analysis also provides some support for a view from the other end of the political spectrum. Marx argued that the private ownership of land is a barrier to investment. The analysis above demonstrates that, at least at one level, this view is correct. Manifestly, investment in the land, the number of cattle grazing on it, would be greater if the land were used communally than if it was privately owned. Nevertheless the analysis also demonstrates that the implication embedded in the Marxian argument, that greater investment would be socially better, is incorrect. Further investment beyond $Q_o$ would not benefit society since although total output might be greater, the costs of achieving that increased output would be greater than the benefit. The Marxian view that more investment is necessarily better does not take into account the fact that there are diseconomies of scale.

Nevertheless the analysis does not wholly undermine a Marxian position. There are some finer points which need to be borne in mind. Suppose that the land which had been farmed communally is taken over by a landlord and enclosed and that he employs the former users of the land. Since investment is reduced fewer people will be employed than used the land before and some will become unemployed and be forced to seek employment elsewhere. Competition for the jobs remaining will almost certainly cause the wages of those continuing to be employed on the land to fall below the incomes they obtained before. On the other hand the profits accruing to the landowner will increase as he reduces inputs to economically efficient levels. Thus although enclosure may be socially efficient if we seek to maximise net social costs, this conclusion is based on the assumption that we can add up revenues, whoever receives them, and compare them with total costs, whoever bears them. But the economic benefits of enclosure accrue to the land owners, not to the workers. From a national point of view efficiency may be increased, and hence net national output, but the income distribution may be worsened, and most of the population may actually be worse off (Evans 1992).

It is worth pointing out what may be forgotten, that both the analysis and the argument depend upon the assumption that, however the land may be owned, each person pursues their own self-interest. Even if the land is owned communally, each of the owners is assumed to act in a self-interested way. While it may be true that a single land owner may do this, it is less likely if the land is owned communally. In that case there is likely to be some communal view as to what is likely to be in the common interest and, probably, some means of ensuring that the community as a whole acts in its own best interests. In one of the few investigations of the way in which common ownership actually operates, Stevenson (1991) found that this was indeed the case. He looked at the operation of the systems used for controlling the grazing of cattle in the Swiss Alps. In this area the system of common ownership had survived yet by no stretch of the imagination could Switzerland be described as having a backward economy.

What happens is that the cattle belonging to the people of a village are grazed on the lower pastures in the winter (or kept indoors), but are taken up to upper meadows, the alps, in the summer. In both cases the land is owned in common by the villagers. The grazing and, in particular, the movement of the cattle up and down the mountainsides in spring and autumn, are not uncontrolled and left to the decision of individuals. There are formal and informal agreements covering the arrangements and procedures for making communal decisions with respect to the timing of the movement of the cattle. These arrangements prevent the over-grazing which might other-wise occur if each pursued their own self-interest. Stevenson also found, though this was not the primary object of his research, that arrangements of a similar kind existed to control the farming of the common lands which existed in England before they were enclosed. Thus common land use and ownership need not be inefficient, but for it to be efficient those farming it have to work together and not pursue their own narrow self-interest. But the evidence is that actually they do, and Stevenson (1991) found that common property in Switzerland could perform as efficiently as private property, but only under fairly restricted circumstances. Thus the conclu-sion is that common ownership is likely to be less efficient, but need not be the tragedy alleged by Hardin (1968). It may also be more equitable (Evans 1992).

Even though the ownership of land in common may not necessarily be inefficient, problems can arise when the two types of land tenure come into conflict. In particular, a society which relies on the concept of ownership in common faces difficulties in any conflict with a society which depends on the concept of individual land ownership. The latter is likely to, indeed has to, rely on deeds, registration, contracts, and other forms of evidence of title. The former need not have such evidence. After all, if the land is owned communally by the tribe or the clan or the village or the nation, who does it need to prove title to? An obvious example of the problem is provided by European settlement of North America. The indigenous peoples did not have anything to prove their title to the land which they gathered food from and hunted over. They were therefore regarded as having no title to it, until, in the end, most land had been settled by Europeans. The process was repeated during the European settlement of Australia. Since settlement there is more recent than in America and aboriginal attachment to parti-cular areas of land remains very clear the right to these lands has become a current political problem, and one of considerable interest and importance in some parts of the country as the (European) owners of leaseholds from the Crown seek to retain 'their' land while the indigenous peoples seek the recovery of 'their' land.

## A libertarian view

At the opposite end of any scale running from communality to individu-alism we find the view put forward by Cobin (1997). He argues that, at least in the United States, the owner of land should owe no duties to the state whatever. Unaffected by planning controls and taxes the owner of land should be free to do whatever he or she wants. Their rights can only be curtailed if they freely and voluntarily enter into agreements with other land owners or with other parties, and Cobin expresses the belief that where this is necessary the market will ensure that the right mechanisms exist, but that where they are not necessary no government should be available to impose controls or constraints. Thus each land owner becomes a kind of miniature autonomous state.

In fact Cobin appears to go further than this. He seems sometimes to be arguing not only that land ownership should involve no rights and responsibilities other than those freely entered into by private treaty, but also that, in the United States, by virtue of the revolution against British rule, land actually is held in this way, if only the legal position were correctly interpreted. The argument is based on the point that we made at the beginning of this chapter, that in the United Kingdom it is theoretically the position that land is owned from the Crown. When, therefore, the Americans rebelled against the Crown they asserted their right to own their land independently, and this also implied that they held it independently of any duty to their new state or their new president. We can leave aside this legal question since it does not concern us, and the position as it is currently interpreted in US law is likely to continue. Of slightly greater interest, however, is the extreme libertarian view put forward by Cobin that land ought to be owned in this way, and although with typical American solipsism he does not say so, he presumably feels that land should be held in this way outside the United States as well as within it.

His justification for this view is based on a faith in the market. The market will ensure that agreements would be made between land owners to control the use of land if these agreements were thought necessary by them, and if they are not thought to be necessary then they will not be made. Implicit in this conclusion is an assumption that the views of the owners of land coincide with the wants of society so that if agreements are not thought to be necessary by the owners of the land then they are not necessary for the protection of the rest of society.

Cobin's argument is prefaced and defended by a discussion of the necessity, or otherwise, of building regulations using empirical evidence. He shows that despite the increase in the number of regulations dealing with fire safety in Baltimore, MD, the number of fires has increased disproportionately. This, of course, fails to recognise that most fire regulations are aimed at preventing the spread of fires and consequent loss of life and property since fire prevention would be impossible. He shows that in a region in Virginia some counties enforce building regulations but some do not, but that houses built in the latter areas are built to the same standards as those in the former. This demonstrates, he argues, that building control by government is unnecessary. He goes on to argue that if it were thought necessary, the private sector would supply it, and points out that in the field of numismatics (coin collection) independent experts, for a fee, certificate the authenticity of coins.

All of this fails to recognise that it is not the normal builder which may be the problem but the 'cowboy' seeking to cut corners. Also, that while the original buyer of a house may be able to require evidence of good construction, tenants, users of the building, and even the buyers of parts of a building may be in a much weaker position. In other words Cobin presumes a wish to provide a good product. But this wish may not exist. Even when they are meant to be enforced by governments building regulations may be ignored. For example, in Italy about a third of the houses built in the last 50 years have been built without planning permission and outside building control. A result is the occasional collapse of a building. The most notorious recent case was the collapse of a six-storey block of flats in Foggia in the south east of the country in November 1999. At least 67 people were killed. It has been suggested by the research institute Censis that three-and-a-half million dwellings are at risk (Piccinato 2000; Jones 2003, p. 215).

The evasion of government regulations when they exist gives the lie to the view that they would be voluntarily obeyed by builders and developers if they were not legally enforceable. In this respect it is odd that Cobin claims that the collapse of a department store in Seoul in 1995 provides an argument against government regulation. After all the owners had illegally constructed an extra storey and installed a swimming pool on the roof. Given that they had evaded the legally enforceable government regulation there seems no reason to suppose that they would have complied with any voluntary code.

An accessible example of the problem of enforcing quasi-voluntary regulation is available in the market for rented housing in Britain. After a number of deaths from poor maintenance of gas fires and heating the landlords of rented properties are now required to show that gas appliances have been checked for safety if asked by a prospective tenant. While nearly all landlords are happy to comply I have been told by Reading students that it is not unknown for a landlord to refuse to comply and also to refuse to let a house to those asking to see such a certificate regarding them as obvious trouble makers who are likely to be difficult tenants.

It is argued that in Italy the periods when houses have been built most badly have been boom periods when the demand is greatest. It is precisely when the demand for space is greatest that builders and developers are most likely to cut corners, and also that would-be occupiers are in a weak bargaining position in demanding certification (Piccinato 2000). It is precisely because there is a high demand for rented accommodation in southern England that landlords can refuse to comply. After all, in their view, eventually someone will come along who doesn't ask questions.

It is unlikely that many people, other than American economists, would have such faith in the powers of the market as to believe that no government intervention in the market for land and property should be either required or permitted. Nevertheless what we have tried to show is that this faith can be misguided. Even when governments try to enforce controls they may be evaded, buildings may collapse and people may die. Such deaths may be thought by some to be a price worth paying to have less government intervention, but this is unlikely to be a view held in western Europe.

## Summary

What we have tried to do in this chapter is to show that land – and hence the market for land, the use of land, the ownership of land, is not some abstract economic good or factor of production. Land has social and political importance. Its ownership may give political power. The ownership of land and property may cause people to behave differently and to have different political views.

Furthermore, land may be owned and used in different ways. Apart from owner occupation and the occupation of property by a tenant paying rent to a landlord, there is also the possibility of ownership of the land in common by a group. If property is owned in common then the group is likely to construct rules to regulate the way in which the property is used. An obvious example is the meeting of all those who own properties in a condominium to decide on the maintenance of the exterior and grounds for the following year. A similar modern example is the time-share agreement set up by the agent with respect to a holiday villa or apartment.

Finally, we argued that land and property cannot be owned apart from the rest of society. As John Donne memorably put it 'No man is an island'. The ownership of land involves responsibilities towards those who might live in it, or visit it. It also involves responsibilities towards those who live nearby. But a discussion of these would take us into the economics of town planning and that is part of another book.

# 10

## Ownership and Control: Monopoly

### *'Baby, you're a rich man'*

### Introduction

The assumption generally made in mainstream neoclassical economics has always been, as we have stressed, that land will be rented out or used by its owner to obtain the highest possible current income. Nevertheless in classical economics there were perceived to be situations in which this assumption might not hold. This chapter and the next consider two of these.

In this chapter we consider the possibility that a landowner may be able to extract a higher total income from a property if the use of part of it is restricted, so that a higher rent may be extracted from the remainder. To achieve this the landowner has to have some kind of monopoly power over the product or service derived from using the land so that the additional income can be called monopoly rent. The idea of monopoly rent was put forward by Adam Smith, and was discussed by a number of classical economists, including Marx. The concept was always applied by them to the agricultural land market, and to the production of vintage wines. We show that it has a wider relevance and can be applied to modern urban uses such as shopping centres where a single land owner can exercise control over and limit uses so as to maximise the total rent from the centre.

### Monopoly rents and wine production

The concept of monopoly rent appears in Adam Smith's *An Inquiry into the Nature and Causes of the Wealth of Nations* and in the work of numerous other classical authors. It even appears in the work of some twentieth century authors such as Chamberlin, and was rediscovered and reintroduced by the radical geographer David Harvey in the 1970s. I have explored this history elsewhere (Evans 1991). What is clear from this literature is that there is a problem of definition. Sometimes the term is used to mean that if owner A obtains a higher rent for his or her land than owner B does for a similar urban site then he or she has obtained a monopoly rent because A has a 'monopoly' of the site. This is suggested by Chamberlin (1933), for example. But actually the difference in rent usually arises because A's site is better located than B's site, for example they are both sites for shops but more pedestrians pass A's site than B's. The difference in rent is then an example of 'differential rent' and to call it monopoly rent is misleading.

In the 1970s the term was sometimes used in a way which was tautological and therefore virtually meaningless. Harvey (1973), for example, argued that since each piece of land could be distinguished from any other piece of land, the owner of any piece of land had a monopoly in respect of this land. It followed that the land owners as a group or class had a monopoly over the land that they owned since they were the only suppliers of land. Defining all land owners as the class of land owners it then followed that the rent that they received was a monopoly class rent. In this argument the terms 'monopoly' and 'class' are merely being introduced because of their pejorative connotations. The terminology adds nothing to our understanding of the land and property market. The rents described remain differential rents.

The situation where a true monopoly rent might be obtained was described by the classical authors who usually used wine as an example. The argument, as it has been developed, can be demonstrated using Figure 10.1. Land area is measured along the horizontal axis and rents are indicated on the vertical axis. The area of land owned by a single land owner is represented by OQ on the horizontal axis. This land can be used for growing some ordinary product which we can call corn. The market price of corn is independent of the amount grown on this land, so the market rent of the land if corn were grown is given by OP on the vertical axis, with a horizontal demand curve PP'. The land can also be used for growing grapes for wine production, and the wine produced from grapes grown at this location is assumed to have qualities which make it distinctive. The wine can therefore be labelled by its district of origin. In the terms used in the French wine industry it may be regarded as an 'Appellation Controlee'.

A monopoly rent can be extracted if the demand curve for this wine is downward sloping so that the less that is produced the higher is the price obtained for it. It follows that if less land is used for wine production the higher the rent that can be obtained and if more land is used for wines the lower the rent. The demand curve for land for wine therefore slopes downward and is shown in Figure 10.1 by the line marked AR.

If this area of land were owned by many small land owners, who all behaved competitively, then this competition would ensure that the income or rent for each hectare would be the same whether corn or wine was produced. In the figure the intersection of AR with the horizontal line PP′ at Y determines the allocation of land to each use – OT, on the horizontal axis, is used for wine, and the rest, OTQ, for corn.

If, however, a single land owner or landlord owns the whole area the uses to which the land is put can be restricted, either directly, as the occupier and user of the land, or indirectly, as the landlord, through constraints in the contracts with tenants. If then the amount of land used for wine production is restricted, a higher price can be obtained for the wine and a higher income or rent from the land. The argument can be demonstrated using the figure. The downward sloping line marked as MR indicates the additional revenue obtained from allocating each further hectare to wine production. This falls faster than the demand curve AR because as each unit of land is added the price falls both for that unit and for the land already used for wine production. The land owner's income is maximised if the allocation of land between the two uses is determined by the intersection of curve MR with the horizontal line PP′ at X. It is worth allocating or allowing additional land to wine production so long as the additional or marginal revenue is greater than or equal to the income from using the land for growing corn. In the

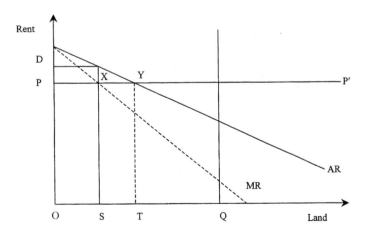

**Figure 10.1**

figure the allocation of land is shown along the horizontal axis – OS is used for wine and SQ for corn. OS is, of course, less than the amount of land which would be used for wine if land ownership were fragmented and competitive.

In the figure the rent or income from the land used for wine production is indicated by the point D and OD is higher than the rent of land for corn production, OP. The difference PD can be called a monopoly rent. It should be noted, nevertheless, that this monopoly rent is achieved by withholding an area of land, ST in the figure, from the use which would appear to be more profitable. As we have said, this may be achieved by restrictive agreements, if the land is tenanted, or by the owner's own actions if he or she is the user. It is also possible, of course, for small owners to enter into cooperative agreements to mutually restrict the output of wine from their area. It has been suggested that this may happen in France (Loyat 1988). In whatever way it is achieved, while a monopoly rent is obtained for some land, other land is not allowed to be used for its 'highest and best use'.

## Monopoly rents and shopping centres

While it is clear that the concept of monopoly rent can be used in the analysis of the land market in wine growing areas, it is very difficult indeed to think of other agricultural products where restrictions on the use of land would allow a monopoly rent to be extracted. It is no accident that the classical economists always used wine production as an example in their discussions of monopoly rents. And if it can only be applied to wine production the analysis of monopoly rent would be very limited in its scope, a curiosity.

It is, however, possible that the analysis of monopoly rents can shed some light on the operation of the land and property market in other areas where all the sites are under the control of a single owner. An obvious example is the modern commercial shopping centre, often a single building or a complex of buildings with a surrounding car park, the North American shopping mall or the French 'centre commercial'. These differ from normal town centre shopping in that in the town centre the sites will be owned and controlled by numerous companies and institutions each seeking to obtain the highest possible income from their properties, not by one company seeking to maximise its total net income.

For example, using the analysis and diagram in the preceding section, the owner of a centre may calculate that if, say, the number of banks in the centre is limited then a higher rent can be obtained from each bank allowed to operate in the centre, possibly only one bank, because there is less competition. And that this rent would be higher than the competitive rent which could be obtained for the other sites used by ordinary shops, and that this will be unaffected by the number of competing banks.

The situation can be made more complicated, but possible more realistic, if it is assumed that there is a downward sloping demand curve for each use but that the demand for one use, banks say, is less elastic than the demand for, say, clothing stores. This is because people go in for comparison shopping in the case of clothing so there is actually some advantage if there are many of them. They do not do so in the case of uses such as banking. Diagrammatically the position is as shown in Figure 10.2. The area of the shopping centre is represented along the horizontal axis and the total amount of space available is then OQ. For simplicity we assume that there are only two uses, B and C, or banks and clothing. Rents are represented on the vertical axes at O and at Q. The demand curve for space for B slopes downward to the right from the left-hand vertical axis and the demand curve for space for C slopes downward to the left from the right-hand axis.

If the sites were owned by a number of competing owners the position would be as it was analysed in Chapter 2 using the marginalist or neo-classical model and Figure 2.3. Equilibrium would be reached when the rents for all the space were the same. This is indicated in Figure 10.2 by the intersection of the two demand curves at Y. The equilibrium rent would be

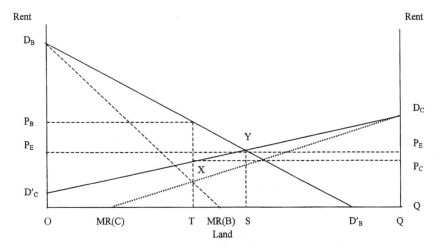

**Figure 10.2**

as indicated by $P_E$, the amount of space used for B would be OS and the remaining space, SQ, would be used for C.

Suppose, on the other hand, that all the sites are owned by a single landlord, and competition from sites outside the shopping centre is restricted, by distance for example. The owner can then price discriminate. The result can be demonstrated using Figure 10.2. The marginal revenue curves for each use are drawn as dashed lines sloping downward below their respective demand curves. Each curve shows the (net) additional revenue, from sites in this use, which would be obtained from allocating an additional unit of space to this use. The profits of the owner are maximised when the marginal revenues from site reallocation are the same so that profits cannot be increased by taking a site away from one use and reallocating it to the other. In the figure this is indicated by the point of intersection of the two marginal revenue curves.

To maximise profits the owner restricts the amount of space allocated to the use with the less elastic demand, reallocating it to the other. So in this case use B is restricted. Only OT is allocated to it, less than the amount OS which it would occupy in a competitive market. On the other hand use C occupies TQ, a greater amount of space than SQ which it would occupy in a competitive market. The rent for space used for C will be lower, $QP_C$ instead of $QP_E$, while the rent for the use with the inelastic demand will be higher, $OP_B$ instead of $OP_E$.

That something of this sort occurs is clear from the evidence relating to the distribution of different types of uses in different types of shopping centre. For example Table 10.1 is derived from research by West, Von Hohenbalken & Kroner (1985) into the distribution of uses in 'planned' and 'unplanned' shopping centres in Canada. The table divides the uses into two groups. One group consists of those uses where more shops might make more people visit the centre in order to make comparisons, and the other group consists of uses such as banks and pharmacies where comparison shopping is neither usual nor, generally, beneficial to the shopper. The evidence indicates that, generally, there are proportionately more of the former kind of use in 'planned' centres than in 'unplanned', but there are proportionately fewer of the latter. Thus the evidence tends to confirm the view that the owners of shopping centres price discriminate, charging higher rents to uses with inelastic demands and restricting the proportion of the total space that they occupy.

Nevertheless the evidence does not actually confirm that the owners are engaged in exploiting their monopolistic position to extract monopoly

**Table 10.1** Average numbers of different types of stores in planned shopping malls and unplanned regional shopping centres, Edmonton (1977).

| | Multipurpose shoppers (Smaller customer base) | | | Multipurpose shoppers (Large customer base) | | | Comparison shoppers | |
|---|---|---|---|---|---|---|---|---|
| | Planned mall | Unplanned regional | | Planned mall | Unplanned regional | | Planned mall | Unplanned regional |
| Restaurants | 6.00 | 5.00 | Bank | 2.11 | 2.75 | Sporting goods | 0.67 | 1.37 |
| Drug | 0.89 | 1.12 | Music store | 1.44 | 1.25 | Men's clothing | 3.44 | 0.38 |
| Beauty shop | 1.33 | 2.37 | Book store | 1.11 | 1.00 | Women's clothing | 7.89 | 0.50 |
| Barber shop | 0.78 | 2.00 | Florist | 0.89 | 0.88 | Shoes | 4.22 | 0.63 |
| Dry cleaners | 0.78 | 1.00 | Liquor store | 0.67 | 0.13 | Misc. apparel | 1.00 | 0.38 |
| Supermarket | 0.89 | 0.63 | Shoe repair | 0.22 | 0.25 | Jewelry | 2.78 | 0.50 |
| Petrol station | 0.22 | 0.63 | Meat and fish market | 0 | 0.50 | Travel agency | 0.67 | 0.88 |
| Grocer | 1.11 | 1.12 | Gift and novelty | 3.11 | 1.00 | Department store | 1.67 | 0 |
| Bakery | 0.22 | 1.25 | Candy and nut | 1.22 | 0 | Variety store | 0.44 | 0.25 |
| — | | | Hobby, toy and game | 1.22 | 0.38 | Family clothing | 2.00 | 0.13 |
| — | | | Cigar | 1.33 | 0 | Camera | 0.67 | 0.13 |
| — | | | Misc. food | 1.00 | 0.25 | Luggage | 0.33 | 0.38 |
| — | | | Stationery | 0.22 | 0.13 | Sewing | 1.00 | 0.38 |
| — | | | News dealers | 0 | 0.13 | Women's accessory | 0.67 | 0 |
| — | | | Film developers | 0.22 | 0.13 | Children's clothes | 0.78 | 0 |
| — | | | — | | | Furriers | 0.11 | 0.25 |

Source: West *et al.* 1985, p. 114

rents. The owners of shopping centres may engage in discrimination for other reasons. For example, it is well known that the developers of major shopping centres seek to let a section of their space to an 'anchor' store and that they try to let this space first of all. The view is that people will visit the anchor store whatever other shops are located in the centre. Once some of the space has been let to such a store it becomes easier to let the remaining space since the tenants can be guaranteed that there will be some passing trade.

The developers of centres may therefore let space to an anchor store at a discount. Indeed it is not unknown for the rental for an initial period to be zero, even for a premium to be paid by the owner to the tenant to ensure their presence in the centre. Clearly this is price discrimination and equally clearly it can only occur because the whole centre is owned and controlled by a single landlord. It could not occur if the ownership of the centre was split up and numerous land owners competed with each other.

Nevertheless this behaviour does not appear to be explained by the monopoly rent analysis. It would appear that in this case the situation is explained by the fact that one use, the anchor store, generates trade for other uses, that is it creates positive externalities. The differences in rents, and the possibility of premiums being paid, can be explained in economic terms as the internalisation of these externalities. Monopolistic behaviour implies a welfare loss. The internalisation of positive externalities does not, indeed implies a possible welfare gain, so that a more refined analysis of the theory and the evidence would be necessary to decide the welfare benefits or losses incurred through price discrimination by the owners of shopping centres.

## Summary and conclusions

In this chapter we have analysed the concept of monopoly rent. The term is sometimes used mistakenly, to refer to what is actually differential rent, and sometimes used pejoratively to refer to any or all rent. We have tried to show that monopoly rent can arise with a product such as wine which can only be produced on some land and where the rent or income obtained can be increased if production is reduced by limiting the amount of land used for production of the good.

We have also showed that the idea of monopoly rent can be applicable to urban uses where a single land owner has control over a large development such as a shopping centre. The owner can then price discriminate charging higher rents for some uses and restricting the amount of space available for those uses. Although this behaviour may not result from an attempt to extract monopoly rent but from an attempt to 'internalise externalities', both result in some space being let for less than it might and some other space being let at a higher rent than it would have been. In either case, therefore, the price of land is not determined solely by the market, and some land is let for less than its 'highest and best' rent.

# 11

# Ownership and Control: Minimum Rents

## *'Wait'*

---

## Introduction

In the previous chapter we looked at the ways in which the owners of land may behave monopolistically. In this chapter we look at a second way in which the owners of land may restrict the use of land which they own so that it is not used for the activity which would yield the highest current income. In the case considered here this can only occur if the land is occupied by tenants and rented to them by landlords. In this respect it is related to discussions in Chapters 7 and 8 which were also concerned with the landlord–tenant relationship. It is argued that if land is owned by landlords who let it to tenants then there is a minimum rent which landlords would be willing to accept and that they will refuse to rent land to tenants at any rent below this minimum. Moreover, this would be so even if the land would be used, rather than left unused, if it were occupied by the owner who could derive a positive income from its use.

The concept of a minimum rent was put forward by Marx, who called it absolute rent. Marx himself did not give any clear reasons why absolute rent should occur. Nevertheless, whatever may have been the reasons that he had in mind, we demonstrate that modern economic analysis, using the concepts of transaction costs, monitoring costs, and risk and uncertainty, provides an explanation for the existence a minimum rent, although this minimum may vary from landlord to landlord, from use to use, and from site to site. More extensive discussions of Marxian absolute rent and of a modern interpretation are given elsewhere (Evans 2000a, b).

## Minimum rents

The idea of a minimum rent was put forward by Marx in a very lengthy discussion in *Capital* (Marx 1894/1962, Chapter 45). Typically, as with much of the rest of the book, the discussion is rather opaque. Most historians of economic thought, for example Blaug (1997), have interpreted Marx as arguing that 'absolute rent' occurs in agriculture because investment in agriculture is lower than in other industries. As a result there remains a surplus which is appropriated by the landlord. However, this interpretation is difficult to reconcile with Marx's stress on the fact that, in his view, land will be farmed if it is owner occupied, provided the net income from doing so is positive, even when this net income is less than the minimum rent that a landlord would require. Or that such land might be rented out by a landlord if it could be associated in the tenancy agreement with other land which could be rented out at a rent greater than the 'absolute rent'.

In the light of these examples I have argued that he can be interpreted as saying that landlords will not rent out their land for less than some minimum for other reasons, as he says, they will not be philanthropic. Thus less land is let to tenants and so investment in land is lower because less land is being farmed. So the lower investment in agriculture is caused by the existence of a minimum rent rather than vice versa. Of course, to accept this argument one has to accept that Marx had insight into why landlords would be unwilling to let land below some minimum even though he could not explain why. And that this was because the economic reasons which are necessary to an explanation – transactions costs, monitoring costs, risk and uncertainty – were not concepts current in classical economics and only came to prominence in economic analysis in the second half of the twentieth century.

For our present purposes the history of the idea might be regarded as irrelevant. This is true, except for the fact that the concept is met with, to my knowledge, nowhere else and the discussion by Marx provides some evidence that the phenomenon of a minimum rent could be observed in practice at that time, even if its existence could not be satisfactorily explained. Here, therefore, we are concerned with providing an explanation for the existence of such a minimum rent, and with its possible relevance to the land market of the present day.

The reasons for the existence of an absolute or minimum rent are, as we have said, threefold. The first is the cost of setting up the agreement between the landlord and the tenant, the transaction costs. The letting of a property by the owner requires the expenditure of time and money to negotiate an agreement, and may involve paying others, lawyers or land agents in particular, to make sure that it is legally watertight. These transaction costs are to some extent a fixed cost associated with any letting. Because of this it is evident that no landlord would be willing to let a very small area of land at a very low rent because the income generated would not pay the costs of the transaction. It is also evident that if the land were occupied by the owner no transaction costs are involved – no agreement needs to be drawn up or put into force. So land which would be used if it were owner occupied might not be let out by a landlord.

The second reason is the cost of monitoring the operation of the agreement, that is the use of the land by the tenant. It is in the interest of the land owner that the tenant treats the property in such a way that it is worth at least as much at the end of the lease as it was at the beginning. In the case of farmland the land should not be made less fertile or otherwise degraded. Buildings have to be kept at a certain level of repair. The buildings, the land, and the way that they are used during the period of the lease have to be monitored by the landlord, or by an agent. In agriculture, in Britain, this agent is called a land agent and land agency is a branch of the surveying profession. The role of the land agent is to act on behalf of a large land owner both in setting up the tenancy and in ensuring that the tenants stick by their agreements. The cost of employing the land agent to monitor a tenancy has to be covered by the rent received. It follows that if the rental which is likely to be received from letting a piece of land is too low to cover these costs then letting the land out is not worthwhile. Once again, if the land were owner occupied the land would be used. The problem of monitoring does not arise since, in effect, the owner monitors his or her own activities as occupier.

The third reason why landlords may be unwilling to let land at a very low rent is the problem of risk and uncertainty. Or rather, the interaction between uncertainty as to the future income which can be derived from the property and the tenant's requirement that the property should be let for a reasonably lengthy period to provide security. In much economic analysis it has been the assumption that the future is predictable and that there was therefore no uncertainty. This assumption was certainly implicit in the work of the classical economists. It may be a useful simplifying assumption to make in many circumstances but it may also sometimes be misleading since the future is not certain and people make provision for this uncertainty. Therefore some features of economic life may only be explicable if the future is assumed to be not certain, of which the idea of a minimum rent may be one.

Suppose, for example, that a would-be tenant of a piece of land can estimate the average future profit that can be made from the use of a piece of land, recognising, however, that this is an average of a distribution of possible returns, some higher, some lower. To simplify matters considerably let us assume that there is a 50% probability of good weather, and that if the weather is good the tenant's profit, before rent but after providing a reward for his labour, would be $D + 50$. There is a 50% probability that the weather is bad and if this is so then the tenant's profit, similarly calculated, would be $D - 50$. It follows that the tenant's expected profit would be D and that a rent of up to that amount could be offered by the tenant. In most circumstances D would be greater than 50 and the landlord would be expected to accept the offer. Thus, suppose a tenant offers D and that the landlord can either accept D or wait until it becomes more certain what the weather conditions will be. If D were greater than 50 the landlord would have no incentive to wait. For if conditions are good the rent offered later would be $D + 50$, if bad $D - 50$, and the average rent received would be the same as that originally offered but the landlord would bear the risk not the tenant.

Suppose, on the other hand, that D is low and in particular that it is less than 50. The landlord then has an incentive to wait. If the weather is good the tenant offers $D + 50$, but if the weather is bad the tenant does not make an offer because the expected profit of $D - 50$ is less than zero. The return to the landlord is the average of zero and $D + 50$ which is greater than D since D is less than 50. It follows that if D is high the landlord will accept the tenant's original offer but if D is low this offer will be rejected. The landlord then bears the risk of waiting and may either receive a rent more than double the original offer or not let the property. It is evident that there appears to be some rent below which the landlord will not let the property out.

Of course, if the tenancy is for one period and the uncertainty is not resolved by the time the period starts neither the landlord nor the tenant can afford to wait any longer and the landlord may accept the amount offered, low as it is. The situation is different, however, if the standard tenancy agreements commit the landlord to leasing the land to a tenant for two or more periods. Conditions may change. The rent currently on offer from any tenant is small. If the landlord waits conditions may improve and a rent may be obtained which would be much higher than the current offer. On the other hand conditions may not improve and may get worse so that no rent at all can be obtained in the future, but very little has been lost by waiting because the current offer was so low.

In effect the landlord's best strategy is to state some minimum below which the land will not be rented. Lower offers can be rejected, at small cost since they are so small, in the hope or expectation that at some time in the future, when economic or other conditions improve, a much higher rent can be obtained. The more substantial rent received in the later periods will be expected to more than cover the (small) losses made earlier when the land was left unoccupied.

Note that if the land were owned and occupied by the same person it would be used. This bears out Marx's insight mentioned at the beginning of this section. It is the landlord and tenant system, coupled with the need for a lease to be for a reasonably lengthy period, which can result in land being left idle and unoccupied because some minimum rent cannot be obtained. The need for a lease to be of some length is in the interest of both landlord and tenant but primarily in the interest of the latter. The tenant makes a commitment to the site and an investment which may be financial, but which may be mainly in the form of the 'human capital' invested in acquiring a knowledge of the land and the property. And this is in addition to the social attachment to the location which we discussed in Chapters 7 and 8.

Note also that this minimum rent is likely to be highly variable, varying from area to area and site to site. There will not be some standard minimum 'absolute' rent below which no property will be let. After all, to cite a rather extreme example, it is evident that the huge ranches in the Australian outback may be let at a rent per acre which would be regarded as derisory in most of western Europe.

Whatever its level, some minimum rent is likely to be set by each landlord for each piece of land. Therefore some land which would be farmed if all of it were owner occupied would be left unused if it were owned by landlords who would wish to let it to tenants. Thus the landlord–tenant system will itself affect the way the land is used. The argument is demonstrated using Figure 11.1. Rent per unit of land area is indicated on the vertical axis and distance from the market is shown along the horizontal axis. The figure shows a standard Von Thunen/Alonso relationship between the rent of land and distance from the market, with the rent of land falling at a decreasing rate as distance increases. In the case of agriculture the slope of the curve is a consequence of the cost of transporting the produce of the land to the market. In the figure the lower of the two curves shows the position if all the land is owner occupied. In this case the 'rent' is implicit being the return to the occupier after meeting all costs including implicit cost of the owner's labour. This 'rent' declines to zero at the margin of cultivation.

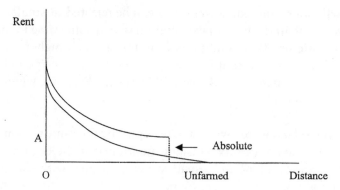

**Figure 11.1**

If the land is owned by landlords and leased by them to tenants then the land will not be let at less than some minimum rent. We assume that this can be regarded as the same for all the land at the margin of cultivation and so shown as OA on the vertical axis in Figure 11.1. In the figure the upper of the two curves shows the rent gradient if all land is owned by landlords. Some land at the margin will not be cultivated which would have been if it were owner occupied, so that the margin of cultivation is closer to the city than it would otherwise have been. The demand for produce is the same at the market as it was, but less land is now cultivated. This land therefore has to be farmed more intensively. The restricted supply of land means that rents will be higher throughout the area of land which is cultivated, although, as can be seen from the figure, not by as much as the level of the minimum rent.

It follows that the prevailing system of tenure can have real effects. It can affect the way in which land is farmed and its intensity of use. It can also affect the level of rents and because this increases costs the price of the goods produced will be higher. Nevertheless we would not expect the effects to be large. The very fact that only Marx among the nineteenth century economists commented on the existence of a minimum rent suggests that even then it was not very noticeable and therefore not very large.

Finally we may note that Marx thought that the landlord tenant relationship would result in investment in agriculture being lower than it might have been, since investment would not take place on the marginal, untenanted, land. But the analysis based on Figure 11.1 shows that though less land is farmed, the land which is farmed is farmed more intensively. This means that investment in this land will be greater than it would have been in owner occupation. This higher investment will compensate in whole or in part for the investment which does not take place on the marginal land. Conceivably, therefore, the landlord and tenant system could result in greater agricultural investment not less.

## Minimum rents in an urban environment

The discussion in the previous section related to agriculture and to the system of tenure in agriculture. Clearly the question has to be raised, and will certainly have been asked by the reader, as to the relevance of the discussion to industrialised economies. Even in nineteenth century England there was a margin of cultivation (Chisholm 1968) but nowadays, in countries such as those of western Europe, almost all land is cultivated and there is virtually no margin of cultivation.

Nevertheless the concept is applicable and can be useful in explaining some features of the land market. A practical modern example of such a minimum rent is the rent charged for laying cable across land or for erecting aerials for cellular telephone networks. Theoretical economic analysis which neglected the arguments set out in the previous section would be likely to reach the conclusion that competition between land owners for rents would cause the rent charged to fall to almost nothing. In fact, the rents charged are not small. In Britain the Country Landowners Association and the National Farmers Union currently suggest to their members that the rent that they charge should be at least 35 pence per metre per annum or £350 per kilometre per annum equal to £560 per mile. Of course, it might be argued that in making such a recommendation the CLA/NFU are, in effect, rigging the market, except that the rate suggested is just that, a suggestion, and so there is no reason why competition should not cause the rent actually charged to fall below it.

In this case the most important reason why rents do not fall below some minimum level would seem to be transaction costs, in particular the cost of negotiating agreements with the various owners of contiguous pieces of land in order to set up a route for the cable. If land ownership is fragmented, negotiation with large numbers of land owners in order to find the least cost route may be lengthy and costly, and the delays and the costs of negotiation may wipe out any savings achieved through lower rents. From the points of view of both the telephone companies and the landowners a recognised rate is likely to simplify and speed up the process of negotiation.

For a piece of evidence which supports this view we only have to look at the position in the early 1980s when competition was introduced into the

British telephone market by the government. Mercury, the first competitor allowed into the field, wished to lay cables between major cities in order to transmit telephone signals in competition with British Telecommunications. The important thing to note from our point of view is that Mercury did not set out to arrange deals with a number of land owners in order to lay its cable. It entered into an agreement with a single landowner, British Rail, to be allowed to lay cable alongside its rail tracks. The rate which was agreed to be payable was equivalent to £2000 per mile per annum at current prices. This rate was significantly higher than the rate quoted earlier as that recommended by the CLA/NFU. Moreover, BR gained in other ways from the deal in that it could use part of the cable capacity for its own purposes so the 'real' rent was higher than the nominal rent. From Mercury's point of view it would appear that there was an advantage in negotiating a single agreement with a single landowner, even if this resulted in the firm paying a premium rent. This was preferable to trying to reduce the rent payable by negotiations with a large number of land owners. The transactions costs were kept down but the rent paid was higher.

Another example of minimum rents comes from the same industry. To set up cellular networks for mobile phones the companies need to locate aerials at suitable points across the country. If these aerials can be sited on the top of existing tall buildings then this saves the companies the cost of constructing towers. Once again, particularly where there are a number of such buildings, an economist might predict that competition between the owners would cause the rent paid to be close to zero. In fact, at the time of writing, the rent paid is likely to be at least £5000 per annum. Once again it is less costly for the companies to pay. Trying to save what, for them, would be a relatively small amount by negotiation with a number of building owners would be costly in terms of time and possible delay, if nothing else. Similarly, on the building owners' side, it is not worthwhile leasing the site for a very low rent, again because of transaction costs, monitoring costs, and risk.

We have argued that minimum rents exist, and that they exist because of transaction and monitoring costs, and because of the interaction between risk and uncertainty and the need for some security and permanence of tenure on the tenant's side. This interaction can also affect changes in use, not just the change from 'unused land' to 'used land'. An example of the way in which this interaction can affect land owner behaviour even when the property is far from the margin of cultivation is given by the early history of Centrepoint in central London. Built at the junction of New Oxford Street and the Tottenham Court Road in the mid-1960s the office block became notorious because it lay empty for many years. The left-wing argument, which was influential at the time, was that the owners were deliberately leaving the property empty, as well as others that they owned, in order to create a shortage of office space and force up rents. In fact, it required little thought to realise that this was not very plausible if the owners were behaving rationally. It would have been better from their point of view to buy up the land and delay constructing offices rather than constructing a very expensive and prominent building and leaving it empty. If the intention was to restrict supply what was done was both more expensive than the alternative of not building and it drew more attention to itself.

The real explanation appeared to be that the owners did, in fact, behave rationally but that the end result, leaving the building empty for nearly ten years, was not what they had expected or intended. The office space was intended to be let under the terms of a normal lease. Under these terms the initial rent would be fixed for a number of years, probably five or seven, with a rent review at the end of that period after which the rent would be fixed for a further period. During the late 1960s and early 1970s rents in central London were rising rapidly, from about £4 to about £20 per sq. ft per annum in 1973. It appears that in each year the owners of the property, Oldham Estates, correctly anticipated the rent obtainable in the following year would be higher than could be obtained in the current year. So if the current rent was £8 they asked, say, £10, on the grounds that if they accepted £8 they would be locked into this rent for the rent review period. They preferred to ask a higher rent, the rent which they expected to get next year anyway, even though there was a risk that they did not let the property in the current year.

In each year they were correct in their expectation that the rent in the following year would be substantially higher. On a year-to-year basis they were therefore correct in asking for a higher rent in the current year. Overall, of course, although they were consistently right in the short term, they were wrong in the long term. This is made absolutely obvious by the fact that the building was left unlet for a length of time which was longer than the normal five or seven-year rent review period. Thus they could have let the building for this period and still have obtained the higher rent after the rent review. Thus they certainly lost the rent for that period. Nevertheless what is clear from our point of view was that the owners were asking a high 'minimum' rent because of their anticipation that economic conditions would be better in the future and because of any tenant's need for a long-term contract. But it was the interaction between these factors which we argued in the previous section was an explanation for the existence of minimum rents in agriculture.

The same factors can affect the property market even when properties are to be sold rather than rented, though it is the permanence of development rather than the tenant's security which is then the factor interacting with risk and uncertainty. Capozza & Helsley (1990) demonstrate this in relation to rural land at the margin of urban development. The questions at issue are the time at which development will occur and the rent from the developed land at that time. In Chapter 5 we assumed that the future was risk free so that the rents obtainable from the land either used for agriculture or developed were known with certainty. The position is shown in the upper part of Figure 11.2. Time is shown on the horizontal axis and rent on the vertical axis. The horizontal line marked $R_F$ shows the expected income from agriculture, while the upward sloping line $R_1$ shows the expected income from urban development. The expected date of development is marked as $T_1$ on the horizontal axis since the income from the urban use is greater than the income from farming after that date, but lower before it.

Suppose, however, that the future is uncertain and that the rent from an urban use varies from year to year in an unpredictable way. The would-be developer may be able to observe the general trend and predict that urban rents will increase, on average, over time so that urban development would be profitable at some date. The questions are, again, what will be the date of development and what will be the rent from developed land at that time? The situation *ex post*, that is as revealed by the data after the event, is shown in the lower part of Figure 11.2. Time is shown on the horizontal axis

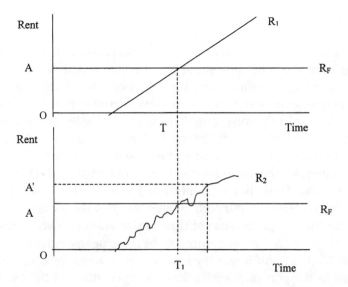

**Figure 11.2**

and rents on the vertical axis, as in the upper part of the figure. The agricultural rent is assumed not to vary and is, again, the horizontal line $R_F$. The rents from developed land are shown by the irregular line $R_2$. As in the upper figure this line first intersects with $R_F$ at time $T_1$, but development does not now occur at this time. That is because the developer does not know whether rents will stay above $R_F$ or drop below it again. Since development is irreversible, if they do fall, as is possible, even probable, then immediate development would result in a lower current income in the near future. To avoid this risk the developer will develop the site only when the rent obtainable is securely above the agricultural rent.

Because of uncertainty development takes place later than it would do otherwise and when the urban rent is higher. In the figure the urban rent at which development takes place is marked as OA' and this is substantially higher than the agricultural rent OA. At this level it is unlikely that the urban rent will fall below agricultural rent for very long, if it does so at all. The difference between the two rents, AA' in the lower figure, is analogous to the minimum or 'absolute' rent analysed earlier and it arises for similar reasons. In this case, however, the minimum is not the minimum rent needed to ensure the land is used but the minimum difference between rents required to ensure a change in the use of the land. The main difference between this and the analysis in the first part of this chapter is that this minimum does not depend upon the landlord–tenant relationship but on the permanence and irreversibility of change.

An example of the way in which the owners of land may require a price much higher than its current use value is provided by the situation in the London docklands after the docks themselves had closed. At that time, in the 1970s, the buildings were derelict, many sites were contaminated, and there was little demand for sites. But the then owner of much of the land, the Port of London Authority, was asking prices for their land which were thought unnecessarily high, given that the value of the sites seemed to be zero or near zero. But there was no advantage to the PLA in giving the sites away by selling them for nothing. By asking a higher price they lost nothing and could hope to get this price if and when the market improved, as in the end it did, after intervention by central government both in making tax relief available for location there, and in financing infrastructure construction.

The examples and analysis given above show that the concept of a minimum or absolute rent is relevant to an understanding of the operation of the land market in a modern economy. It is clear, nevertheless, that much more needs to be done to fill out the picture of the way in which uncertainty and irreversibility, whether temporary or permanent, interact with each other and delay the development or redevelopment of land.

## Summary and conclusions

In this and the previous chapter we have discussed two approaches to the analysis of land ownership which derive from the work of the classical economists. In this chapter we have looked at the way in which the owners of land may choose not to rent out (or, possibly, sell) their land at less than some minimum rent or price. This means that some land will not be used to yield its highest possible current income because tenants (or purchasers) will not be willing to pay this minimum. The result is land which is vacant or underused.

There are three reasons for the existence of this minimum rent or difference. The first is the cost of negotiating the contract, the second is the cost of monitoring its operation, and the third is the uncertainty of the income derivable from the property. This uncertainty interacts with the fact that any change is not immediately reversible. Land owners are therefore reluctant to accept an offer which is too low in case economic conditions change but the commitment that they have made prevents them accepting a new and better offer.

The problem of risk and uncertainty has been of major importance in explaining why minimum rents may exist, and it is a topic which we have touched on at various points so far in this book. In the following chapter we discuss the uncertainty caused by lack of information in the property market and show the way that this affects both the way the market operates and the way that buyers and sellers behave.

# 12

# Information, Uncertainty and the Property Market

## *'Magical mystery tour'*

### Introduction

The received theory of the market for land and property is basically a simple exposition of the theory of supply and demand. The presentation of the theory may be based on the Ricardian assumption that the land has one use and no alternative use, or it may be based on the neo-classical assumption that there are a number of alternative uses, or it may even be set out within the Marxian framework as a theory of differential rent. The alternative methods of presentation are, however, based on similar assumptions as to the workings of the market. These are that the market clears at all times and that the owners of the land will rent or sell it to the bidder who expects to derive the highest current income from it.

Implicitly or explicitly an associated assumption is also being made, namely that the participants in the market have full information as to the alternatives available. After all if this were not so, in one way or another, the owners would not be able to sell or rent their land to yield the highest current income. At a minimum, then, even if sellers do not know of the possible prices which buyers would be willing to pay, buyers must be aware of all the properties which are available, of their qualities and character-istics, of their suitability for the buyers' purposes, and hence are able to calculate the prices which they might be willing to offer for these proper-ties. Through some kind of bidding process then, the various properties are each bought, it is assumed, by the highest bidder.

Clearly this assumption is unrealistic. As we showed in Chapter 4, properties are heterogeneous. The property market is not like a stock market with a centralised trading floor, even if only a virtual or electronic one, on which, say, central London office space is continually and continuously traded. Sellers, as we have tried to demonstrate over the past six chapters, have differing attitudes toward the land that they own. They may be unwilling to sell, may even be unaware of the price of their land if they were to sell, and the prices that they ask will differ as they have differing perceptions of the value and uses of the land that they own. Therefore buyers and sellers cannot have full information, and to ignore the way this lack of information affects the way the market operates can only be misleading and lead to misleading, or even incorrect, conclusions. The aim of this chapter is to outline the effects of this lack of information, or uncertainty, on the way that the market operates.

We start, in the next section, by outlining the way in which economists have tried to analyse and model this situation. Buyers or sellers of some good search for information, it is argued. This search costs time, money, and resources. The buyers and sellers seek to optimise this process of search so that they do not carry on searching beyond the point where the cost of search would be greater than the likely benefit from further search. The changes in the behaviour of market participants in response to changes in the market environment or in response to changes in the searcher's own characteristics are set out in the third section of the chapter. In the fourth we present some empirical evidence relating to the way in which house buyers and house renters search for properties.

We then go on to outline the way in which the housing market as a whole will respond to changes, in particular to increases or decreases in demand. We show that one would expect to find, as one does, an inverse relationship between the number of properties on the market and the rate of increase in prices. When prices are rising rapidly there will be few properties to be found for sale, while falling prices will be associated with large numbers of properties advertised for sale.

Finally, we look at the market for land for development. Developers also have to search for land, and we show that when the amount of land which is available, that is the amount of land over which they can search, is limited by planning constraints, then if the limitation is effective, it will result in higher land and property prices. Moreover, this will be so even when there will appear to be much land available for development. Empirical evidence to support the argument is found in the effects of 'urban growth boundaries' declared in the state of Oregon where even with a potential 16 years land supply available, the price of land had increased.

## Modelling the search for information

The consequences of a lack of information amongst buyers and sellers have been explored in other areas of economics for some time, particularly labour economics (see, for example, Pissarides (2000)). The first attempt to deal with the problem was made by H.A. Simon (1959) who argued that it was clearly unrealistic to assume that consumers optimise when making decisions. They could not optimise, he argued, because they lack the necessary information on all the alternatives which might be available. In many cases, therefore, consumers must be unaware of goods and services which they would have preferred, if they had known about them, to those that they actually chose. Moreover, from the consumer's point of view, spending the time and resources necessary to find out all the alternatives available would be wasteful since, in many cases the choice made would remain the same, and in most other cases the improvement in 'welfare' would be negligible. Simon's view was that consumers should be regarded as 'satisficing' rather than 'optimising'. They did not attempt to make the best possible purchase, only to find something which was satisfactory or suitable enough for their purposes.

Simon's approach was not widely adopted, possibly because it assumed that consumers did not optimise. An alternative approach that was put forward by George Stigler (1961, 1962) is in some respects similar but assumes that consumers still behave rationally and optimise, and this has been the approach generally adopted. Consumers, and other buyers and sellers, are seen as searching through the environment that they inhabit to find what alternatives are available. The crucial assumption made by Stigler is that the process of searching and acquiring information is itself costly. Consumers therefore optimise by taking these costs into account and balancing the costs of further search against the possible benefits resulting from the acquisition of further information. Optimising is therefore not seen to be finding out all the alternatives available and choosing amongst them. The cost of search has also to be optimised. Finding out all the alternatives available would usually be sub-optimal because of the excessive cost of obtaining all this information. Potential buyers will therefore limit the extent of their search.

The other side of this particular coin is that would-be sellers need to provide information so that it is available cheaply to the buyer, otherwise buyers might not consider products, not because of their high price or low quality, but because it would not appear to be worthwhile expending resources finding out about them. In the context of search theory, if you build a better mousetrap, the world does not necessarily beat a path to your door. It only does so if you advertise the fact that you have built it, and even then it might be better to take it to the possible buyers rather than asking them to come to you. Sellers therefore advertise, employ agents and representatives, use marketing techniques, and otherwise ensure that their product is known to buyers.

Stigler modelled the behaviour of buyers with what has become known as the 'fixed sample rule'. Buyers take a sample of the products available and choose the best of that sample. For example, someone who needs a new tyre for their car might look up firms selling tyres in the area in the Yellow Pages. Then the would-be buyer would telephone, say, five of them and ask them to quote their prices for the tyre required, taking the car to the workshop of the firm quoting the lowest price. Note that the telephone is used to reduce the cost of search – the car owner could have gone to each of the firms, or written to them, or e-mailed them.

The fixed sample rule proposed by Stigler quickly gave way to a slightly more plausible model which does not assume that the size of the sample is fixed beforehand but that it can be changed (Pissarides 1985). The size of the sample is then itself determined by the information being obtained in the course of the search. Buyers carry on searching until they find the product at a price at which further search appears not to be worthwhile. The 'sequential optimal stopping rule', as it is called, assumes that buyers search, that search takes time, and that they consider whether or not to accept each option as it is found. In the original theoretical work there was no possibility of recall. For example, to continue with the motoring theme, the situation being modelled was like that of a car driver who needs to fill up with fuel and is driving along a road. Every mile or so there is a filling station displaying the prices it charges. As each one is approached the driver has to decide whether to stop there to fill the fuel tank. Passing the filling station means rejecting the price offer, and carries the possible benefit that a lower price may be found further down the road, but also carries the risk that either the car will run out of fuel, or that the prices found later will be higher. Recent theoretical work explores the implications of the more realistic assumption that some recall is possible, that is a combination of the two rules.

The theoretical work which is carried out is often based on the assumption that the buyer knows beforehand the distribution of prices, so that in the example above, the likely petrol price distribution is known through travel along similar roads elsewhere, and can be presumed to apply on this road as well. The essential concept in modelling the situation is that of the 'reservation price'. The buyer is assumed to set out, knowing the price distribution and with a reservation price in mind. In the example above, the car driver has a price in mind and will not pay more than this but will carry on searching until this reservation price is found. In practice, of course, and in some theoretical work, the buyer tends to find out the nature of the price distribution in the course of the search. So, for example, the car owner looking to buy a new tyre may conclude after ringing up the first three or four firms that they are all quoting very similar prices so that further search is unlikely to turn up anything very different. If, on the other hand, the first few calls reveal a fairly wide variation in the prices asked, the likely conclusion is that further search is likely to be worthwhile, since it may turn up a still lower price than that already found. Obviously in this example it is realistic to assume that it is possible to go back to and accept earlier price quotations.

The theory of search has mostly been developed with respect to the economic analysis of the labour market. The situation modelled is therefore frequently that of someone seeking a job. What the job searcher has in mind is therefore not a reservation price which is the highest that will be paid, but a reservation wage which is the lowest which will be accepted, that is the searcher is a seller rather than a buyer. Nevertheless the theory is obviously applicable to the property market, because, as in the labour market, information is not widespread and can be costly to obtain so that buyers, and sellers, have to search to find what they want. There is now a considerable literature, by both geographers and economists, exploring the ways in which house buyers search the market. Thus there is plenty of evidence, if it is needed, that buyers do search, that they obtain information in different ways and from different sources, depending on their circumstances, and that some search more intensively than others, and we will review some of this evidence later in this chapter.

What we are concerned with here, however, is not whether buyers search, or the modelling of their search behaviour – it is accepted that they do search and that their behaviour can be modelled. Our concern here is with the implications for the land and property market of a lack of freely available information and the search behaviour which seeks to overcome this lack. We therefore take over results from the findings for the labour market, changing only the idea of the reservation wage – the lowest acceptable to that of the reservation price – the highest payable.

## Information, search and the property market

Potential buyers must search through the properties which are offered for sale. As we argued in Chapter 4, the properties which are available on the market are heterogeneous, and vary in their characteristics. Inevitably all properties vary in their location, that is their spatial relationship with other properties and activities at other locations. The potential buyer has to take into consideration distances from places of work and from shopping centres, as well as distances from, for example, railway stations, bus stops and major roads. The buyer of commercial property has to consider things like ease of access for customers, and for trade vehicles, and for the workforce. Apart from location other factors will differentiate one property from another. The house buyer will be interested in the size of the plot, the characteristics of the physical structure, and the character of the environment. The buyer of a commercial property will be concerned with its configuration and the coincidence between form and potential function, as well as its potential obsolescence. The planning constraints and zoning regulations which affect the site will be important to both kinds of buyer.

As we also argued in Chapter 4 property prices are not definitively fixed by the market, but are determined by haggling between a potential buyer and the seller. Thus the final price at which a transaction takes place will not vary solely with the characteristics of the property but will also be affected by the bargaining abilities and positions of both the buyer and the seller. The buyer searching the market will therefore be confronted by asking prices which depend not only on the property but also on both the seller's desire and willingness to sell and the seller's perception of future market prices. On the one hand the executors of an estate or someone who is moving to a job in another part of the country may ask and accept a 'reasonable' price. On the other hand someone who has lived in a house for many years and has no immediate plans to move may ask a very high price of any developer who wishes to redevelop the site, and be unwilling to accept anything lower. Sellers' asking prices are also likely to be affected by what they expect to happen in the future. A seller who expects prices to fall is likely to set a lower asking price than a seller who expects prices to rise.

Thus the potential buyer faces a market in which all properties are different and in which prices are not completely determined by the characteristics of the properties. Property developers, moreover, as potential buyers of land, will have frequently to discover developable sites for themselves and then persuade the owners to sell. They may have to physically search for sites. Even if the market is less complex, if all the details of all the properties are gathered together and displayed in one place, so that the buyer does not have to search for this information, as may happen in some cities in Scotland or in the US, still any property which might be seriously considered has to be visited and inspected. Finally, before a buyer actually purchases a property it is usually be advisable to pay a building surveyor to check for faults which would only be recognised by an expert.

The buyer therefore has to search through the properties which are or might be available and the process of search is expensive. What we now have to consider is the way in which the buyer's search process interacts with the market. In particular, we are concerned with how changes in the market, as they are perceived by potential buyers, affect the prices that they expect to pay, i.e. their reservation prices.

Most of the findings are fairly obvious, once it is accepted that we are dealing with a market with heterogeneous properties about which it is difficult to obtain information. The first conclusion is that a continuation of search leads to the reservation price being raised, or, alternatively, if the amount the buyer can pay cannot be increased, the quality of what is sought may be reduced. In terms of prices, the buyer will start searching with a sum in mind as to the price that he or she is willing to pay for a property. As the buyer acquires more information about the properties which are on the market, it may become apparent that the initial reservation price is too low. Given the prices of what has been seen already, it will be perceived that it is unlikely that anything of the desired quality could be found, even after an extended search, at the initial reservation price. The buyer then has either to raise the reservation price or, particularly in the housing market, to reduce the quality or quantity of the housing that is being sought, that is, move down market.

The reverse should also apply of course. A buyer finding almost immediately what is wanted at the reservation price or lower may decide to lower the reservation price. In effect the potential buyer has to decide whether this is luck or whether it is because the overall price distribution is lower than originally thought. This is implicit in the second finding, however. That is that if some or all of the asking prices are reduced, that is the price distribution is generally lower, then the potential buyer will reduce his or her reservation price. In effect the buyer comes across lower prices than initially expected as the market is actually being searched, and so decides that the distribution of prices must therefore be lower. It follows that the initial reservation price was too high, given the buyer's assessment of the cost of search, and could be reduced. Again, in terms of the housing market, the buyer may also choose to buy 'more house' and continue to borrow the amount previously agreed with the mortgage lender.

The third finding is more difficult to apply to the property market. It is that an increase in the amount of price dispersion leads to a reduction in the reservation prices of buyers. This can best be understood if we think of a situation in which all prices are the same. No search is worthwhile and buyers pay what is effectively the fixed price. If now some variation in prices occurs, search becomes worthwhile to find the lower price. Some buyers, primarily those with low search costs, will lower their reservation prices and search for longer to find the lower priced product. The wider the distribution, or, to put it another way, the greater the variation, the lower the price that can be achieved by a sufficiently long search. To use again the example of someone driving along seeking to fill up with petrol, if there is no or very little variation in prices it becomes worthwhile filling up at the first available station when it is seen to be necessary. If there is greater variation, the salesman whose expenses are paid may still do this. On the other hand the impecunious student driver may start looking earlier for cheaper petrol, and fill up early, or late, if a garage advertising lower prices comes into view.

Finally, and importantly for the property market, an increase in the number of properties for sale, per searcher, leads to a reduction in the reservation price. Because there are perceived to be more properties on the market, it is also perceived by the searcher that there is a greater probability of finding what is wanted at a reasonable price. Therefore, buyers will be less willing to accept any given property at its asking price than they would have been before.

Conversely, of course, a decrease in the number of properties for sale per would-be buyer leads to an increase in the buyers' reservation prices. There are fewer properties on the market so the potential buyers perceive that there is a decreased probability of finding the kind of property they want at the kind of price they can afford. They therefore have to lower their sights, either by increasing their reservation prices, or, what comes to the same thing, seeking to buy a smaller or lower quality property.

The findings that we have outlined above are expressed in terms of the searches carried out by potential buyers, and their responses to market conditions. But the same arguments apply to sellers. They are searching for buyers willing to pay their reservation price. So, for example, an increase in the number of properties on the market is seen by buyers as a reason for dropping their reservation prices. From a seller's point of view, however, what is perceived is that there appear to be fewer potential buyers per property. In the face of this scarcity of buyers, the lower number of buyers per property will cause the sellers to reconsider their strategies and lower their reservation prices.

The above analysis relates to the situation in the market and changes in the character of the market. The position of the searcher, whether buyer or seller, and changes in their situation, can also be analysed. First, and as one would expect, a fall in the cost of search serves to reduce the buyer's reservation price, and, conversely, to increase that of the seller. Similarly, we would expect that a buyer for whom the cost of search was low would have a low reservation price. It follows that those with high search costs will try to minimise the length of the search process and will tend to pay higher prices than those with low search costs.

Second, the more risk averse buyers will tend to have higher reservation prices than the less risk averse. This will be most evident when it is not possible to go back to accept previous offers. It can be most easily understood from consideration of the car driver travelling along a road. The more risk averse drivers will be more worried about the possibility of running out of petrol than the less risk averse. They are therefore likely to want to fill up with fuel sooner, and therefore to be willing to pay a higher price than the driver who is less risk averse and therefore more willing to take a chance that they may in the end be stranded with an empty tank.

Third, buyers who benefit more from search will have lower reservation prices, and those who benefit less will have higher reservation prices. To use once again the example of the car driver travelling along a road seeking to fill the car's fuel tank. If the car has a small tank the driver will be more willing to pay a higher price per litre than the owner of a car with a larger tank, and this will be true even if the costs of continued search are the same for both and they are both equally risk averse. This is because the possible gain for the first driver of, say, one or two pence per litre on 30 litres is smaller than the possible gain for the second of one or two pence per litre on 50 or 60 litres.

Clear examples of this effect drawn from the property market are difficult to construct because those who benefit more from search, those buying large houses for example, are usually those for whom the cost of search is high, because they have higher incomes. So it could be argued that the large firm seeking land to develop, or a property to occupy, is likely to search longer and to try to get a better bargain than a smaller firm, simply because the total benefit of obtaining a lower price per square foot or per acre is worth so much more. Other factors complicate the analysis, however. The search cost for the smaller firm may be higher, because managerial time has to be diverted into searching for property. On the other hand, the search costs of the larger firm, a supermarket chain for example, may be lower because they will be able to employ people on a permanent basis to search for sites.

One fairly clear cut example drawn from the property market is the difference in the search patterns of renters and buyers in the housing market, which we discuss in the next section.

## Searching for housing in practice

Over the past 20 years or so there have been a number of empirical studies of the way in which people go about searching for a property which is suitable for them at a price they can afford, and on the way in which the owners of property go about finding buyers or renters.

The way in which people search may differ depending on the information that they have to start with and the cost of search. In this respect Maclennan & Wood (1982) looked at the information sources used by students at Glasgow University and found significant differences between the sources used by students already resident in the city and those coming to live in it for the first time. As Table 12.1 shows, the newcomers to the city tended to use the more formal sources of information – the University lodgings office, newspaper 'small ads', and estate agents. They also viewed fewer alternatives, 11 flats or houses against the average of 14 viewed by those already living in the city, presumably because the cost of search was lower for the latter. The students who were already there were more likely to use relatively informal sources of information – information from friends or relatives, and cards in shop windows. Maclennan & Wood found that the information sources of each group tended to differ most at the start of their searches, but the difference tended to become smaller as they continued. The continuing students used the lodgings office more while newcomers used contacts and shop window ads more. Presumably the continuing students had to start to use more formal channels when they were unsuccessful with the informal ones, while the newcomers found out about less formal sources as they continued to search.

Maclennan & Wood's research deals with groups who start off with differing levels of information and differing costs of search, so that the differences in their search methods are relatively easy to explain. Differences between groups in the way that they search may sometimes be more difficult to explain and may depend not on differences in the groups but on where each is searching. Harriet Newburger (1995) looked at differences between black and white house buyers in Boston, Massachusetts. The most noticeable difference was that white buyers looked at twice as many houses as black buyers, 18 as opposed to 9. In part this could be explained by the high number of houses viewed by whites buying in the

**Table 12.1** Relative frequency distribution and information source use. New and continuing students by stage of search (number of searches currently made).

| Sources | Continuing | | | | Newcomers | | | |
|---|---|---|---|---|---|---|---|---|
| | 1 to 4 searches | 5 to 8 searches | 9 to 12 searches | 13 to 16 searches | 1 to 4 searches | 5 to 8 searches | 9 to 12 searches | 13 to 16 searches |
| Friends/relatives | 7.1 | 19.8 | 16.9 | 6.3 | 0.2 | 1.4 | 3.5 | 5.4 |
| Other landlords | – | – | – | 0.3 | – | – | – | – |
| Lodgings office | 13.2 | 6.7 | 8.7 | 15.5 | 26.7 | 24.2 | 15.3 | 16.1 |
| Shop window | 30.6 | 31.0 | 29.8 | 38.4 | 2.3 | 10.7 | 24.5 | 31.2 |
| Newspapers | 42.1 | 30.3 | 31.7 | 24.3 | 47.1 | 42.3 | 37.7 | 29.0 |
| Estate agents | 7.0 | 10.2 | 12.9 | 15.2 | 23.3 | 21.4 | 19.0 | 18.3 |

Source: Maclennan & Wood (1982, p. 149).

suburbs, over 20. Nevertheless there was still a significant difference between the number of houses viewed by white buyers searching within the city of Boston, 17 houses, and the number viewed by black buyers. These differences appear odd given that each racial group searched for about the same period of time, about six months, indeed black buyers searched for longer on average, though the difference was not statistically significant.

Newburger found significant differences between the groups in the search methods used. Over a third of black buyers used no more than one information source, usually real estate agents, while less than 10% of white buyers did so. There were differences in the newspapers used as sources, as one might possibly expect, though the same proportion, 90%, used estate agents. The greatest difference between the groups was that white buyers were more than twice as likely to visit 'open houses' as black buyers. (An 'open house' is a form of sale which is not much used outside the United States. A house which is for sale is stated to be open to prospective buyers on a particular day, when the real estate agent will be present, and the agent's board advertising the 'open house' is displayed outside.)

The explanation put forward by Harriet Newberger for the differences between the two groups is that they tended to be searching in different areas within the urban area and within the city, and that the methods used to advertise properties for sale differed between the areas. That is to say, the search methods used by buyers differed because the search methods used by the sellers differed. She found, for example, that there very few 'open houses' to be seen in the predominantly black areas of the city, and there were few boards put outside houses to advertise that they were for sale. The reasons why the sellers of properties used different search methods in the different areas remain unexplained, however.

A study by McCarthy (1982) looked at differences between the ways that renters and buyers searched. As Table 12.2 shows renters looked at far fewer properties. Nearly 60% of the renters surveyed looked at three or less, and a third looked at only one property. On the other hand, two-thirds of the buyers looked at four or more properties with a substantial proportion viewing more than 17 properties.

As might be expected the difference in the number of properties looked at was reflected in a difference in the time spent searching. The average (median) time spent by renters was about two weeks while the average for buyers was about two months, and a third spent four or more months.

**Table 12.2** Comparison of search effort by renter and owner households (Brown County, Wisconsin and St Joseph County, Indiana).

| | Percentage distribution by tenure and site | | | |
| | Renters | | Owners | |
| Search characteristic | Brown County | St Joseph County | Brown County | St Joseph County |
|---|---|---|---|---|
| *Length of search:* | | | | |
| 1 week or less | 42.6 | 37.9 | 17.9 | 22.3 |
| 1–4 weeks | 39.3 | 34.3 | 20.2 | 18.4 |
| 1–3 months | 13.9 | 18.8 | 25.1 | 29.1 |
| 4+ months | 4.2 | 9.0 | 36.7 | 30.2 |
| Median (days) | 11.3 | 14.8 | 59.2 | 53.3 |
| | | | | |
| *Alternatives examined:* | | | | |
| 1 | 39.5 | 30.5 | 21.1 | 25.5 |
| 2–3 | 18.5 | 26.3 | 12.6 | 7.6 |
| 4–6 | 21.4 | 26.2 | 20.2 | 28.7 |
| 7–11 | 13.0 | 11.5 | 16.4 | 19.7 |
| 12–16 | 4.2 | 2.9 | 11.5 | 8.1 |
| 17+ | 3.4 | 2.6 | 18.2 | 10.4 |
| Median | 2.1 | 2.5 | 6.4 | 5.8 |
| | | | | |
| *Percent using source:* | | | | |
| Friend or relative | 70.0 | 82.5 | 79.0 | 68.7 |
| Newspaper ad | 79.7 | 77.8 | 75.6 | 71.8 |
| Looking at properties | 31.8 | 46.1 | 64.4 | 74.0 |
| Real estate or rental/agents | 23.9 | 27.9 | 68.0 | 66.2 |
| Mean number of sources | 2.05 | 2.34 | 2.87 | 2.81 |

Source: McCarthy (1982, p. 45).

The fact that buyers searched more thoroughly can also be seen in the way that they used more sources of information than renters. The latter mainly used personal contacts, while a substantial proportion of the buyers also used real estate agents and 'looking at properties', for example visiting 'open houses'.

The differences in the search patterns occur because the actual cost of moving is higher for buyers than it is for renters. Buyers have to pay costs which renters need not pay, in terms of legal fees for example. Renters may therefore rent for a short period, may even try out a property, in a way that a buyer would not. Because buyers are more committed to any property they buy their search is likely to be more thorough than the search carried out by the average renter.

## The housing market

In Chapter 4 we set out to demonstrate that the property market is imperfect and not 100% efficient. Prices are not wholly determined by the market, but are partly determined by factors which will differ for each transaction, for example the need the buyer has to sell. In this chapter we have set out to show that one of the features of the market, and one of the characteristics associated with its imperfection and inefficiency, is the lack of knowledge of the alternatives available. In consequence buyers and sellers operate in an environment where information is scarce and where this information has to be sought. The way in which they search and their response to change can be used to explain features of the property market, in particular the way the market as a whole responds to change.

In the housing market the sellers of houses search for buyers. Usually they do this by asking a price which is slightly higher than they expect to receive and then waiting for offers from potential buyers. In some parts of Britain a price may be indicated above which offers are invited. The buyers determine the prices they expect to receive and set their asking prices on the basis of the information available to them. They will take into account the advice they receive from professionals, in particular their estate agent, if they are employing one, their own knowledge of the market in their area, and other relevant factors. For example, a recent buyer with a large mortgage will be more reluctant to sell at a loss, if prices have recently fallen, than someone who purchased the house many years before at a much lower price and whose mortgage is now a small proportion of the house's value. Again, the price asked may depend on the price of the house to which it is intended to move, and the seller will not sell at all unless this is obtained. At the other extreme the executors seeking to sell the house of someone who has died may want a quick sale and will have no minimum price because the property has to be sold come what may. The price that is finally expected may differ from their initial expectations since information will be obtained as the property is on the market. For example, the initial expectation as to price may be too optimistic and have to be reduced as buyers prove reluctant to pay anything like it.

Buyers also search, but for properties. They search over the properties which are offered for sale using various sources of information. The process of search by buyers, and by renters, has been researched on a number of occasions, and we reviewed some of this empirical evidence in the previous section of this chapter. They will have a price in mind and an idea of the size and characteristics of the kind of property which they hope to be able to buy at this price. They too will adjust their reservation prices, or, what comes to the same thing, the kind of property they hope to buy, as they search.

What we want to look at here is a specific aspect of change in the property market, a change in the purchasing power of potential buyers, and we will use a change in interest rates as a specific example.

Most of the cost of home ownership is represented by the cost of the capital invested, whether actual – the interest paid on the mortgage loan, or imputed – the interest which could have been obtained from the capital invested in the house if it had been invested elsewhere. What happens if interest rates fall? Buyers now feel able to buy more house since they can afford to service a larger debt, they therefore raise their reservation prices. As a result it takes them less time to find what they are looking for, and houses sell more quickly.

Slowly this change in the market environment will work its way through to cause a change in the market. Buyers are now more willing to buy at the prices which sellers have set on the basis of advice, experience, and their knowledge of the prices at which similar properties have been sold in the area. Houses sell more quickly and the number of houses on the market starts to fall. Sellers now find that there are more searchers (buyers) per property on the market and respond, following the principles set out in the previous section, by raising their reservation prices. Buyers, on the other hand, find that there are fewer properties per searcher, and they in turn will have to respond to this perceived shortage by also raising their reservation prices. Thus increasing prices will be associated with fewer properties on the market.

Suppose, alternatively, that interest rates rise. Buyers find that they cannot afford the prices that they could have done before. They reduce their reservation prices and consequently search longer to find an affordable property. Sellers, on the other hand, do not initially respond by reducing their asking prices. As a result the number of houses 'on the market' increases. Estate agents find that they have a lot more properties for sale on their books. There are now more houses for sale per potential purchaser and, conversely, fewer potential buyers per house for sale. Sellers will eventually respond by reducing their reservation prices. Prices will fall but they will tend to fall slowly. Sellers will be reluctant to accept a lower price than they have seen similar properties fetch in the recent past. They may also be committed to obtaining some price on the property they are selling by the price they have agreed to pay for the property they are hoping to buy. What one would therefore expect to find is that falling prices would be associated with an increased number of properties on the market.

Overall one would expect to find the relationship between price changes and the number of properties on the market would be of the kind shown in Figure 12.1. That is it would be similar to the relationship found between the rate of change of wages and the level of unemployment by A.W. Phillips. In the labour market the rate of change of wage rates is inversely related to the level of unemployment; in the housing market the rate of change of prices would be inversely related to the number of properties for sale.

Empirical evidence of this relationship is hard to find because there is little data available relating to the number of properties for sale at any point of time. What is called casual empiricism, however, that is my own personal experience and observation, suggests that the relationship holds. Certainly during the major booms in house prices in the early 1970s or the late 1980s estate agents had few properties on their books, and those that were offered for sale were sold quickly and might even be sold at a price higher than the asking price. The shortage of properties was less evident during the smaller booms at the end of the 1970s and the end of the 1990s, but then since prices were not rising so dramatically this is as one would expect. Certainly at the end of each of the booms it was also evident that properties were on the books of estate agents for longer. Further, while few estate agents' boards might appear outside houses advertising that they were for sale during the booms, since they were sold so quickly, during the downturn forests of boards would appear along suburban streets advertising properties for sale.

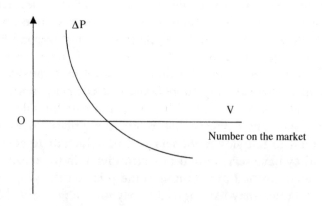

**Figure 12.1**

# The developer and land supply restrictions

Just as a lack of information affects the market for housing, so it affects the market for land for development. The same problem of finding out what is available and at what price affects developers seeking sites for development and potential house buyers. The developer's problem is, however, much worse than that of the house buyer. People who wish to sell houses advertise them for sale and the house buyer can acquire information through routes which are formalised or semi-formalised. Land which might be developed is much less likely to be formally advertised and marketed. Certainly much of it will be. In Britain the pages of the weekly magazine *The Estates Gazette* are filled every week with advertisements for properties of this kind – land which has development potential and is to be sold by auction, by tender, or by negotiation. Sites advertised for sale in this way tend to be expensive and, therefore, usually relatively large. Certainly many smaller sites may also be advertised and marketed in this and other ways, most often through agents, some of whom specialise in industrial or commercial property. But the owners of many smaller sites may not realise that they are the owners of land with, as it is put, development potential. This means that the developer seeking sites for development may have to search much harder than the potential house buyer.

An extreme example can be given of this. At the height of the property boom in the second half of the 1980s, it was not unknown for developers to hire helicopters to fly over the outer suburbs of London to see if they could discover pieces of land suitable for development. They were literally searching for sites, pieces of land which could not be identified from the street or on a map such as large back gardens which could be developed, either on their own or together with adjacent gardens. Obviously this kind of searching is unusual, but it serves to illustrate the nature of the problem. The developer has to find sites, persuade the owners to sell, negotiate terms and conditions, and all this has to be done before arriving at the point that the property is actually sold and the actual process of development can begin.

To summarise, and in short, the developer has to search for sites. It costs time, money, and resources to search, properties have to be found and the owners negotiated with. The price which is asked for the land by the owner will depend upon the characteristics of the site, its location, its size, the nature of any existing buildings, the planning position, etc., and also on the need or willingness of the owners to sell. Thus the reservation prices set by the owners will vary considerably, with the implication that search will be worthwhile, since, as we pointed out earlier, the wider the dispersion of offers, the lower will be the buyer's reservation price, and the buyer will anticipate a lengthy period of search.

An understanding of the nature of the market in land for development is essential in order to understand the effects of constraints on the availability of land for development. The market, as has been stressed, is characterised by a lack of information, information which has to be searched for over time, but also over space. A planning constraint which limits the area of land available for development self-evidently, by definition, limits the area over which the search for suitable land can take place. In terms of the discussion earlier in the chapter the number of possible sites is reduced but neither the number of developers nor the demand for housing is similarly reduced. The effect is therefore to reduce the number of sites to be searched over per developer. In terms of the earlier discussion, since there are fewer sites per developer, the expectation would be that the developers will raise their reservation prices. One would therefore expect that, to the extent that the planning constraint is effective, the prices paid for sites would tend to increase.

This increase in prices will occur much sooner than might be expected if one approaches the question in terms of a standard theory of supply and demand which assumes, amongst other things, that the buyers and sellers have complete knowledge of the alternatives available. Empirical evidence showing how early the price increase can occur is provided by studies of the economic effects of imposing 'urban growth boundaries' around the larger cities in the state of Oregon. These boundaries were intended to prevent urban sprawl. The area of land contained by the urban growth boundary (UGB) and which was not yet part of the built up area of a city was intended and expected to provide a land supply sufficient for the next 20 years of urban expansion and house construction. Only when this was built up, after 20 years, was it anticipated that land outside the UGB would become available for development (Nelson 1985; Knaap 1985).

Standard, received, theories would suggest, as we have indicated, that the price of land would remain fairly constant until the 20-year period was almost over. Certainly I do not think that many in Oregon suggested at the time the scheme was being discussed that it would very quickly lead to higher land and house prices. In fact, the evidence suggests that although there was no noticeable increase in land prices immediately after the UGBs were designated, nevertheless, four years after this the prices being paid for land within a UGB were significantly higher than the price paid for land outside it. And this increase in prices occurred even though a further 16 years' land supply was meant to be available.

Such a rapid response would, however, be predicted by the theory outlined earlier. As we have said, developers are forced to raise their reservation prices because of the scarcity of sites. It is true that a limited amount of land might come on to the market, essentially for life cycle reasons, but the remaining land owners are not 'in the market' and would only be willing to sell if sought out and offered a price which compensates them for selling and moving now rather than later. Land owners on the other side of the UGB who might sell their land more cheaply are not allowed to sell their land for development now, only as farmland and vacant land. The effect is that to find the amount of land which is necessary to accommodate the demand for housing, the prices asked by the less willing sellers within the UGB have to be paid, even though more willing sellers exist the other side of the UGB who would be willing to sell their land for less.

Of course, as land and property values rose within the area contained by the UGB, there were other effects, though ones not strictly relevant to the discussion here. In particular it was observed that increased development occurred on the other side of the area designated as not available for development within the 20-year period. The increase in property values, and the shortage of land available at a 'reasonable' price which was the cause, led development to leapfrog over what was effectively a green belt, and therefore an increase in the amount of commuting across it. The operation of the land market, and in particular its failure to supply land at the market (agricultural) price, on demand, actually resulted in a different kind of urban sprawl, albeit sprawl which was somewhat less than it otherwise would have been and transferred somewhat further from the city (Nelson 1988).

## Summary and conclusions

In the basic elementary economic theory of price, the price is set in the market at the level at which demand equals supply. But this theory makes a number of assumptions, one of the most important of which is that both the buyers and the sellers have full information about the alternatives available. In many markets this may be a reasonable approximation of reality, but in the market for land and property it is not. The goods for sale in the market are too heterogeneous, the participants may buy or sell infrequently, and there is not, and cannot be, one central market. All of which we discussed in Chapter 4 in relation to the inefficiency of the property market. Since then we have shown the way in which the behaviour of owners is another factor affecting the prices which they ask for their properties. The result is that buyers have to search for properties, acquiring information as they do so, and to decide both what property to buy, and, simultaneously, whether the cost of further search would outweigh the possible benefit. Sellers have to search for buyers and make a similar decision as to whether to accept an offer that has been made.

The consequence of this lack of information and the fact that the market is characterised by a search for information, is, we have shown, that price is not set at the level at which supply equals demand. Rather there is a relationship between the rate of change of prices and the amount of property on the market. In the housing market this means that there is an inverse relationship between the number of houses for sale at any time and the rate of change of house prices. When prices are rising rapidly there will be relatively few houses on the market and they will be sold quickly. When prices are falling, on the other hand, there will tend to be a large number of houses for sale, and they will take a long time to sell.

This observable relationship between the number of properties for sale and the rate of change of house prices helps to explain the effects of planning constraints on the amount of land available for development. If the rate of increase in house prices is related to the number of properties on the market, it seems reasonable that, as we show, the rate of increase in land prices should be related to the amount of the land which is on the market. If the amount of land is limited by a constraint imposed by government the implication is that prices will rise. Thus, contrary to a simplistic analysis, the price of land will rise because of the planning constraint even when there is land which is available for development because the constraint does not affect it.

# 13

## Land Availability and Land Banking

*'I want you'*

_____

### Introduction

At this point let us draw together the threads of the previous discussion and try briefly to summarise the argument. We argued in Chapter 4 that the market for land and property is imperfect, that is to say, the price of a piece of land is not determined by the market, except within a range. The exact price at which property is sold will depend upon the characteristics and expectations of both the buyer and the seller. In the ensuing chapters we explored the ways in which the owners of land may rationally choose not to use their land for whatever might yield the currently most profitable income. What we have tried to demonstrate is that the owners of land have a role to play in determining the use of their land and therefore the supply of land for any particular use, most importantly, for development or redevelopment.

Then in Chapter 12, we returned to the question of the imperfect nature of the property market, showing that, because it is imperfect, it is characterised by a lack of information as to the alternatives available to both buyers and sellers. It was argued that this pervasive lack of full information as to prices, the availability of properties, and so on, affects the way the market operates. It means that both buyers and sellers have to search, the buyer to find a piece of land at an acceptably low price, the seller to find someone who will pay an acceptably high price.

The differing expectations, motivations, and characteristics of owners, and their lack of knowledge of the opportunities available, means that the standard assumption is wrong. It cannot be assumed, either explicitly or implicitly, that land will always be used for its 'highest and best' use. This might have been a useful assumption to make in earlier analyses of the economics of the land market but the owners of land, as we have demonstrated, may not know what the 'highest and best' use for their land might be, and, even if they do, they may have other plans for its use. Thus the simplifying assumption is wrong and it is liable to be misleading. It may lead to false conclusions and it may lead to features of the land market being left unexplained, anomalies which are ignored because they do not fit in with the received paradigm.

In this chapter we shall look at two topics, the first, the availability of land for development, being a revision of the received theory, the second, land banking, being one of these anomalies. Land availability has been a subject of considerable discussion in the United Kingdom because the planning system has required local authorities, in each period, to assess the amount of land required for housing and the amount of land available. 'Land banking' is the acquisition of land ahead of development either by construction companies, usually house builders or, sometimes, by central or local government or their agencies.

## Land availability

The British planning system restricts the amount of land available for development, and this causes the price of land, and of housing, to be higher. This is now generally accepted by planners and by government. But it was not the official view up until the early 1990s (and I am not sure that it is understood by the general public even now). As we showed in Chapter 2, it was seriously argued as late as 1987 that the price of land and of housing was unaffected by the restricted supply of land for development which the planning system allowed. Therefore, when house builders argued in the 1970s and early 1980s that there was a shortage of land, a mechanism was put in place to try to reconcile the planners' and the developers' views. In England in each area outside London joint housing studies were carried out to agree the amount of land required and the amount of land available, and to show that the two were more or less equal (Rydin 1998, pp. 216, 218–9).

Of course, the amount of land required for a given number of dwellings depends upon the density of development so that it was always open, in practice, to a local authority simply to increase the density it would permit on the land it believed to be available, and so ensure equality that way. But even if this is a possibility, it still has to be shown why equality in the amount needed with the amount available still resulted in rising, and rapidly rising, land and house prices. The received theory, and the theory implicit in setting up the joint committees, was that if the amount of land available was equal to or exceeded the amount of land required then the policy was non-restrictive and would not, and should not, affect prices.

The model implicit in this argument is not necessarily explicit or, therefore, completely logical. Nevertheless what would appear to be the argument can be demonstrated using Figure 13.1. Land is measured along the horizontal axis and price is indicated on the vertical axis. The demand curve for land for housing is shown as the downward sloping line DD'. The supply of land for housing, as allocated through the planning system, is indicated as OS on the horizontal axis, and by the vertical line SS'. All of this land is not used for housing so there is still some land available. We indicate this on the horizontal axis as VS. The implication is that there is some other use to which land is put, and that the price at which this land is sold, for whatever use, is OP. Given this other use the supply of land can be represented by the horizontal line PP'. It may also be upward sloping but this does not affect the model.

According to this view of the land market, if the supply of land for housing is, in the figure, anything greater or equal to OV, the land allocation is non-restrictive. Of course, if the land allocation were less than OV, it can be seen that land prices, and therefore house prices, would rise. The joint committees were designed to ensure that OS was at least equal to OV.

The problem with this model is that the land which was allocated for housing was rarely being used for uses such as retailing or offices, for which the price of land was higher than the price of land for housing, at that time, or even for industry where the price of land was approximately the same, in southern England at least. Most often the land was used for agriculture, if it was not vacant. Thus in its original, or alternative, use the value of the land was much, much lower than its value with planning permission for residential development.

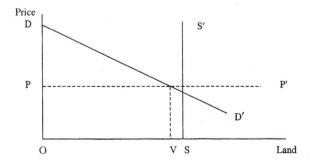

**Figure 13.1**

If the policy makers' model of the land market is of the kind portrayed in Figure 13.1 then there are two pieces of evidence which tend to conflict with any explanation based on it. On the one hand, the existence of a price difference between the price of land for agriculture and the price of land for housing creates a difficulty for those wishing to demonstrate that there is no land constraint. But, on the other hand, the difference between the amount of land available and the amount of land used, what Glen Bramley (1993a, 1993b) has called an 'implementation gap', creates a difficulty for those wishing to argue that there is a constraint.

The truth is, of course, that the model portrayed in Figure 13.1 is not a realistic model of the market. The 'gap' exists because plans may be made by planners but they will not necessarily be implemented by the land owners. The explanation for the gap lies in the imperfect nature of the land market and in the fact that different land owners have differing attitudes towards their land and the price that they would be willing to accept for it.

There is one piece of evidence from the land availability studies themselves which tends to confirm this view of the land market as highly imperfect. Increasingly, local authorities found that pieces of land were being put forward for development, and being permitted to be developed, which had not been earmarked as suitable for development in the authorities' original plans. Indeed, it was found that as much as a third of the housing being built in some areas resulted from these so-called 'windfall' sites. As a result local authorities, in their land availability studies, began increasingly to assume that a substantial amount of land would be brought forward for development in this way, but that it could not be predicted what land this would be. What the existence of these windfall sites demonstrates is the lack of information in the market, that even with considerable resources and the best of intentions, the planning authority for an area cannot know which land owner is likely to want to develop what land. The information as to what land might be available is brought together as developers explore the area and put together deals to buy pieces of land, land which, at the time the local plan was being drawn up, neither the planners nor the owners nor the developers had any assurance could be developable.

Clearly, therefore, the land market is imperfect and characterised by a lack of knowledge and by uncertainty. Developers have to search for sites, and will face differing responses from the various land owners they approach, since each one will seek the best deal, from their own point of view, with respect to the land that they own. The position with respect to differences in prices and differences in quantities can be explained by a theory which takes account of this situation. This must be of the kind set out in the previous chapter, one which is not based on a simple supply and demand model. A diagrammatic model is set out in Figure 13.2. Changes in price, $\Delta P$, are represented on the vertical axis. The difference between the amount of land planned to be available for development, $L_A$, and the amount of land required for development, $L_D$, we shall call D and this is represented on the horizontal axis.

According to the arguments set out in the previous chapter, the smaller this difference is, the more difficult it becomes for developers to find land and the more competitive becomes the bidding for the land which is found. Thus developers will pay higher prices as this difference becomes smaller. Similarly, as the difference becomes smaller, so the owners of land become more willing to ask higher prices. So the smaller this difference relative to the total quantity demanded, or the smaller, proportionately, the implementation gap, the faster prices would tend to rise. The relationship is shown in the figure by the downward sloping curve.

Thus the way of looking at the problem which we attempted to portray in Figure 13.1 was mistaken. The question at issue was not one as to whether there was, in some sense, land available for development, with the implication that if there were then prices would not rise and if there were not prices would rise. At issue was a question as to by how much the amount of land made available for development exceeded the amount of land required with the implication that the rate of change in prices depended on this difference, as shown in Figure 13.2.

Thus a land policy may be restrictive and cause higher land prices even when there would appear to be land available for development because land has been designated as available through the planning system. This is because a margin, possibly a substantial margin, is required to be available

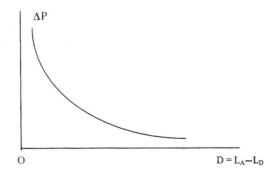

**Figure 13.2**

over and above what is required before price inflation can be prevented. The analogy must be made with the labour market. It is well known, and very well understood, that trying to run an economy with an excessively low rate of unemployment will sooner or later result in wages being bid up. If, on the other hand, the pool of unemployed labour is larger the wage level will be stable or even fall. The same is true, mutatis mutandis, of the land market, with two qualifications. The first is that while the money supply may be expanded to keep pace with wage inflation no such correlation is likely with respect to the land market so that price booms will, in the end, peak. Second, there is almost invariably some alternative use for land, primarily agriculture, so that prices will not fall below a certain level.

Of course, what frequently happens is that the increases in price are blamed on the owners of land and particularly on 'speculators', with the implication that if only they would behave differently and sell their land for less then the planned land allocations would not be restrictive. This has happened in the UK, and it has happened in South Korea, where land supply has been constrained by green belts and other controls (Kim 1993, 1994). But this is equivalent to saying, with respect to the labour market, that an economy could be run with zero unemployment and zero wage inflation if only, when labour was scarce, employees did not seek higher wages and employers did not pay them. It is possible that if the economic institutions were different this might be true, but they are not different and wishing does not make them so.

The scarcity of land for development is created by the planning system, and this scarcity gives market power to the owners of land. With different institutions, as we shall show later in this chapter, land prices might be kept down. Public intervention to ensure that land is available by planning ahead and buying land in anticipation of its development would help to keep prices down. But most planning systems, and certainly that in the UK, are fundamentally negative rather than positive in character. Plans can indicate that an application for permission to develop some pieces of land is likely to be refused, and that an application with respect to other pieces of land is likely to be granted. But while it can prevent development in the one case, it cannot ensure that development takes place in the other. It cannot direct that land will be developed.

Before 1980, of course, in the UK, before the Thatcher government came to power, a substantial amount of new housing was provided by local authorities. An authority's housing department could therefore act in a way which could be coordinated with the plans of its planning department. There was therefore an element of positive planning, particularly if compulsory purchase was used to acquire sites, but this has disappeared as the activities of housing departments have been wound down and sold off. The negative nature of the system which now exists therefore gives great market power to particular owners of land. It is illogical to blame the landowners for exercising this power, rather than examining the workings of the system which gives them this power.

To appreciate, however, that a constraint may have an economic impact even when it is non-binding, it is necessary to understand the way in which an imperfect market like the land market actually works. And, in particular, how its workings differ from those of the perfect market which the teachings of economists have so successfully embedded in people's consciousness. Without this arguments may occur which miss the point. For example, in the discussions which have taken place in the UK over the years between local authority planning departments and house builders about the availability of land, the builders have frequently argued that the sites which had been indicated as available were in the wrong location or of the wrong type. The implication was, of course, that there was a shortage of land of the right type, rather than a shortage of land *per se*, but the difference is basically a question of how a perceived shortage in the market is characterised. Because of their common, but incorrect, theoretical framework both parties were forced to agree that the amount of land indicated as available for development was greater than the amount required, and so to agree that there was no general shortage. Pointing to the type of land which was available was a way of keeping to this framework but indicating that there was still an effective constraint which resulted in higher prices. With the theoretical framework set out here this kind of convolution is not necessary.

## Land banking by private firms

This discussion of land availability leads naturally on to a discussion of 'land banking' by developers, that is the buying up of land for development some time ahead of the date at which the firm will wish to actually build on it. So a firm will buy land for future development and keep it in its 'land bank', a supply of land in its ownership and not subject to changes of mind as to its availability or price by land owners.

Once again the received theory provides no explanation as to why this should occur. It is implicitly assumed that land is freely available at the market price and/or that the location of land does not matter. The availability of land for development is therefore not a problem. Together with this there is a further assumption implicit in the way that the standard theory is presented and that is that each piece of land, each site, is developed on its own in isolation from any other developments: in effect a new 'firm' comes into existence to carry out each development. This comes about because the discussion of land tends to concentrate on individual pieces of land and also upon their continuity, on their use before development and their use after development. But this is not so in the rest of economics. There, it is the firm whose continuity is assured, and the firm is discussed as an organisation for processing resources and delivering products and services. The theory of the firm is non-spatial, but to the extent there is a spatial dimension there would seem to be an implicit assumption that the firm remains at a given location and that resources are brought to it, and goods and services are delivered at or from that location.

With a construction company or a property development firm this implicit assumption is incorrect. One of its inputs or resources is land, and the firm comes to the land not the land to the firm. While the continuing nature of land is important, concentrating on it can be misleading. In some contexts, in particular in this one, it may be more revealing to concentrate instead on the continuing nature of the firm. If we do this then land is seen as resource to be processed by the firm, and it follows that the firm must arrange for continuity in its supply.

Of course, there is an element of truth in the idea that a new 'firm' comes into existence to develop each site. The firm organising the development will hire in resources solely for the purpose of carrying out that particular development. Architects, engineers, and quantity surveyors must be engaged, work subcontracted, labour employed, and plant hired, all solely for that purpose and for the period necessary to carry out the work. But the core skills of the firm, in the management and control of the development, are central to the nature of the firm, and the aim of its senior management will be to keep these core skills, and any synergy between them, so as to maintain the firm in being. One of the economic factors ensuring this continuity, and the need for it, is what is called 'learning by doing'. The management will have learned from working together in the past, and will be more efficient if it is kept together. Thus the implicit assumption that a new firm comes into existence for each development is not realistic. The firms carrying out developments continue in existence but deal with new pieces of land.

The model of the development process which flows from this analysis has been called the 'pipeline' model – sites move metaphorically through a 'pipeline' being processed as they pass through this pipeline, changing over time from being undeveloped to being developed (Barrett, Stewart & Underwood 1978). The purchase of land is, from this point of view, part of the process of acquiring factors to enable the firm to act economically and efficiently, directing its resources to each development in sequence, without any break in activity which would result in resources lying idle.

But the relevance of the discussion of the supply of land so far in this book is that it is apparent that land is not freely available to be bought 'off the shelf'. Suppose that a firm requires a site, A, to develop in year 1, another site, B, in year 2, another, C, in year 3, and so on. At the end of the first year, when development on site A is nearing completion, it is just not possible to ring up or send someone across to the local land wholesaler for a new site. Because of the nature of the land market the developer must start searching for sites well before they are needed. Various factors combine to cause this, factors which we have discussed in earlier chapters. The first is the lack of information as to what sites are or, more importantly, might be available for development. This knowledge has to be acquired. From this flows a second factor, it takes time and costs money and resources to search for and acquire this information. Then there is the heterogeneity of the sites which might be available and the willingness and unwillingness of the owners of the land to sell. These owners therefore have to be bargained with and this in itself takes time. Finally, there are the problems associated with what we might call the degree of reversibility of the search process. A piece of land which may be available at one time may not be available later, because it has been sold to some other firm. Or it may only be available at a much higher price because other competitors are bidding for it and/or the land owner's views as to its value have changed. Complicating the problem of irreversibility is the fact that the firm's bargaining position weakens as its existing developments near completion. It becomes increasingly imperative that the firm acquires new sites to keep the management and the workforce together.

Taken all together these several factors mean that a firm has to begin seeking to acquire land well before it is about to begin work on the site. Of course, if there were a lot of land available, or if land were always available at the market price, as the received theory implies, then there would be no need to hold land banks. But since land is not always available at the market price, and because few sites may be available when they are required, so it becomes necessary for developers to buy and bank land. A 'just in time' policy might increase efficiency in many parts of industry, but it is not likely to do so with respect to land.

Another factor which is likely to affect land banking is the restrictiveness of the planning system and the extent to which planning decisions can be predicted. The greater the degree of constraint and the greater the uncertainty, the greater the need to land bank. If the system is a zoning system of the American kind then it is known beforehand that land is zoned as, say, residential, and in most parts of the country more land is zoned as residential than is required. As a result land banking is less necessary than with a British 'non-zoning' system where the amount of land available is constrained, and planning permission is uncertain. The reasons for this are clear. In the first place it takes time to obtain planning permission, and it is not certain that permission will be granted for what is asked for. In England the process may be long drawn out involving site visits, modifications to the application, negotiations with the planning officers, etc., and can take eight or nine months even if the application is approved by the planning or development control committee without demur. If the application is refused and the developer has to go to appeal or put in a new, more acceptable, application, the process is even more drawn out, and more uncertain. Thus, a restrictive and uncertain planning process increases the length of time required to get from starting the search for a site to starting construction work on it, and so in itself encourages the holding of land banks.

Of course, as we have already noted in Chapter 7, because of the uncertainty of the planning process in England, a system has developed whereby developers buy options on land, particularly rural land. The owner is paid a relatively small sum for the option, and the developer then seeks planning permission for the site. The developer only actually buys the site if and when planning permission is obtained. In this way the length of time between actual acquisition and starting work is reduced, so that the size of the developer's land bank is reduced. Nevertheless there is still uncertainty as to whether and when permission will be obtained so that developers are still likely to need to hold land banks.

Further, even if the uncertainty of a planning system can be reduced through the use of options, it is still going to be true that a restrictive planning system encourages land banking for a second, but less obvious reason. Because the land which is available for development is limited, developers are competing with each other for a scarce supply of sites. This is likely to result in rising land prices, as we argued in the first part of this chapter. But another consequence is that it encourages developers to buy land ahead of development to make absolutely sure of their own land stocks while, at the same time, making it more difficult for their competitors to find land on which development would be permitted.

Thus, constraints on the availability of land will tend to lead firms, for their own self-preservation, into seeking to buy land for future development well ahead of actual development, so increasing the impact of the constraints both on prices and availability. In this way the constraints themselves are part of the reason for what we referred to earlier as the 'implementation gap', the difference between the amount of land planning authorities believe to be available for development in a period, and the amount on which development is actually taking place.

The situation as far as the developer is concerned is illustrated in Figure 13.3. The time taken from starting the process of search for a site to an actual site being available for development is shown on the horizontal axis. The probability that it will actually take this period of time is indicated on the vertical axis. The probability distribution is drawn as a conventionally bell-shaped curve. In most economic situations it would be the average which mattered. If we are interested in the effects on the consumption of bread of an increase in its price, then what is actually measured is the mean. The fact that some will reduce consumption considerably more than the mean and others considerably less is unimportant. In the acquisition of land for development, however, it is the longest period that this might take, even if it is unlikely, which becomes important. The process must be started leaving a period of time before land has to be actually acquired which is well above the average. But this means that, because of the need for certainty, it must in fact be highly probable, indeed almost certain, that the process of acquisition will be completed well before the site is actually needed. The uncertainty as to the length of time that acquisition will take leads to the possession of land banks.

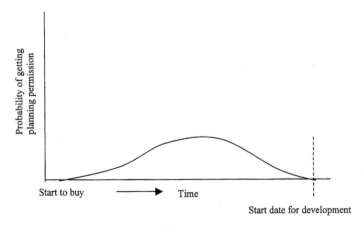

**Figure 13.3**

Of course, the risk and uncertainty associated with land acquisition can be minimised. The obvious way to do this in this case is to adopt a portfolio approach, so called because the risks associated with owning a single share can be reduced by owning a portfolio of shares. In this case, therefore, a company which can afford to do so can set out to acquire a number of pieces of land. This will reduce the possibility that it will be left without a site to develop, and, conversely, it increases the probability that the firm will acquire at least one site within the maximum possible period. But this approach reduces the scale of the problem in one way only by, possibly, creating a different, though more manageable, problem. As it becomes less likely that, after a given period, the firm will have no sites, so it becomes more likely that, after a given period, it will have several sites. The portfolio approach makes it less likely that the firm has to hold one or two sites for long periods before they are needed, but only by making it more likely that it has to hold a number of sites for short periods, and that some may have to be disposed of.

It follows that if a planning system makes the process of acquisition more uncertain, as the British system does, then firms are more likely to land bank and likely to hold larger land banks than they would with a more certain system. The strategy adopted, however, will vary with the size of the firm. A large firm can adopt the portfolio approach because it will have, or will have access to, the capital necessary to finance a large land bank, if that is necessary. On the other hand, a small firm is less likely to have access to this kind of capital and will have to pursue a different strategy, even though this carries the risk that it may find itself without a site.

A study by White (1986) provides some empirical evidence on the situation amongst British firms in the 1980s. He found, indeed, that some smaller firms could find themselves in a situation where they owned no land ready for development. Some of these, he reported, then had to make what he described as 'suicidal bids' for land with planning permission in order to stay in business, in the short run at least.

He found further differences between large and small firms. The smaller firms tended to be more 'production oriented', while the larger firms had wider interests, often financial. Many of the larger firms had found that obtaining planning permission was often more profitable than actually building. Thus the larger firms could, whether accidentally or deliberately, find themselves with more developable sites than they needed, and these surplus sites could be sold on to other, usually smaller, firms.

White also found that the ownership of a large land bank could be a mixed blessing for a firm. A large land bank represents a large capital investment but until it is developed it yields virtually no income. The shares of companies owning overly large land banks could therefore be under priced with the result that firms which were short of land could launch take over bids seeking to acquire the land bank of the target firm.

One further point should be made with respect to private land banking, that is the cost of holding a land bank will vary in the course of the economic cycle. White, as I have said, was reporting the situation in the 1980s. The research was done during a period when house and land prices were rising strongly, a boom which ended a few years afterwards. During the period of the boom the cost of land banking was low since the increase in the value of the land was likely to be greater than the cost of financing any loan raised to buy it. Since the cost of owning land was probably negative, this in itself would encourage firms to build up land banks, even apart from the scarcity of sites for which planning permission could be obtained.

The situation was very different in the early 1990s during a period when land prices and house prices were falling in most areas of the country. During this period holding land became extremely expensive, even though interest rates were lower than they had been. Thus the cost of land banking, and the incentive to do so, can change drastically over the cycle, exacerbating the boom and bust nature of the house building and construction industries.

## Public land banking

In this and previous chapters we have stressed the level of uncertainty in the land market. Owners may not wish to sell, developers may have difficulty finding the right site at the right price. But one feature of the land market to which we have so far attached little importance is the need for sites which are to be developed should be favourably related to each other in their configuration, possibly being contiguous. But if the likelihood of a piece of land being put on the market depends solely on the owner's preferences, then the sites which are sold for development are unlikely to consist of sites located adjacent to each other at a favourable location. Development is likely to sprawl in a quasi-random way across the landscape, sprawl which was seen in Britain between the wars and which continued to occur in countries like Australia and the United States after the Second World War.

This urban sprawl is difficult to avoid without some form of planned intervention in the land market. The usual approach is negative. In Britain, for example, the growth of the major cities, and some other smaller towns, has been limited by green belts. Green belts have also been used to limit the growth of South Korean cities. The intention in both cases has been that development is only likely to be permitted on land within the inner boundary of the designated green belt, or at specific locations on the other side of it. A looser form of constraint is provided by the Urban Growth Boundaries favoured in the State of Oregon which are not designated as permanent, even though the intentions are the same, to prevent urban sprawl and to try to ensure contiguity in the development which does occur.

An alternative, positive, approach to the problem of urban sprawl has been adopted in some countries, notable Sweden and the Netherlands, where central or local government buys up land well ahead of the anticipated development, and sells it to developers, in effect, off the shelf, as it is required. The practice appears to have grown up for historical reasons in the Netherlands. Since much of the land was reclaimed from the sea by government action, this land began in government ownership, and could be sold by government as it wished without raising any political objections. It was then natural to adopt the same practice with respect to land which was not reclaimed land but which was already in existence and owned by someone. Local governments could therefore buy up agricultural or other land ahead of expected urban growth using if necessary, though in fact very rarely, its powers of compulsory purchase. The land would then be retained by the local authority until it was due to be developed, possibly being let to a tenant in the meantime. The local authority would plan the area, providing the infrastructure and setting aside land for parks and other such uses. The remainder of the land, about half, would be sold for development at a price which covered the cost to local government of this infrastructure and of the land which was not sold, but which did not yield a profit, in effect at cost. The system is described in more detail by Needham (1992). The system in Sweden was similar to that in the Netherlands, although there the system appears to have grown up during the long period of control by the Social Democratic Party in the middle part of the last century (Duncan 1985). It may be worth noting that the intention of the Labour Government which introduced the 1947 Town and Country Planning Act was that a somewhat similar system should operate in the United Kingdom, and this also appears to have been the intention of a later Labour government with the Community Land Act of 1975. In both cases, however, the election of a Conservative government at the next election meant that these intentions came to nothing.

Although this degree of government intervention in the land market may

being diverted further out. The economic and planning advantages of public land banking seem clear. Nevertheless the political, libertarian, objections to government intervention in the land market, and indeed objections to government intervention generally, mean that public land banking operates in very few countries.

Moreover, where it does occur its existence would seem a historical accident. For example, Hong Kong, as a Crown Colony, had a system under which all the land started off in the hands of the government of the colony. The sale of this land for development was integrated into the planning system, since the sale of a site was controlled by a contract which laid down how it should be developed, controls which would elsewhere be part of the planning system (Bristow 1984; Staley 1994). The example of Hong Kong, however, illustrates also that public land banking need not result in low land prices. Land prices in Hong Kong were notoriously high, and the government derived a considerable part of its income from land sales. It is clear that it did operate a policy of constraint, possibly for planning reasons, but also because the flow of land sales generated a revenue for the government in a politically painless way. Nevertheless, negative methods of constraint if the government did not own the land would have resulted in land and prices which would have been at least as high, while generating capital gains for private land owners and no revenue for the government.

## Summary and conclusions

In this chapter we have looked at the problem of the availability of land for development in the light of the previous analysis of the economic effects of uncertainty and lack of information in the land market. We have shown that if planning is negative then local planning authorities may designate land as being available for development but they cannot force land owners to sell. Would-be developers must still search to find sites which owners are willing to sell at what the developer regards as a reasonable price. If the land designated as available only exceeds the amount required by a small margin then the constraint on the availability of land will still result in prices being higher than they would be with a more relaxed regime.

We also analysed the ways in which firms ensure that land is available as and when they require it. Because the process of acquisition may be uncertain and long drawn out, firms need to embark on the process of finding and buying land well before they require the land for development. As a result firms will frequently hold 'banks' of land which are not yet required. Where the planning process is uncertain, as in Britain, the process of acquisition may take even longer and 'land banks' are likely to be more frequently held and larger. Moreover, since one way to reduce the risk that the developer will be left without developable land is to acquire a 'portfolio' of developable sites, risk reduction favours larger firms but encourages even higher levels of land banking.

Finally, we looked at the way in which in some countries, most notably Sweden and the Netherlands, government may intervene in the process of land acquisition, buying land ahead of development and selling it, when it is needed, for development. This process controls urban sprawl while leading to lower land and house prices than other 'negative' methods of preventing sprawl through constraints on development. Government control of the supply of land may, however, result in manipulation and constraint by the government to ensure that the price received is high.

In the next three chapters we look at a feature of the land market which distinguishes it from all others, the problem of contiguity.

# 14

## Contiguity: Site Assembly

### *'I want to hold your hand'*

---

### Introduction

Probably the most important way in which land differs from other factors of production is that the location of a piece of land is fixed and cannot be changed. This fixity of location affects the market in a number of ways some of which have already been mentioned, for example the value of a piece of land depends on its location relative to the location of economic activities such as shopping centres and workplaces. One important characteristic of land has only been touched on briefly, however. Not just relative location but the actual adjacency or contiguity of pieces of land can be important. In particular, if a firm wants to construct a large building then it has to have a large site to do so, and to have this large site it has either to have bought it or to have assembled it, putting together a number of contiguous sites.

This problem of contiguity is of considerable importance, and accounts for a number of peculiarities in the way land is treated in law. The nature of the problem can be succinctly stated using the same example that we used in Chapter 1. If a company wishes to build a railway, then it can advertise for labour and assemble a labour force from those who respond. It can approach investors and banks for capital, seeking only to obtain the total sum required at the lowest possible cost, not caring as to who actually puts up the money. But it cannot simply advertise for land, not caring from whom it buys and seeking only to obtain it at the lowest price. The very idea of buying land in this way without caring where it is located is obviously absurd.

Clearly a company seeking to build a railway between one town and another has to put together a set of contiguous sites which form a continuous strip of land between the towns on which the railway can be built. Equally clearly it may be difficult to do this. The firm may find, having negotiated with a number of land owners, that while it can put together most of the strip, it is not completely continuous because one particular land owner is seeking an excessive price. As we noted in Chapter 10, in the discussion of minimum rents, because of this problem and the difficulty and cost of negotiating with numerous land owners, a firm may offer a price, in some circumstances, which is intended to be acceptable to all so that it is not held to ransom. This may not be possible in all cases, however. An alternative is that owners may be compelled to sell. It is because of this problem of contiguity that powers of compulsory purchase, or, as it is called in the United States, eminent domain, are allowed to be used by governments and by public utilities.

The problem of contiguity also arises where there are economies of scale in a development, for example in the construction of a shopping centre or a housing estate. Powers of compulsory purchase may sometimes be available and we shall discuss the economics of compulsory purchase in the next chapter. More usually, however, the developer has to put the site together without such assistance. In this situation the developer has to decide the tactics to employ to minimise the total cost of the land. This can be considered as a problem in game theory, and it is with this kind of problem that we start this chapter.

## A game theory approach

Game theory as a branch of mathematical economics was formulated by Von Neumann & Morgenstern in their book *Theory of Games and Economic Behaviour* first published in 1944. Game theory tries to analyse the moves which might be made by those who are in some way competing against each other. These might be rival firms trying to capture larger market shares or ensure higher profits, or, as in the case we are trying to analyse, buyers and sellers each trying to ensure that they get the best available deal.

One of the first uses of game theory to analyse the process of site assembly was by Wolfgang Eckart (1985), and it is his analysis which we use as the basis of our discussion here. In his study it is assumed that there is a single would-be developer who wishes to buy an area of land, the ownership of which is split up amongst a number of different people. To model the 'game', Eckart assumes that the first move is made by the developer who makes an initial offer to buy all the land at a price of $p_0$ per hectare. This offer price must be at least as great as the basic 'market' price of the land, say the price it would normally be sold for use in agriculture, $p_a$, and will probably be greater. This price, $p_a$, is therefore the value of the land to the owner, per hectare, if it is not sold to the developer.

Once the developer has made an initial offer it is up to the owners of the land to make their move. Eckart assumes that they each independently, without consultation, make a counter offer. This is $p_i$ for each of the $n$ owners, that is $i = 1, 2, \ldots, n$. If each land owner's proportion of the total site is $k_i$, then the average price to the developer implicit in the landowners' counter offers is given by:

$$p = \sum_{i=1}^{n} k_i.p_i$$

There is a probability, $\theta$, that this counter offer will be rejected by the developer. Obviously if $p = p_o$, the original offer by the developer, the counter offer will be certainly accepted and $\theta = 0$. On the other hand there must be some ceiling price $p_{max}$, at which, and above which, the developer would certainly reject the counter offer, so that if $p = p_{max}$, then $\theta = 1$.

Each land owner has to choose a price $p_i$ which is their counter offer. They also have to bear in mind that if the land owners' counter offer is rejected they will be left holding the land and it will only be worth its basic 'agricultural' value $p_a.k_i.L$, where $L$ is the total area of the land being bid for. Obviously if their counter offers are accepted then each will receive the price asked so that the amount each receives will be $p_i.k_i.L$.

Each land owner is assumed to try to maximise the expected value of their land, and this can be represented mathematically as $\theta.p_a.k_i.L + (1-\theta)\,p_i.k_i.L$. Clearly what each land owner expects to receive depends upon their own counter offer $p_i$ and on the total of the counter offers made, since this total determines the probability that the counter offers will be accepted.

A basic assumption which can be, and is often, made in game theory is that there is no collusion and that each participant, each land owner in this case, assumes that their counter offer will not affect anyone else's counter offer. From this assumption we can arrive at what is called a Nash equilibrium.

We do not need to go into the mathematics here since the results obtained are to some extent obvious, given the assumptions. The main result is that small land owners will tend to be more aggressive in their counter offers than large land owners. The implication is that the average price asked in the counter offer will increase with the number of land owners involved in the deal. The reasons for this would seem to be fairly intuitive. A small land owner who owns a very small proportion of the total land being bid for will tend to think that the price that he or she asks will not really affect the probability that a deal will go through and so will tend to ask a high price. Since all the small land owners can be assumed to think in this way, the more there are, the higher will be the average price asked as part of the counter offer.

A large land owner, on the other hand, is in a different position. He or she will be very aware that the price asked in the counter offer will certainly tend to affect the average price and will itself, therefore, help to determine the probability that the counter offer will be acceptable. So large land owners will be more likely to ask 'reasonable', i.e. lower, prices than small land owners. They will be more concerned to ensure that a deal goes through and that they don't get left holding land which is only then worth its agricultural value.

Obviously the assumptions made in Eckart's analysis simplify the problem considerably in order to make it mathematically tractable. It is unrealistic to assume a single bid and counter bid, and not very realistic to assume that owners will not take into account what they think others will ask. Nevertheless the analysis does give an insight into the nature of the land assembly problem. It is useful to know the way in which land owners may behave in the given circumstances. The predictions can be tempered by reality if necessary.

So, given these theoretical results, one can see that if a site were owned by two people, one owning a large part of the site and one owning a very small part, then, even if they took account of each other's actions, the former would tend to ask a lower price than the latter. The small land owner would be very liable to ask a high price, figuring, as above, that the price asked for a very small part of the site would not significantly affect the chances of the deal going through. It is in this way that we get what are called 'hold outs' in Britain and, more graphically, 'price gougers' in the US.

It can also be seen that if the several owners of a site get together, 'collude', in setting their counter offer this collusion is likely to lead to a lower average price being asked than if they didn't collude. The several colluders are put into the position of having to act like, and therefore think like, a single large land owner, so they, together, have a greater incentive to set a price which will ensure that the deal goes through. Of course, it is also always feasible for one or two small land owners to refuse to collude and, by acting independently, to try to 'hold out' for a higher price.

Finally, looking at the process from the developer's point of view, it can be seen that a developer might prefer to encourage several small land owners to get together and to act in collusion, since the price asked jointly is likely to be lower than the average price asked severally. This is not always likely to be true, however. In the case analysed it is assumed that each land owner knows that the developer is seeking to acquire a large number of sites. In this case the owners are likely to discuss things anyway, and the paradox is that one would have thought that a developer might wish to discourage collusion, trying to deal independently with each owner.

The theoretical analysis suggests that this would be true if the developer can conceal from the owners that a large site is being assembled of which each owner's land is only a small part. If each can be negotiated with separately independently, each owner has to act as though they were the sole land owner, and indeed believes that they are. So each has to ask a price which is 'realistic' to try to ensure that a deal goes through. They do not know that their piece of land is only a small part of the whole and therefore have no incentive to hold out for a high price.

The analysis helps to explain why developers may see advantages in concealing their plans. In practice this may be achieved by having a number of different 'front' companies and agents apparently acting independently in seeking to acquire different parts of the whole site. Only when all the land has been purchased can it be revealed that there was, in fact, only one development company assembling land for a single large development.

Activities of this kind by developers are necessarily not widely publicised, so that although such tactics may be talked of they can rarely be confirmed. One of the few descriptions of such a process operating in practice is given by Oliver Marriott (1967) in his book *The Property Boom* (pp. 160, 161) describing the boom of the 1950s and 1960s.

> The next step was to buy all the land as quietly as possible. The site stretched for a quarter of a mile between the underground stations at Warren Street, and Great Portland Street, along the north side of Euston road, ... Behind the frontage to Euston road ... was a collection of decaying late Georgian terraces and sad little shops .... At the same time as Sidney Kaye was finding out what density of offices and of shops the LCC would allow ... Joe Levy was forming a consortium of estate agents.

He knew that if his firm alone were to attempt to buy from all the many different owners, freeholders, leaseholders and sub-leaseholders, his intention might become apparent and there would be two great dangers. Owners might dream up an exaggerated idea of the value, to him, of their properties or some small-time property dealers might compete against him in order to hold him to ransom. In either case his ultimate profit on the redevelopment could be either sharply slimmed down or wiped out entirely. Levy brought in three other agents to help his strategy....

Joe Levy never put up an 'Acquired through D.E. & J. Levy' notice board on the site at all. He dictated the policy and held the reins, while the other three agents reported to him. They hoisted their notice boards as they bought.

The bulk of the properties was bought in a four-year period between 1956 and 1960 and the total number of separate deals added up to around 315....

The prices paid for the land varied wildly. In Diana Place were two adjoining semi-derelict cottages, worth in themselves about £1,000 apiece. One was bought for £1,800. The other, owned by a shrewd Cypriot, cost Joe Levy £45,000. A small factory belonging to a cast-iron welder cost £360,000.

What Marriott's description makes clear is that the process of land acquisition and site assembly takes time. It may take considerable patience on the part of the developer to put together the site. The game theory model collapses the process of acquisition into a limited number of moves which are essentially timeless. An alternative approach which we discuss next stresses the importance of the time element.

## A question of time

In earlier chapters in the book we argued that, for a number of different reasons, the value of a piece of land to its current owner will tend to be higher than its current market price. We also argued that this is particularly likely to be so if the owner is also the occupier and user. Owners will have differing views, however, as to the price that they would accept for their land, some will be very reluctant to sell, some will want to move immediately. The result, as we showed, is that the supply of land for a particular use at a point in time can be best represented by an upward sloping supply curve.

While this supply curve represents the situation at one point in time, it is evident that the position will change from one year to another as the situation and views of the owners change. So sites which were not on the market at one point in time are likely to come on to the market at a later date. To give an extreme example the elderly couple, who would not sell their home at any price because it holds too many memories, will eventually die, and their executors will want to sell the house quickly and so be willing to accept the best price available. In this way and in other ways every piece of land will come onto the market in the long run, but the long run may be very long indeed, and, as Keynes famously remarked 'In the long run we are all dead'.

The situation is represented, if rather schematically, in Figure 14.1. The area of land which could be used for the development is represented along the horizontal axis and prices or costs are shown on the vertical axis. The diagram is derived from a figure used by Munch (1976) in her analysis of the economics of eminent domain. The increase in the value of the development to the developer from any increase in its size, that is the marginal value product, is shown by the curve marked MVP. The curve slopes upwards when the area of the development is small indicating that there are economies of scale, though it slopes downwards beyond a certain point because of the inevitable diseconomies of scale.

The horizontal line indicates the price which is quoted as the market price of land at that location. Some of the land which a developer would wish to acquire for any development would be available at this price at this location, and other sites would be available elsewhere at this price, but all of the land required for a development at this location cannot be bought there at

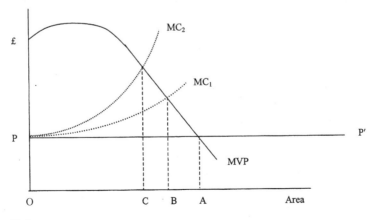

**Figure 14.1**

this price at this time. Nevertheless, if, of course, the developer had infinite patience and could wait, if necessary for ever, all of the land could eventually be acquired at this market price. The area of the development which would be 'optimal' is shown by the intersection of the MVP curve with the horizontal line PP', so the area developed would be OA.

Of course, no developer can wait for ever, and few can wait for any very long period. The analysis above presumes that waiting is costless. Since this is not true it is evident that developers have to act more precipitately than is assumed above. It is difficult to represent a possible rate of acquisition since development may take place more or less rapidly and the greater the rate of acquisition the higher the prices that are likely to have to be paid. Making the assumption that there is some 'normal' rate of acquisition the curve marked $MC_1$ can be drawn indicating a schedule of prices which would have to be paid. Some pieces of land will be on the market and can be bought at the market price. Over time more can be bought at or only slightly above this price, but as the developer continues buying a higher and higher price will have to be paid. Thus $MC_1$ curves upwards. Given that this curve indicates the additional cost of adding each additional piece of land, the most profitable size for the development is now OB, somewhat smaller than OA, the size when all the land can be acquired at the market value. Finally, if the developer is impatient to finish the development still higher prices will have to be paid, as indicated by the curve marked $MC_2$, and the most profitable size for the development will be still smaller at OC.

## Conclusion

In this chapter we have looked at the problem of site assembly using two different approaches. The first, the game theory approach, assumes away the problem of time but concentrates on the strategies adopted by the land owners in responding to an approach by a would-be developer. The second, apparently more conventional, diagrammatic approach concentrates on the fact that it takes time to assemble a site and that the size of the development may be affected by the developer's willingness to wait.

One tactical problem for the developer is revealed by this approach but is concealed by the game theory approach because of its timelessness. In acquiring land the developer has to lay out funds ahead of the development. If sites are left vacant after acquisition then this can be costly if the development is delayed for long. If, on the other hand, they are let, the developer may have difficulty removing the tenants when the other sites have been acquired. Thus the speed of acquisition of the land becomes a tactical problem for the developer. A faster rate increases the prices which have to be paid for sites bought later, but reduces the opportunity cost of the investment in the sites which are bought earlier.

Another tactical problem is one that was thrown up by both the diagrammatic and the game theory approach. Can the developer price discriminate or does the same price have to be paid to all sellers? The curve showing purchase prices in Figure 14.1 is drawn as it is on the assumption that the developer is able to price discriminate in dealing with sellers. It is assumed that 'market prices' can be paid for some sites, higher prices for others, and still higher prices for the rest. Can this be done? What happens if the owners find out what is afoot and attempt to get together. In this analysis it is evident that this is likely to lead to a higher price having to be paid.

In the next chapter we return to the discussion of the length of time that is necessary to acquire a site, and show how and why compulsory powers may be used to ensure that large scale projects can be achieved.

# 15

## Contiguity: Compulsory Purchase and the Scale of Development

*'I need you'*

---

### Introduction

It is because of the problem of contiguity that powers of compulsory purchase or eminent domain are used by governments and by public utilities. Moreover, these powers of compulsory purchase with respect to land are unusual in that they are generally regarded as acceptable in a democratic society, whereas powers to direct labour or the use of capital are not. With respect to capital and labour such powers are only likely to be used in time of war, or, in peace time to compel young people to spend a period of time in military service. Otherwise they are regarded as illiberal and not to be used by governments in democratic societies.

The problem of contiguity arises in the construction of railways or roads and similar public activities. The problem also arises where there are economies of scale in a development, for example in the construction of a shopping centre or a housing estate. Powers of compulsory purchase may sometimes be made available in these cases, for example if the housing is being built by a local authority, or a shopping centre is being built by a developer in partnership with a local authority. The intention is that with such powers economies of scale may be achieved in the development which could not be attained if land had to be purchased slowly through the market, negotiating with each owner and having to deal with the problems of 'hold outs' mentioned in the previous chapter.

While the use of compulsory purchase may be widely accepted it is still necessary to establish that the social benefits of its use outweigh the social costs, and in the second part of this chapter we attempt to deal with this question. The conclusion that we reach is that its acceptability largely depends upon the time scale. Rapid implementation of a scheme may impose costs which a more measured approach does not.

This problem of scale is looked at in a different way in the third part of this chapter. Here we use the development of a housing estate to show why a large scale development may not only be more profitable to a developer but may also be different to a collection of smaller scale schemes. Nevertheless, if the differences in the level of profitability of large and small schemes are not great, developers will not be willing to expend resources in putting together sites. The pattern of development will then depend upon the ownership of the land. History will therefore affect the pattern of development. Areas of land owned by a single individual or firm will be developed in one way, areas where the ownership is fragmented in another.

## Compulsory purchase and the speed of acquisition

The nature of the problem referred to immediately above is illustrated in Figure 15.1. The diagram was used by Munch (1976) to demonstrate not only the tactical problem facing a developer wishing to acquire a number of contiguous sites, but also the reasons why powers of compulsory purchase or eminent domain may be taken and used by central and local government.

Figure 15.1 is similar to Figure 14.1. The area of land which might be developed is represented along the horizontal axis and costs and prices are

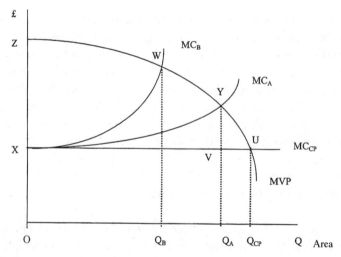

**Figure 15.1**

indicated on the vertical axis. The marginal value product is represented by the line marked MVP and originating at Z on the vertical axis. The market price of land is OX on the vertical axis. If all the land required for the development could be bought at this 'market price' then this would indicate the marginal cost of each additional unit of land. But this is only possible if either the developer is prepared to wait for an indefinite time to buy land as it comes on the market, as we discussed above, or powers of compulsory purchase or eminent domain are available to the developer. If these powers can be used by, or on behalf of the developer, then the land can be bought compulsorily at the 'market price' without waiting. The horizontal line starting at X on the vertical axis is therefore marked $MC_{CP}$. If powers of compulsory purchase can be used then the optimal size of the development is marked as $OQ_{CP}$ on the horizontal axis and is determined by the intersection of the MVP and $MC_{CP}$ curves at U. Beyond this point the additional cost of extending the size of the development would be greater than the revenue received from doing so.

For a developer who does not have access to any powers of compulsory purchase then, as we showed earlier, the price that has to be paid will tend to increase as the quantity purchased increases. Suppose that the prices which would have to be paid can be represented by the curve marked $MC_A$. As we noted in the discussion of Figure 14.1, such a curve assumes that the developer can price discriminate. Some land can be bought at the market price OX and the price of each additional unit is represented by points lying along $MC_A$.

Since the developer has to pay a price greater than the market price to purchase most of the additional units the optimal size of the development is likely to be smaller. This optimal size is indicated in the diagram by the intersection of MVP and $MC_A$ at Y. The most profitable size of the development is $OQ_A$ which is less than $OQ_{CP}$, the size if powers of compulsory purchase can be used.

Suppose now that the developer finds it impossible to price discriminate. Suppose that the owners of land are aware that someone is trying to assemble a site and that they collude together by passing information around as to the prices which are being offered. As a result the price that has to be paid to any one land owner has to be paid to all of them. In that case the curve $MC_A$ does not represent the marginal cost curve. It does not represent the schedule of prices which would have to be paid for each of the pieces of land making up the site. It is now a different kind of price schedule in that any point on it now represents the price which has to be paid for all the pieces of land making up a development of that size. Thus, if we consider a development of size $OQ_A$ on the horizontal axis, the point Y indicates the price which would have to be paid for all the land used for the development. If price discrimination had been possible, however, the points on the curve between X and Y would represent the schedule of prices and Y would indicate the highest price which would have to be paid for any land.

The problem for the developer is then that any higher offer to any single land owner raises the price which has to be paid to all the others. The additional cost of increasing the size of the development is now higher than the price which has to be paid for the extra, marginal, land, because the higher price has to be paid for all the other 'infra-marginal' land. The marginal cost curve which faces the developer is then not $MC_A$ but a curve which can be derived from it, $MC_B$, lying above $MC_A$. Because it does lie above it so that the additional cost of increasing the size of the development is everywhere higher, the optimal, profit maximising, size of the development is smaller. So in Figure 15.1 the marginal cost is equal to the marginal value at W, where $MC_B$ and MVP intersect, and the size of development which maximises profits shown as $OQ_B$ on the horizontal axis, less than $OQ_A$, which in turn is less than $OQ_{CP}$.

This analysis based on Figure 15.1 demonstrates two points. The first we discussed in the previous chapter. It is clear that a developer may have a strong incentive to try to price discriminate. If, by using front companies or several agents or any other methods, owners of parts of a site can be made to believe that each of the sales in the area is being made to a different buyer then a larger, more profitable, development can be built.

The second point is that the use of compulsory powers would enable the completed development to be larger. It could also be built more quickly, since the various parts of the site could be bought quickly without having to wait and negotiate. It would also mean that the development would be even more profitable. This can be demonstrated using the figure. Suppose that the developer can price discriminate but has no powers of compulsory purchase. The cost of the land is represented in the figure by the area $OXYQ_A$. The value of the whole development, on the other hand, is represented by the area under the MVP curve, that is $OZYQ_A$. The difference between the two areas in the figure is XYZ. This represents the amount available both to pay the costs of all the other factors of production, and to provide a profit, if possible.

Suppose, now, that the land can be bought using powers of compulsory purchase. Assume that the area purchased remains at $OQ_A$, then the cost of the land, in the figure, falls to $OXVQ_A$. The area XYV represents additional profit. Of course, it might be true that the development would not actually be profitable if it had to be carried out without these powers so that they might be necessary in order to allow it to be viable. This is, after all, the reason why local authorities enter into partnership agreements in the UK, particularly for the creation of major shopping centres in urban central areas which the local authority wishes to revitalise. Thus the analysis shows how powers of compulsory purchase can turn a potentially loss making development into one that is profitable, and make one which is already likely to be profitable even more so. It will also allow the development to be larger than it otherwise would be, since $OQ_{CP}$ is greater than $OQ_A$. Moreover, this potential increase in the size of the development from $Q_A$ to $Q_{CP}$ further increases its possible profitability. The additional revenue, which, of course, has to cover the additional costs of the increase in size, is shown by the triangle YUV in the figure.

Although a development built with the aid of compulsory purchase may be more profitable, the question has to be raised, however, as to whether this increase in profitability is achieved at the expense of the previous owners of the land. What are the social costs (and benefits) of using compulsory purchase. At one extreme, with respect to some public activities such as road widening, certain pieces of land are essential to the scheme which cannot otherwise be carried out. Most people would feel that giving the owners of these pieces of land the right to ask whatever price they think the public purse will pay would be wrong, since this would really give them a 'monopoly power'. (Not all would agree, however. Many on the libertarian right would regard any state compulsion even of this kind as wrong – and I have been shouted down during a discussion of the economics of town planning at one libertarian economic institute for daring to defend it.)

Nevertheless, we have argued at length in earlier chapters that the 'use value' of a piece of land to the owner may really be higher than its 'exchange' or market value. That is to say the difference in the figure between the two marginal cost curves, $MC_A$ and $MC_{CP}$, can represent a real value to the owners and expropriation can therefore impose a social cost. This is most likely to be true for people who live on the site whose homes are being expropriated but it may also be true for small businesses whose operations are disrupted and who may be forced out of business by the disruption caused by the move.

A factor which would appear to be important in determining these social costs would seem to be the time element. Imrie & Thomas (1997) investigated the acquisition of land in Cardiff for a development which was brought from the conceptual to the implementation stage very quickly, indeed within two years. The small businessmen whose land had been purchased were generally unhappy about the process and the price received. At the other extreme Lin (1999b) looked at the acquisition of land for a road improvement in West London which had been initially proposed in 1958. When he carried out his interviews in 1997 he found that the UK Highways Agency (and its predecessors) had purchased sites over a long period of time as they came on the market. Furthermore the remaining land owners had largely anticipated that the land would eventually be compulsorily purchased. This expectation was largely factored into both the price of the properties and their owners' valuations. People, and the market, had had time to adjust so the social costs appeared to be low.

In this case the process of adjustment was assisted by the British system. So owner occupiers receive the market price of their house plus 10% in compensation for having to move, businesses can also receive compensation for disturbance. Moreover, an authority which has published plans to acquire land can be forced to buy sites well ahead of the planned date for compulsory purchase if the owners cannot sell them on the open market. In some other countries the price paid if a property is compulsorily purchased may be well below the market value, so that compulsory purchase becomes a threat to back up an offer to purchase at the market price. Thus in Taiwan the compulsory purchase price is the price at which the land is assessed for taxation which is lower than market value. In Italy the formula is complicated but the result is that the legal compulsory purchase price is usually well below market value (Ave 1996). The US system allows for recourse to the courts to settle the price. Munch (1976), in one of the few empirical studies of the economics of eminent domain, found that the costs of going to law appeared to affect the price paid. The owners of smaller sites received a price which appeared to be less, on average, than what she assessed as true market value, while the owners of larger sites received a price which appeared to be greater. She attributed this differential to the fact that the owners of larger sites would be able to pay for more, and better, advice than the owners of smaller sites.

Leaving aside variations due to differences in legal systems and returning to the question posed earlier as to the balance between the social costs and benefits of compulsory purchase, my own assessment would be that it depends on the rate at which sites are purchased. The benefits will tend to exceed the costs if the rate of acquisition is relatively slow. The faster it proceeds the more likely it is that people will be forced to sell at a time and at a price which imposes a real cost on them. The slower it proceeds the more likely it is that some people would wish to sell anyway during the period, and that the others will have had time to adjust.

If there has been little empirical investigation of the economics of compulsory purchase there has been rather more discussion of theoretical aspects, in great part, I suspect, because of the possible interesting interaction between economics and the law. Thus a welfare problem which has been discussed is the extent to which the knowledge that a property is to be purchased (compulsorily) at full market price in the near future sends a misleading signal. Blume *et al.* (1984) argue that while full compensation at market value would appear to be ethically correct, the knowledge that full compensation is to be paid may lead to over-investment from a national point of view.

The argument runs as follows. A firm which owns a property which it plans to demolish and redevelop in a few years time will not invest money in the property which will not be recouped during its expected life. If, on the other hand, the firm knows that the property is to be compulsorily purchased in a few years time, and that full compensation is to be paid, then the firm will be more likely to make major investments in improving and maintaining the property since it will get the money back. Therefore, it is argued, when compulsory acquisition is independent of the current use of the site, as it might be, for example, with respect to a road widening, full compensation is not (socially) efficient. On the other hand, if the site's current use is taken into account, then it may be both fair and efficient. This would be so because, for example, when the route for a new road is being determined it will be deliberately sited so as to minimise the cost to government and to avoid knocking down too many expensive buildings.

In fact, it would seem to me that while there may be a theoretical problem of equity and efficiency it does not appear to be one that is important in practice. Governments do decide their development schemes at least partly on the basis of what each will cost and will try to avoid buying expensive buildings only to demolish them. Owners do not appear to over-invest in buildings which they expect to be compulsorily purchased. Rather the reverse, the problem is more likely to be that once plans for the future development of the area have been published by the local authority the area becomes blighted as the owners fail to invest or adequately maintain their properties. This was, after all, the reason why the law was changed in Britain to allow owners to require a public authority to buy their properties ahead of any actual compulsory purchase.

Finally, it is difficult to see why possible over-investment should be regarded as a particular problem caused by compulsory purchase. Properties are bought every day at full market price by developers who will demolish them to make way for some new development. Since little time may elapse between the first approach by a developer and the sale and demolition of the building it is evident that over-investment, from a social point of view, is likely to have occurred. Since this is not regarded as a problem with respect to the large number of sales in the private sector, there is no reason to suppose that it is any greater problem when properties are acquired by the public sector where the number of transactions is very small indeed. There may be a theoretical case to be made but it is not a problem in practice.

## Scale economies, acquisition costs and history

The question of scale and hence the size of the area to be developed can be approached in a different way. The analysis in the first part of this chapter, and in the previous chapter, shows that, if land can be acquired relatively easily, the scale of development will tend to be bigger than if a large site can only be put together by patiently negotiating with numerous small land owners. But the land available for development will then often be a question of history. In some places there may be a large site owned by a single land owner, indeed several large sites. In other areas the ownership of the land may be fragmented and no large sites may be available to be purchased. Whether it is worth putting together a large site in the latter case depends then not only on the costs of acquisition but also on the possible economies of scale. If the economies of scale possible from proceeding with a large development are not very great then it will not be worthwhile expending time and resources in trying to put together a large site. It follows that the pattern of development in an area if it is under the control of a single land owner is likely to differ from what it would be if the ownership of the land were fragmented. In the first case large-scale integrated developments are possible, in the second case they are not economically feasible.

The argument can be illustrated by considering the optimal kind of residential development, from the developer's point of view, if owner occupiers prefer lower residential densities to higher in the area in which they live. The empirical evidence suggests that they do in that econometric studies of the factors affecting house prices indicate that for any given dwelling its price will be lower the higher the residential density in the surrounding area. On the other hand the price differences are not very great.

The position is illustrated in Figure 15.2. Prices and costs are represented on the vertical axis and residential density on the horizontal axis. We assume initially that the area to be developed is large and that the development is under the control of a single firm. The line marked AR is the average revenue curve and indicates the relationship between the average price

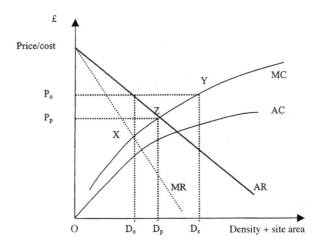

**Figure 15.2**

which can be obtained for a house on the site and the residential density of the area. It slopes downwards because the higher the density of development the lower will be the price. The average cost of construction of a house is assumed to increase with density and is shown by the curve marked AC.

The developer determines the optimal, profit maximising, density of development, however, not from AR and AC but by balancing the additional cost of an additional dwelling against the additional revenue which can be obtained from building it. These two factors are indicated by the curves MR and MC. The curve marked MR indicates the additional, marginal, revenue from an extra house. MR lies below AR because from each additional house the developer gains the price of the house but loses the small falls in price on all the other houses because the density of development is increased. MC lies above AC because the marginal cost is the cost of building the additional house plus the increase in the costs of all the other houses because of the additional density.

The developer's profits are maximised when marginal revenue equals marginal cost, in the figure, at the intersection of MR and MC at X. Increasing the density of development is profitable up to this point but beyond it the cost of an extra unit is greater than the additional revenue received. The intersection of the two curves at X indicates that the optimal density is $D_o$. If the area is developed at this density then the price which can be obtained for each house is indicated on the AR curve as being $P_o$.

Suppose now that a single small part of this area is to be developed. The density of development of the single small site will affect the price which can be obtained very little indeed, it will be affected primarily by the density of development of the surrounding area. To fix the argument, suppose that the area has already been developed at the density $D_0$ and all the houses sold off, but that one of them is shortly after destroyed by fire so that its site has to be redeveloped. The density of development of the surrounding area has already been fixed at $D_0$ and this means that the price which can be obtained for any houses built on the small site is $P_0$, and this price can be got whatever the density of development of this single small site. In effect the developer of the small site faces an (almost) horizontal average revenue curve at $P_0$. To profit maximise the developer now has to build up to the density at which the cost of an additional house is just equal to the price which can be obtained, in Figure 15.2 the point at which the horizontal line at $P_0$ intersects MC, that is Y, with a density $D_s$ marked on the horizontal axis.

It is, of course, obvious that if enough of this kind of piecemeal development were to take place the average density would visibly rise, the environment be seen to deteriorate, and the average price receivable would fall. With piecemeal small scale development each developer faces, or is perceived as facing, a horizontal average revenue curve, although the combination of the developments which take place does affect the average density and there-fore the price which can be obtained. A long-run equilibrium is reached when everyone builds at the same density on their small site as the average density of the surrounding area so that any new building does not affect the average density. This equilibrium density with piecemeal development is indicated in Figure 15.2 by the intersection of the curve MC with the curve AR at Z. The density of development is then $D_p$, and the price per house is $P_p$. That this is the equilibrium density can be seen from the fact that if any site has to be redeveloped it will always be most profitable to build at this density, no higher and no lower.

The argument above demonstrates that when a large area is developed by a single developer for residential use, the residential density is likely to be lower than the density which would result from the piecemeal develop-ment of the area when the ownership is split up and the individual sites being developed are small. There is a further possible difference. Not only may the density be different, the character of the development may also be different because it may be intended for different customers. It seems plausible to assume, and there is some evidence to confirm the assumption, that, in economic terms, the quality of the environment is a good for which the demand is income elastic. That is to say, in this context, higher income households are more willing to pay a higher price for a better, lower density, environment than lower income households. In terms of Figure 15.2, the average revenue curve may slope downward with respect to housing for higher income households but be near horizontal for lower income households. Of course, the relative position of the curves will vary with other factors such as location. Nevertheless, let us assume that in Figure 15.2 the curve AR is the average revenue curve for higher income residents and that the average revenue curve for lower income residents would be a horizontal line lying just above $P_p$. It can be seen that the characteristics of any development will depend upon the ownership of the land. If a large site can be acquired it would be most profitable to develop it as a whole for higher income households at a relatively low density. If, on the other hand, the ownership of the area is fragmented so that it is developed piecemeal by a large number of developers, then it is likely to be developed at a higher density for lower income households.

Of course, the argument assumes an absence of planning controls, and one of the reasons why residential density controls may be imposed is to prevent densities being too high (Evans 1985, pp. 28–31). Nevertheless the argument does help to explain some historical differences in past patterns of development, and this in turn helps to confirm the theoretical argument. To cite an obvious and well known instance, the West End of London was developed for and occupied by higher income households, and the developments were carried out on large estates owned by relatively few families, so that the Bedford Estate covered much of Bloomsbury, the Portman Estate much of Marylebone, and the Grosvenor Estate much of Mayfair and Belgravia. In each of these areas some land was left as open, green, space, obvious examples are the eponymous squares – Bedford Square, Portman Square, Grosvenor Square. Clearly, if the ownership of the land had been fragmented the owners of the land now occupied by these squares would not have left their land idle. This would not have benefited them, only the occupiers of the surrounding houses. A less well known example is provided by Dyos (1961) in his history of the former borough of Camberwell in south London. In Peckham, in the north of the area the ownership of the land was fragmented and it was developed at a relatively high density and occupied by low income households. Much of Dulwich, in the south, however, was owned by a single land owner, Dulwich College, and the land was developed at a relatively low density for high income households. The differences between the two areas remain a hundred and more years later, as the purchase of a house on the Dulwich Estate by Margaret Thatcher on her retirement helps to illustrate.

These examples demonstrate that patterns of ownership will affect what is built. Moreover, since buildings can stand for a very long time, past patterns of ownership can affect what exists on the ground hundreds of years later.

This is because one type of development which uses the economies of scale may only be economic if a large enough land area can be easily obtained. If land ownership is fragmented the costs of acquisition will frequently ensure that the developments which occur are small scale and fragmented. The theoretical analysis and the empirical evidence cited above relate to development for residential use, but there seems no reason not to suppose that the same kinds of argument apply to other kinds of development. As we noted in an earlier section, compulsory purchase is used by local authorities in partnership with private developers to purchase land to create major shopping centres. Obviously there are economies of scale, and equally obviously trying to put together a large enough site by negotiation is seen as not even feasible. I suspect that the arguments can even apply to the development of land for industrial use. I have known the development of a large area of land as an industrial estate to be planned to take place over 20 years, a period, one may note, longer than the usual time horizon of a local planning authority. The aim of the developer was to develop the area slowly and in this way to maintain a high and cohesive environmental standard. Coincidentally, nearby there was another area which had planning permission for industrial development and the developer was concerned that this might have presented serious competition. In the event the other area was developed piecemeal without any overall control being exercised so that, in terms of the quality of the environment it actually could not compete. Thus, even when one might think that it would not matter, in an industrial development, the scale of the development can affect the environmental quality of the result, and therefore how it is used and what locates there.

## Summary and conclusion

The discussion in the current chapter follows naturally on from that in the previous chapter. There we were concerned with the problem of site acquisition. The developer perceives that a large scale development would be more profitable than one at a smaller scale. The large scale development can only be achieved by putting together a large enough site and this may only be achievable by negotiating with a large number of individual land owners. These negotiations may be expensive and time consuming. In the current chapter we show that one way round this problem is for the land to be compulsorily purchased. This was done as part of schemes of urban renewal or comprehensive redevelopment in order to provide public housing, particularly in the 25-year period after the Second World War. In recent years powers of compulsory purchase have more frequently been used by local authorities acting in partnership with private developers to construct large commercial developments, primarily shopping centres with car parks, in central urban areas. The analysis shows why compulsory purchase may be used in these cases as well as in the more obvious cases such as road widening and road building. We also look at the social costs of using powers of compulsory purchase and show that these costs may be minimised if the process of planning and acquisition is long drawn out, but may be much higher if the plans are drawn up with little notice and speedily implemented.

Powers of compulsory purchase are used when there are perceived to be economies of scale. In the final section of the chapter we show that if the possible economies of scale are not very great and the ownership of the land is fragmented, then the costs of acquisition may be greater than the available economies of scale. On the other hand, if the land is owned by a single land owner the cost of negotiation and acquisition will be much lower and a large scale development becomes feasible. Thus the pattern of land ownership will affect what is developed. Fragmented land ownership will result in disjointed small scale schemes. Unified land ownership will be more likely to result in large scale, unified developments.

In the next chapter we look at the way in which some countries have sought to deal with the problem of fragmented land ownership without using compulsory purchase, that is by voluntary schemes for the reallocation of the ownership of land. We also look at the price of land. The implication of the analysis in these two chapters is that larger sites should be worth more than smaller sites. This appears to be true with respect to small sites, but the cost of infrastructure dominates with respect to larger sites.

# 16

## Contiguity: Land Reallocation and the Price of Land

### *'Come together'*

---

### Introduction

The problem of contiguity is most obvious when the pieces of land owned by individual land owners are small and of irregular shape. In some countries this has led to policies to 'reallocate' or 'readjust' the boundaries of the land parcels. In a peasant economy on fertile land the pieces of land may be very small and very irregular. If the land is to be developed for urban use the sites need to be rectangular, more or less, and with frontage onto a road. Land reallocation results in each of the previous owners owning the same proportion of the total area as before, but each site is of a shape and at a location suitable for development.

Land reallocation is discussed in this chapter, together with the evidence concerning the relationship between size of site and land price. We would expect that, *ceteris paribus*, larger sites would sell at a higher price per unit area precisely because the larger the site, the fewer the problems of land acquisition which can arise. The empirical evidence is conflicting, however, and we seek to reconcile this conflict by showing that larger sites cost more to develop because of the infrastructure which has to be put in.

### Land reallocation or adjustment

Laws and policies which allow for the reallocation of the ownership exist in many countries. Schemes of this kind avoid the negative libertarian implications of compulsory purchase since the previous owners still own a piece of land approximately where they did before, and can therefore benefit from its sale. Primarily concerned with rural land such schemes can best be used where the land holdings of the peasant farmers in the area are small and irregular in shape and where the land owned by a single farmer may nevertheless be split up and at different locations. Development which would involve the construction of buildings usually requires the existence of more or less rectangular plots fronting on to more or less straight roads. If the existing land holdings are very irregular this can only be done if either a single developer buys up a large number of holdings and imposes order in that way, or the boundaries of the holdings are all simultaneously read-justed.

Policies which allow for land reallocation are described by Hebbert & Nakai (1988) for Japan, by Dieterich *et al.* (1993) for Germany, and by Lin (1993) and Lin & Evans (2000) for Taiwan. A representative scheme would start from a pattern of land holdings as shown in Figure 16.1, in simplified form, for an area lying outside Taipeh, in Taiwan (Lin 1999a). The end result would be the kind of land holding pattern shown in Figure 16.2. First, the owners of the land have to get together. They may do this voluntarily or a government agency may act as the catalyst. In some cases the threat of compulsory purchase may be used to 'encourage' participation and, in the end, agreement. To allow the construction of roads each owner loses a proportion of their original total holding. They will usually lose a further proportion as some of the land is sold to pay the cost of providing the infrastructure. So, if roads are expected to take up some 10% of the area, and if 5% of the land is sold to cover the cost of road construction, each land owner who starts with a holding of, say, 1000 square metres will hold, at the end of the process, about 850 square metres. An owner of two or more sites will finish up with one single site, and each site will be rectangular and front onto a road. Thus the owner of the piece of land shown shaded in Figure 16.1 before allocation has, at the end of the process, the area similarly marked in Figure 16.2. Astute developers, as Lin (1999a, Ch. 7) has shown, who know that a land reallocation scheme is to take place can anticipate the scheme by buying up scattered land holdings in the knowledge that they will finish up with unified developable sites after reallocation has taken place. This may be easier than waiting until readjustment has taken place and then trying to buy up adjacent sites.

The main disadvantage of land reallocation is signalled by this discussion of the strategies that developers may adopt. It results in the tidying up of the boundaries of land holdings and it allows the infrastructure to be built, but it does not necessarily, or even very often, create large developable sites. Furthermore, since the sites which do result are handed back into the ownership of the peasants they can continue to hold on to their land,

**Figure 16.1**  Representative land reallocation scheme. Land holdings before implementation of reallocation scheme with road plans shown in outline (Source: Lin, 1999).

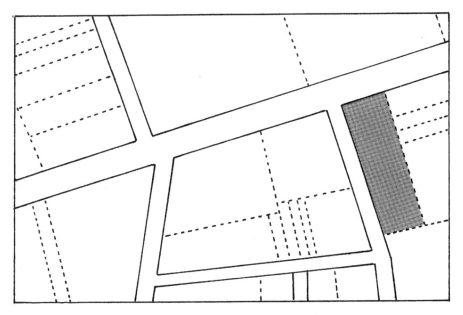

**Figure 16.2**  Representative land reallocation scheme. Land holdings after implementation and reallocation scheme. The owner of the area shown as shaded was the
owner of the (larger) area shown shaded in Figure 16.1 (Source: Lin, 1999).

farming it if they wish, until their family circumstances or the price available persuades them to sell.

Hebbert & Nakai (1988) point out that in Japan peasant landowners frequently continue to hold on to their land, possibly selling a part of their holding when they require some capital, for example on the marriage of a daughter. The Japanese system allows owners to arrange amongst themselves land reallocation schemes to allow for urban development, and even permits this as the only form of urban development allowed in Urban Control Areas where, as the name implies, urbanisation is supposed to be prevented. The result is that the process of land reallocation appears to condone and even encourage urban sprawl. The urbanised area is extended as land reallocation schemes are carried through, roads and other infrastructure are put in, and some land is developed, if only to pay for the infrastucture. A high proportion of the rest of the land may remain undeveloped, however, the owners anticipating, or speculating, that the price will remain high and may be even higher in the future.

The problem would appear to be compounded by the fact that the high demand for urban land means that there is little land coming on to the market in the region for a peasant farmer to buy and transfer to. Selling one's land therefore implies retirement, not a shift in one's occupation from one location to another. In these circumstances peasant farmers may be even less willing to sell, treating their land as an investment which can be finally cashed in at the time of retirement but not before. Small pieces of 'farmland' can and do therefore remain woven into the urban fabric even though their continued operation as 'farms' would seem uneconomic.

Land reallocation is not a policy used in all countries, it is not used, for instance, in the United Kingdom, the United States, or Australia. The reason would seem to be that in these countries the holdings of land by farmers or other land owners are generally quite large. Thus the sale of a piece of land by one owner, whether the whole or a part of a farm, will supply an area of land suitable for most forms of development. Nevertheless, land reallocation is a policy which might be considered relevant to the redevelopment of existing urban areas where ownership is fragmented. Certainly it gets round the main argument against compulsory purchase, that it results in the forcible expropriation of land which imposes a cost on the owner. Since the owner of a site before reallocation continues to own a site afterwards this objection falls. But, of course, land reallocation still leaves land ownership fragmented and most compulsory purchase schemes are intended to achieve economies of scale which are believed to be available only from a unified and large site.

# Size of site and the price of land

Since site assembly is a problem one would expect the price paid for sites to be affected by their relationship with other sites which may be developed at the same time. Sometimes this may mean that particular pieces of land which are absolutely necessary to a proposed development are sold at prices which appear excessive, given their other characteristics. Sometimes the crucial position of a particular piece of land is realised, or, indeed, arranged, beforehand. A land owner may sell most of an area of land but retain ownership of a so-called ransom strip – a piece of land essential for the development of the rest of the land, and given the name because the owner of it can metaphorically hold the owner of the rest to ransom.

Variations in the price of land because of their spatial and locational relationship to other pieces are difficult to explore systematically, since the price variations depend upon the local situation. One kind of variation can be analysed, however, and that is the variation in the price paid for land (per unit of area) as a function of the size of the piece of land being sold. If the market for land were completely perfect and contiguity was not a problem then one would expect that the price would be the same whatever the size of the piece being sold. On the other hand, since the market is imperfect and since site assembly is difficult then one would expect the price to increase with the size of the site being sold.

A great many empirical studies have been carried out, almost all of them relating to the land market in North America, and almost all of this empirical research has found the reverse of this, the price per unit of area tends to be lower, the larger the area of the piece of land being sold. The explanation for this would appear to lie in the fact that the variation in the size of the sites being studied was in most cases very large indeed. In the development of very large sites it is evident that infrastructure has to be provided and, in addition, a high proportion of the land area has to be used for roads and circulation space and cannot be sold on. On the other hand a small site fronting on to an existing road can be developed and sold as a whole and no infrastructure costs need be incurred.

The way in which the cost of providing infrastructure impacts on the price of land is made clear by Needham (1992) in a paper reporting on the economics of public land banking in The Netherlands. He found that the price of land for agriculture (around 1980) was about 5 Dfl per m$^2$, although local authorities paid about 10 Dfl when they purchased it from farmers for future development. The cost of providing infrastructure came to about 40 Dfl per m$^2$ so that in order to cover its costs the local authority would have had to sell the whole land holding at about 50 Dfl. The amount of land which can be sold for development is, however, reduced by the amount of land which is used by the community for roads, cycle tracks, foot paths, parks and other open space, etc. In the end only about half of the land which was originally purchased by the local authority could be sold for development. To cover its costs the price it obtains for this has therefore to be at least 100 Dfl per $m^2$.

The Dutch evidence indicates that a large area of land may be bought for development at one price per $m^2$ but much smaller sites may be sold for 10 times that price. Thus in a study such as that by Brownstone & De Vany (1991) where the size of the sites which were part of the data set varied from one acre to 19,000 acres, and where the price varies between less than $10,000 per acre to over $1,480,000, the explanation for these large price differences must be the differing infrastructure requirements of the different sized sites. Some explanation of this kind is necessary since other kinds of explanation ignore the fact that sites can easily be split up and sold separately. Thus Brownstone & De Vany themselves refer to the greater risks involved in holding large sites as a possible explanation. But if the owner of a large site thought that the price could be increased if the site were split into two or more parts then there is no reason why this should not be done. The land would then be split up into the number of sites which would maximise the total amount received. Since this was not, and is not, done, the lower prices of larger sites cannot be explained in this way.

On the other hand, while sites can be split relatively easily, they can be joined together less easily. So, as we suggested earlier, where infrastructure needs are the same, all the sites are relatively small and front on to a road, for example, one would expect that larger sites would sell at a higher price per hectare than smaller sites. Two studies of the price of smaller sites have found such a positive relationship between price per unit area and size. One looked at the price of sites in Osaka in Japan (Tabuchi 1996). In this case the sites were scattered through the city. The other was a study of the price of sites in an area outside Taipeh, Taiwan (Lin & Evans 2000). In this case the sites were being sold by the government to cover the cost of infrastructure in a land reallocation scheme. All the pieces of land being sold were at more or less the same location and were sold at auction at more or less the same time. Thus apart from differences in size and in their specific location within the area covered by the scheme the sites were otherwise identical. The authors found that price per unit area clearly increased with size.

The difference between the North American studies and the two Far Eastern studies can generally be explained, as we have already remarked, by the fact that the former generally considered larger sites and a much larger variation in the size of sites than the latter. The implication would seem to be that the true, underlying, relationship between price per unit area and size of site is one in which the price initially increases with size and then decreases. However, one US study by Colwell & Sirmans (1988) did consider sites as small as those considered by Tabuchi and Lin & Evans but found that price decreased with size, a result which could be seen as consistent with the results of the other American studies. It may be that this is a 'sport' result and not to be relied on. An alternative possibility, put forward by a referee of Lin & Evans (2000, p. 393), is that because sites in the US are generally large, so that the infrastructure effect dominates in determining the price schedule overall, it still tends to dominate even when sites are relatively small. That is to say, the general market structure, determined by competition for sites, results in a price schedule where the price per unit area falls as size of site increases. On the other hand in countries such as Taiwan and Japan, the areas of land owned even by farmers on the urban fringe are small, and, as we showed in the first half of this chapter, land policies such as land reallocation schemes exist to deal with the problem. Thus large sites are scarce and may therefore carry a premium for that reason. The competitive price structure which results is therefore one where price per unit area increases as size of site increases. Evidently our understanding of the relationship is still not complete.

## Summary and conclusions

The need for a site to be of a particular size and shape to be developed profitably and economically is obvious. Most work in urban economics has concentrated, however, on the question of location; how does the price of land vary with its location relative to the rest of the urban area is a question fundamental to modern urban economics since the subject became a recognised branch of economics in the 1960s.

From a developer's point of view, however, the most important question is not that of location but one of putting together a site at a location which can be developed profitably. In these past three chapters we have looked at this problem from a number of different points of view starting with this question – if the developer has to negotiate with the owners of a number of different pieces of land in order to put together a site with the right size and shape, how will this affect the price paid? Would it be advantageous to use 'front companies' so as not to reveal that a single developer is seeking to acquire all the sites?

This latter question arose when we considered the purchase of sites over time. It appeared that purchasing sites over a longer period of time would allow them to be bought more cheaply and would be less disruptive. The importance of the time element was used to show how compulsory purchase became necessary when a large number of sites needed to be acquired for some public utility or other use within a relatively short period of time.

The use of powers of compulsory purchase can impose a cost on those who are forced to move. If plenty of notice could be given, then, over time many of the sites could be acquired voluntarily and so without imposing this cost since the owners and/or occupiers would wish to move anyway.

In the first half of this chapter we pointed out that in some countries the use of compulsory purchase can be avoided by the use of land reallocation or land readjustment schemes. These are particularly useful for dealing with fragmented land ownership at the urban fringe, particularly when the boundaries of the land holdings are extremely irregular. The schemes regularise the pattern of land holdings and allow the construction of roads and the installation of infrastructure, although the land ownership may still be fragmented after the scheme has been implemented and the owners may still be unwilling to sell, speculating that a higher price may be available in the future.

In the second half of this chapter we argued that a pattern of small sites which have to be amalgamated to create a site large enough to be economical to develop should result in a price structure in which smaller sites were sold at a lower price per unit area than larger sites. It was shown that the empirical evidence confirmed this view with regard to small sites in Japan and Taiwan, but that the large number of US studies established that when sites were large and very variable in size the price per unit area decreased as size increased. It was argued that this was because infrastructure had to be provided for these larger sites, and that a part of the site could not be sold on but would have to be used for roads, recreational space and other forms of communal activity.

# 17

# The Taxation of Land and Development Gains

## *'Taxman'*

### Introduction

At the beginning of this book we said that, since the time of Ricardo, it has been thought that the taxation of land is one of the most efficient forms of taxation, possibly the most efficient. On the basis of the classical analysis it has been accepted that the taxation of land will not affect the price of land, nor the supply of land. Thus land taxation will not distort the economy in the way that, say, an income tax will affect the supply of labour, or a tax on the income from capital will affect the rate of saving and therefore the availability of capital for investment. Moreover, while people can emigrate and capital can be transferred abroad land is fixed in its location.

This view of the economic advantages of land taxation has been held to this day, and has had considerable political influence. However, the theory set out in this book suggests that this classical view of the effects of land taxation, even though it has been deeply held and influential, is in fact wrong. We show that taxes on land can be passed on in the form of higher rents and can affect the uses to which land is put. Thus land taxes can distort the economy in the same way as taxes on other factors of production.

In this chapter we discuss the differing attitudes towards land taxation which have prevailed over the years, and explain why stringent forms of land development taxation, such as the 100% Betterment Levy imposed in Britain following the Town and Country Planning Act of 1947, will distort the market, even bring it practically to a standstill. This breakdown was observed at the time but explained then in political terms.

## The undeserving land owner

The nineteenth century view of the merits of taxing land seems to have been driven as much by considerations of equity as of efficiency. It was felt by many economists that economic growth and population growth resulted in increases in the value of land which the owners of the land had done nothing to deserve. The labourer invested time and effort in a job. The new industrial entrepreneurs saved up their capital, abstaining from spending it on their own pleasure, and risked it in investment in their undertakings. The owner of land, on the other hand, did none of these things but merely continued to own the land that had probably been handed down to him by earlier generations. So, as J.S. Mill put it, the land 'increases in value while the landlord sleeps'.

Diagrammatically the situation they described is represented in Figure 17.1(a) and (b). In Figure 17.1(a) we have the Ricardo model. Land is represented along the horizontal axis and the rent of land on the vertical axis. There is a given quantity of land, OQ, indicated by the vertical line QQ' representing the fact that the supply of land is assumed to be fixed. The demand for land is represented by the downward sloping demand curve DD'. Equality of quantity demanded with quantity supplied fixes the rent, in the figure, at OP. If the demand for land increases because of economic growth or population growth, then the demand curve shifts upward to, say, $D_1D_1'$, and the price of land to $OP_1$. No further land is brought into use by the increase in demand because, by assumption, the quantity of land is fixed. Therefore, as a consequence of the argument and its assumptions, the owner of land has done nothing.

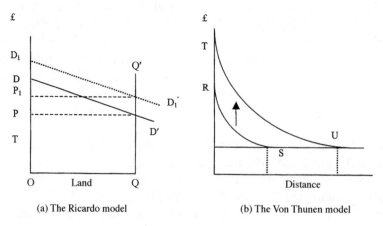

(a) The Ricardo model       (b) The Von Thunen model

**Figure 17.1**

The conclusions are virtually the same if we view the situation in the light of the Von Thunen model as in Figure 17.1(b). Here distance from the market is represented on the horizontal axis, and rent on the vertical axis. The existing rent gradient is shown by the downward sloping line RS. Rents decline at a decreasing rate as distance from the city increases, falling to zero at the margin of cultivation. An increase in the prosperity or the population of the city will lead to an increase in the demand for land and a shift upward in the rent gradient to a new equilibrium level, TU. Land within the previously cultivated area is cultivated more intensively, and, at the edge of the cultivated area, the margin of cultivation is pushed outward, from S to U in the figure, and so new areas of land are brought into cultivation, that is, a ring of land of width, in the figure, SU. Once again the landlord has grown wealthier because of the increase in demand, but does not appear to have done anything to deserve it.

In fact, this view is less easy to justify with the Von Thunen model than with the Ricardian model. With the former it is evident that, in most cases, bringing land into cultivation requires extensive investment in clearing the land and fencing it. Moreover, even within the previously cultivated area, as its price rises, so it is farmed more intensively and alterations have to take place to accommodate, say, a change from arable to pasture and dairying. It is evident that such changes require extensive work and investment by both landlords and tenants. Indeed Marx himself extensively discussed what came to be called 'differential rent II', the increases in rent related to the intensification of the use of land (Marx 1894/1962; Ball 1977; Evans 1992).

Nevertheless the analysis, particularly that based on the Ricardian model, seemed to justify both what one might call the political view that landlords did little to justify the rent they received, and the economic view that taxes on land would not distort the economy. Taxes on land seemed therefore to be uniquely justified. The apotheosis of the idea that land should be taxed especially heavily is set out in Henry George's book *Progress and Poverty* and its arguments support what came to be known as the 'Single Tax Movement'.

The views of Henry George and his followers are, in effect, based on the Ricardian model illustrated in Figure 17.1(a). Given a demand schedule represented by the line DD', and a fixed supply with a vertical supply curve QQ', the price of land will be OP, as we have said. Suppose now that a proportion of the rent is taken in tax, say PT, with a 30% tax rate. It is evident, as we showed in Chapter 2, that the rent of land will remain the same and that the quantity of land supplied will, of course, remain the same. Therefore, a tax on land does not affect the allocation of resources and does not distort the economy. Moreover, it is clear that the tax could be set at any rate, up to 100%, and would still appear, on the basis of this analysis, to have no effect on either the rent of land or the supply of land, or, by extension, on its use.

On the basis of this premise, it could be argued that a high tax on land would deal with the problem of the landlord 'growing richer while he sleeps'. A high rate of tax would capture increases in the value of land since the tax would capture most of the increases in rent. Note that one must be careful to distinguish between the value of land, the price at which it can be sold, and the rental income. If a differential tax is imposed on rents then the value of the land will be reduced even though the rent paid for the use of the land remains the same.

George could also argue that, as a matter of fact, given the level of government expenditure in the United States in the late nineteenth century, a tax on land at a suitably high rate would be able to generate enough income to cover all this government expenditure. Thus since it could generate the same income as all the other taxes put together all these other taxes could be abolished. So a political platform could be, and was, constructed on the basis of heavy taxation of the income from land and the abolition of all other taxes. This platform became known as the 'Single Tax Movement'.

Henry George was one of the few economists to generate a political programme and to have a following. In part this may be because he was not an academic economist but a trade union organiser, so that he was interested in the implementation of ideas as well as the ideas themselves. It also seems to be true that the idea that land should be taxed differentially has a popular appeal. George's book, *Progress and Poverty* (1879), was a best seller in its time. Moreover, George still has followers. His intellectual inheritance can be seen today in the journal *Land and Liberty* or, say, in the book *The Power in the Land* by Fred Harrison (1983), a journalist (and sometime Liberal Party Candidate for Parliament) who has also been editor of *Land and Liberty*.

The Henry George programme has a problem, even taken on its own terms and on the basis of the analysis set out above. This has already been hinted at. A high rate of tax may not affect the rent paid but it does affect the capital value of the property. The higher the rate of tax the lower will be the value of the land. If the rate of tax is 100% and all the income is taxed away then the landlord will receive no income from the land, and can expect to receive nothing in the future, if the tax is expected to be permanent. It follows that the value of the land falls to zero. This may be seen as a good thing by those hostile to landlords, and it might not matter if the economy was static. But no economy is static, and the most profitable uses for a piece of land change over time. If all income is taxed away, however, the owner of the land has no incentive whatsoever to respond to price changes. So, for example, the owner of a piece of rural land adjacent to an expanding city has no reason to respond if an offer is made for the land by someone wishing to develop it for housing. The landlord's income will remain, as before, zero. Thus the 'Single Tax' at 100% would freeze the use of land. The presumption that the rate of tax will not have this effect is based on a view that the landlord does nothing. But this assumes away the fact that in a changing economy, rather than a static economy, land owners do have some role to play even if it is only responding to changes in prices.

Logically, of course, the problem could be solved by nationalising all land and taking over to the state the role that land owners would otherwise play in organising change. Since a 100% tax would result in land having no value whatsoever, it would seem obvious that land might as well be nationalised since the private land owner has no interest in maintaining its value. Curiously this logical step seems not to have been taken by George or his followers. In part this would seem to be a matter of image. While taxation appears consistent with capitalism, nationalisation would represent socialism, and would therefore be a step too far, for most Americans at least. Primarily, however, it would seem to be because to nationalise land for this reason would be to accept that land owners have a role to play in trying to ensure that their land is used efficiently by responding to economic change. But it is not possible to hold this view and at the same time believe that land owners do nothing but hold land 'which increases in value while they sleep', implying that they have no economic role to play. The two views are mutually inconsistent.

## Betterment

A major theme in the argument for taxing land differentially was that public investment in infrastructure benefited the owners of land affected by it and so they should contribute to the cost of providing it. A number of historical examples can be cited where theory was put into practice and which are reviewed by Alan Prest (1981) in his monograph on the taxation of urban land. So the draining of Romney Marsh, on the south-east coast of England, was, at least in part, financed in this way. The construction of sea walls to protect the land from flooding and erosion was often, again at least in part, financed in this way. It was evident in such cases that those being required to contribute would be the primary beneficiaries from the existence of the sea walls, and that their properties would be worth more because of the improved sea defences. Thus a levy on local land owners was both efficient and equitable. Government, in these cases, was acting to coordinate an investment which the land owners might have done for themselves if they acted together. Government's involvement, however, if nothing else, made the investment more likely by circumventing the notorious 'free rider' problem of this kind of investment – the fact that each land owner has an economic incentive to try to avoid contributing, since if the scheme goes ahead anyway, he or she will necessarily still benefit, because of its public good characteristics, but at zero cost.

Difficulties arise when the benefits of public investment are more widespread and it is less obvious who the beneficiaries might be. At the end of the nineteenth century and the beginning of the twentieth attempts were made to finance the construction of Tower Bridge, and the Aldwych/ Kingsway road improvement, both in central London, by imposing betterment levies on the owners of land located nearby (Prest 1981). In practice the revenue raised was very low, and much was dissipated in legal argument as to who should be charged and how much. The problem was similar to that raised in the previous section – if the putative beneficiaries paid a betterment levy then this would reduce the benefit they received, possibly eliminating it entirely. Indeed, if the levy was pitched too high then the land owners would actually be worse off. Since the amount of the benefit to land owners was less certain and therefore less measurable in cases like these than it was in the case of sea defences, legal argument over the level of the benefit and the amount of any levy was virtually inevitable.

The view that the owners of land benefited from public investment and that this benefit should be appropriated to pay for the public's investment was nevertheless one that continued to have some emotive and intellectual support. The argument was the basis for the imposition of a 100% betterment levy in the British 1947 Town and Country Planning Act. Unlike the tax proposed by the Single Tax Movement this was not a tax on the income from land but a tax on a change in its capital value. So, for example, when a piece of land was sold to a builder for residential development, under the Act the difference between its 'current-use value', that is its value solely as agricultural land, and its value as housing land would be taxed away. It was held that the difference resulted from economic and population growth, the basic argument in the previous section, and from public investment in roads and other infrastructure which made the development profitable. In neither case, it was believed, was there any reason why the land owner should benefit, nor had the land owner done anything else to deserve a reward so that the whole could, and should, be taxed away.

Not surprisingly the effect of the betterment levy when it came into force in 1948 was to 'freeze' the land market. Land owners saw no reason why they should sell their land if they were to gain absolutely nothing from the sale, and therefore chose not to sell unless they had to. Understanding of the situation was complicated by the position of the Conservative Party, then in opposition. Their declared policy was that if and when they formed a government they would repeal the levy, which they did after their election in 1951. Thus, on the left, it could be claimed that the land market was not brought to a standstill by the levy itself, but by the owners of land speculating on the election of a Conservative government. After all, if they held on to their land for a few more years they might not have to pay any tax or levy at all, let alone one of 100%, since there was no capital gains tax in Britain until the 1960s. The Conservative Party policy was libertarian in spirit, and was not based on any theory of the land market. The economic reasons why a heavy tax on land betterment would freeze the land market, even in the absence of any speculation about the future, were not understood at the time, though we can set them out now.

## Economic theory and taxes on development

The way in which taxes on land will affect both the use of land and its price can be demonstrated using Figure 17.2. The analysis deals with the imposition of a tax is in the form of a betterment levy or any other method of taxing the profits arising from the development of land. In this figure, as

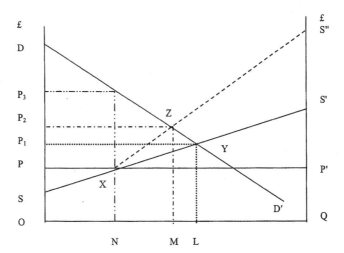

**Figure 17.2**

with the previous times this figure has been used earlier in the book, a quantity of undeveloped agricultural land lying just beyond the edge of the built up area of a city is represented on the horizontal axis as OQ. The price of the land is represented on the vertical axis. In agricultural use this is OP, so that the horizontal line PP' indicates current use value, the price at which the land can be bought and sold in its current use. The upward sloping line SXS' represents the schedule of prices at which the current owners of the land would be willing to sell. It is therefore the supply curve. For the reasons set out in Chapters 6 and 7, some owners, largely for life cycle reasons, would be willing to sell at, or even below, current use value, the price of land for agriculture. Most owners, however, would be unwilling to sell at this price but would require a higher price, sometimes a much higher price, hence the upward slope of this curve.

This higher price may be required in order to compensate the owners for leaving a location, and selling a piece of land, to both of which they have some attachment because of their familiarity with the area and the knowledge of the land that they have acquired over the years. In some cases selling may mean premature retirement because there is no suitable land nearby which is for sale at an agricultural use price and which they could then buy and continue farming. It will also be true that the upward slope of the supply curve is additionally a consequence of the land owners' uncertainty about the future and expectations with respect to the course of future prices.

The demand for land for urban development in the area is represented by the downward sloping line DD', representing the prices that developers are willing to pay, given the availability of land in the area in the period. The diagram indicates that, given this demand schedule, the price paid for land for development would be $OP_1$ and OL would be sold for development. In the diagram the 'current-use value' of the land is represented by OP and the difference between this and the market price $OP_1$ represents the profit that the owner would make on selling the land to a developer. Thus $PP_1$ on the vertical axis represents the difference between market price and current use value.

Suppose, now, that a 100% betterment levy is imposed so that the amount received by the owner of land on its sale can never be greater than OP because $PP_1$ is taxed away. It follows that only those willing to sell at that price will do so. In terms of the diagram only ON is sold and no more. It follows that the supply of land for development is represented by a vertical line at N. Given the limited supply of land for development the price will rise and the equilibrium price, in the period, will be $OP_2$.

Actually the situation could be worse. The amount received by the seller is exactly the same whether it is sold for development or sold to another farmer who wishes to buy more farm land. In these circumstance it is possible, indeed probable, that the existing farmers will sell land to their friends and fellow farmers rather than to builders and developers. The market price might then be even higher than $OP_2$, with very little land being sold for development. Thus the imposition of a levy of this kind could bring the market to a virtual standstill, and this could happen even in the absence of any speculation as to the likelihood that the levy might be repealed in the near future.

Curiously, it was perceived that there might be a problem at the time. The then Home Secretary, Herbert Morrison, wrote to Lewis Silkin, the minister responsible for the Act bringing in the levy, saying:

> Whilst we leave the actual land in private ownership we take away the incentive which the owner has to develop or allow development by taking away the increased value which at present he gets as a result of development. Thus we are in danger of getting ... private ownership without the incentives which a system of private ownership needs to operate (Cullingworth 1975 p. 212).

Thus at least one politician recognised the danger that a 100% levy would prevent the market functioning properly through removing incentives, even if the economists of the time could not. What would be the effect of a tax levied at a lower rate, however? An indication of the possible effect of a levy at a rate of 50% is also shown in Figure 17.2. The market price of land in the absence of any levy would be $PP_1$ and, as above, the line XS' represents the minimum price at which owners would be willing to sell, so that this indicates the level of compensation they require for having to move. If a 50% levy is now imposed, and the market price were to remain at $OP_1$, the owners would receive a return over current-use value of a half of $PP_1$ rather than the whole. Obviously many would be unwilling to sell at this price, the supply of land for development would fall and its price would rise. The new supply curve is the dashed line XZS". Its slope is twice that of XYS'. This means that any price marked on it would, after payment of the levy, yield the amount shown by the point vertically below it on XYS'. For example, on the right-hand vertical axis, S"S' is equal to S'P'. Thus the owners, on selling, would receive the compensation, after paying the levy, necessary to induce them to sell.

The new equilibrium is shown by the point Z. Less land is sold than would have been sold if there had been no levy, OM rather than OL, and the price of this land is higher, $OP_3$ rather than $OP_2$. The tax is not neutral and it affects the use of land and its price. In particular, the fact that it causes higher land prices means that at least part of the impact of the tax is passed on to the final consumer in the form of higher prices. What this analysis, and this diagram, makes clear is that incidence of the tax is very different to that found through arguments and analysis based on Ricardian theories. The Henry George view was that taxes on land of this kind would be borne by the owners of land and that they would not affect either the price or the use of land. This analysis shows that, on the contrary, a tax of this kind need not be borne by the owners of land, that it does affect the supply of land, and that it can be passed on to the final user in the form of higher prices.

Of course, the extent to which it is passed on will depend upon the circumstances. We showed earlier that the supply of land, the slope of the supply curve, will depend upon whether the land is owned by its occupiers or owned by landlords and let to tenants. Again, the price at which owner occupiers will sell depends not only on their attachment to their land but also on their views as to the price which can be obtained in future, and their uncertainty about the future. The imposition of a levy will affect both their views and their certainty about the future. One cannot be precise as the quantitative effect of the imposition of a levy. Nevertheless, in qualitative terms the likely effects are clear. The episode of the 100% betterment levy in the late 1940s is either evidence supporting the theory, or, if preferred, given the time sequence, the theory provides an economic explanation of this episode in British planning and taxation history.

## Land taxation in recent British history

It was not immediately evident, but the betterment levy imposed under the 1947 Act was the last British attempt to try to capture increases in land values on the grounds that they arose through economic and population growth and the provision of public infrastructure. After that the operation of the Town and Country Planning Act became itself, over time, the most important determinant of the value of land. This was because the constraints on the availability of land for development, coupled with unforeseen increases in the demand for such land, resulted in significant, and sometimes astronomical, increases in the value of the land for which planning permission for urban development either had been or was likely to be obtained. As a result it became evident that the most important determinants of land values were not the same as they had been in the past. Although as we showed in Chapter 2 it was not generally understood that these constraints were a cause of the higher prices, the price differences between land with and without planning permission were certainly evident and attributed to demand rather than supply. The owners of land were seen to gain a disproportionate reward from obtaining planning permission. Before it had been thought unfair that the value of their land should increase because of the provision of infrastructure or economic or population growth, now it was thought unfair that the value of their land should increase because of the grant of planning permission by the community.

When the differences between the value of land with and without planning permission first began to become obvious, in the late 1950s and early 1960s, Britain had no system for taxing capital gains, whereas the taxation of income was at rates which could reach 80%. Leaving aside the problems of taxing profits from land sales, this was a situation which could not last, and a capital gains tax was introduced by a Labour Government in 1967, after an initial attempt to tax short-term capital gains introduced by the Conservatives in the early 1960s. In 1967 the Wilson government also set up the Land Commission. This was intended both to acquire land for the implementation of local and regional plans and to secure 40% of any gains in land value through a 40% betterment levy. In the event the Land Commission did not last long and was abolished by Heath's Conservative government in 1971. The capital gains tax remained in existence, however, so that the profits from land sales were taxed, albeit, at that time, at a lower rate than 40%.

A few years later the increasing value of land and property and particularly the spectacular profits attributable to the office building boom of the early 1970s led the Heath government to propose a tax on development gains. This tax actually came into existence under the Labour government elected in 1974, but was quickly replaced by a Development Land Tax in 1976. This provided for a tax or betterment levy at a rate of 80% but it was envisaged that it would eventually be increased to 100%. At the same time the Community Land Act 1975 provided for a system of development under which local authorities would acquire land net of tax and either develop themselves or sell it on to developers at the market price. What was envisaged was a form of public land banking on the Netherlands model, as described in Chapter 13. Whatever was envisaged for the future, the Community Land Act was repealed by the Thatcher government soon after its election in 1979. But the Development Land Tax did continue in existence, though the rate of tax was reduced from 80% to 70%, and it was not abolished until 1985, when the then Chancellor repealed it on the grounds that the cost of collecting the tax was too high relative to its yield to the Treasury. Land sales continued to be subject to capital gains tax, and the maximum rate had been increased now to 40%, the same rate as the top rate of income tax and inheritance tax.

It is sometimes said, by unwary journalists for example, that the attempts to tax land were introduced by Labour governments and repealed by Conservative governments on their election. There is an element of truth in this but it is misleading. The taxation of development gains was proposed by the Conservative in the 1970s before Labour came to power, and Labour's Development Land Tax was continued by the Thatcher government for six years after it was elected. The Tax was actually in operation for a longer period under the Conservatives than it had been under Labour, and was finally abolished, not on ideological grounds, but on the grounds that it wasn't worth the trouble of collection. (This may have been a misjudgement – the sums collected during the land and house price boom which occurred in the late 1980s, after its abolition, would have been substantial.)

One reason for the longevity of the tax would seem to be that, first, it was set at a rate lower than 100%, and, second, the situation had fundamentally changed since the late 1940s because of the operation of the planning system itself. The position was now, particularly in southern England, closer to the pure Ricardian situation than ever before. Figure 17.3 illustrates this. On the horizontal axis OQ still represents an area of land on the edge of an urban area, and on the vertical axis OP represents its price for agricultural use. However, the land which is permitted to be developed, OA in the diagram, is differentiated through the planning system from land which may not, AQ. There is a demand for land for, say, housing represented by the demand curve DD', and this sets the price for housing land, given the

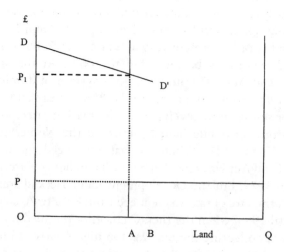

**Figure 17.3**

supply, at $OP_1$. Price differences are less in other parts of the country but in southern England, at the time of writing, the price of housing land, $OP_1$, is likely to be greater than £1 m per hectare, while the price of agricultural land, OP, is about £5,000 per hectare. In this situation land which can be developed is likely to be. The preferences of land owners are more likely to relate to the timing of development than to whether the price is high enough to persuade them to sell and compensate them for moving.

Suppose that in this period local authorities designate an area of land, AB on the horizontal axis, as land which can be developed to accommodate a projected increase in the number of households. Given that the land will be sold at a price $OP_1$, or £1m per hectare, against the current use value OP, or £5,000 for a hectare, it is evident that while tax rates near to or at 100% would inhibit development, rates of 40%, or even 60% or 70%, would not. The amount left over for the land owner after payment of the tax is likely to be more than enough to persuade an owner of land to sell it for development if that is possible.

In practice what has happened is that local authorities have sought to gain some advantage from giving planning permission. Over the years, and particularly since the abolition of the Development Land Tax, the practice has grown up of requiring developers to pay for infrastructure and make other contributions, which may, or may not, be related to the development for which permission is being sought. These payments and contributions came to be called planning gain or, more recently, planning obligations. These planning obligations, like impact fees in the US and Canada, may be meant to cover the cost of associated infrastructure, but as governments and local authorities have sought to make the payments cover other things they have begun to resemble a betterment levy. For example, in 1995 the then Conservative government proposed that, when large housing developments were mooted, up to 30% of the new housing which was built should be required to be 'affordable'. If this housing was not provided on site then the developers could be required to contribute to the cost of providing 'affordable' housing elsewhere in the area. Such a proposal makes it explicit that planning obligations are a form of taxation of development gains, albeit the rate of tax may be (more usually) negotiated with the local authority rather than laid down by central government as a fixed rate.

## Summary and conclusions

In this chapter we have reviewed the attitudes which have been expressed in the past regarding the taxation of land. It has been frequently argued, explicitly or implicitly, that the owners of land had no significant economic role to play, they merely had to allow their land to be used in the way which yielded the highest current income. They did nothing, it was said, but grew rich while they slept as their land increased in value because of economic or demographic growth or the public provision of infrastructure. The argument has been used to support various schemes for the differential taxation of land, some of which have been put into practice. Most evident have been schemes to try to capture some or all of the increase in the value of the land when it is developed or redeveloped, of which the most stringent was the 100% betterment levy imposed in the UK between 1948 and 1953.

Various arguments have been put forward earlier in this book to show why the owners of land may want to keep their land and may be unwilling to sell their land even if the price offered appears to offer a substantial profit. This reluctance to sell means that a tax on the increase in value occurring at development, a betterment levy, will discourage selling. Contrary to the received theories, a betterment levy can be passed on in higher prices and may reduce the supply of land, effects which were both observed in Britain in the late 1940s and early 1950s.

# 18

## Annual Taxation and the Nationalisation of Land

### *'Yesterday'*

___

### Introduction

The forms of taxation which we discussed in the previous chapter were largely concerned with the taxation of any increase in the value of land at the time of development. More important than any development taxes, however, at least in terms of the revenue actually raised, are the taxes which are imposed annually on land and property.

In this chapter we discuss the various forms of annual taxes on land, taxes based on the capital value of the property, both land and buildings – the property tax, taxes based on an assessment of the annual rent which is or might be obtained from the property – the rates; and taxes based on an assessment of the highest income which might be obtained from the land alone – site value taxation.

The last of these has become associated with the Single Tax Movement and as such it is sometimes advocated that it should be at a very high rate, that it should not merely be a revenue raising tax but should be high enough to affect the use of land. High rates of tax may mean that the owners lose the incentive to ensure that their land is used efficiently. Proposals for heavy taxes on land can therefore easily lead on to proposals for the nationalisation of land, so that the state takes over ownership and control. Unfortunately if there is no land market there are no price signals at all so that the state is likely to be less efficient than a heavily taxed land owner.

## Property taxes and the rates

Annual taxes on property may be of various kinds. One kind, and that predominant in the United States, is a tax imposed as a percentage of the current capital value of the whole property, that is both land and buildings. In the United Kingdom the tax currently imposed on residential property, the council tax, is a form of property tax, but it is deliberately regressive since the rate charged is higher on low-value properties than it is on higher-value properties, although, of course, the amount paid per house is lower for the former than it is for the latter. This regressiveness reflects the fact that it was designed for political reasons as a way out of the debacle of the Community Charge, or 'poll tax' which was imposed as a rate per person in the late 1980s and which, because of its unpopularity, led to Mrs Thatcher's enforced resignation in 1990. Thus it is not as regressive as a poll tax but it is, nevertheless, not proportional either to property values or to incomes.

Before the introduction of the Community Charge, residential property was subject to a 'rate' charge which was a tax based on an estimate of the rent which might be obtained if the property were let. The problem with this was that the 'rateable value' had to be estimated periodically and that this was costly. As a result governments tended to postpone valuations to reduce expenditure. This meant that revaluations, when they occurred, reflected large changes which might have occurred over the previous 10 or 15 years rather than the small changes which might have occurred over the previous 5 years. The Community Charge was introduced after the political row caused by the revaluation which took place in Scotland in the mid-1980s, the first carried out for 15 years. Although the overall effect of a revaluation should have been neutral, the gainers, those whose property had fallen in value relative to the average, tended to keep quiet but the losers, those whose properties had risen in value relative to the average, made a fuss. Since a similar revaluation in England would have caused the same kind of political fuss, but on a larger scale, the Community Charge appeared to be a way of avoiding both a revaluation and a political furore. The cure, of course, turned out to be worse than the disease.

Non-residential property, that is industrial and commercial property, has always been, and continues to be, subject to a rate charge in Britain. Revaluations have evidently been less contentious, probably because they have directly affected far fewer voters, and also because any tax would have to be proportional, in some way, to the size and value of the property. No form of poll tax is possible. The only change which occurred at the time of the imposition of the Community Charge was that the rate of tax which could be charged was not left at the discretion of each local authority, but was set as a Uniform Business Rate by central government.

It is worth noting that both the property tax and the rates tend slightly to distort the pattern of investment. This is because they are taxes imposed on capital invested in buildings which are not imposed on capital invested in things which are not part of a building. Thus machinery such as a lift which is part of a building is subject to a rate charge, but a crane which is placed in a building is not. The problem is illustrated in Figure 18.1 (a) and (b). In (a) investment in plant and machinery is measured along the horizontal axis, cost and prices are indicated on the vertical axis. In (b) costs prices are still measured on the vertical axis but investment in buildings is represented on the horizontal axis. In each figure the marginal value product (the increased revenue arising from each additional unit of investment) is indicated by the downward sloping line marked MVP, and the cost of capital is indicted by the horizontal line CC'. A profit maximising firm would be expected to invest so long as the marginal value product exceeds the cost of capital, that is up to the point that MVP cuts CC' in each figure. In the absence of a property tax the optimal investment in plant and machinery would be $Q_M$, and the optimal investment in buildings would be $Q_B$. But the rates or a property tax raises the cost of investment in buildings to the level indicated by the dashed line RR'. Investment in buildings is therefore more costly and investment in buildings would be less, at $Q'_B$. So investment which might reduce the running cost of the building is deterred.

Of course, in practice, the valuation of property is not accurate. As we demonstrated in Chapters 4 and 5 the property market is inefficient and the

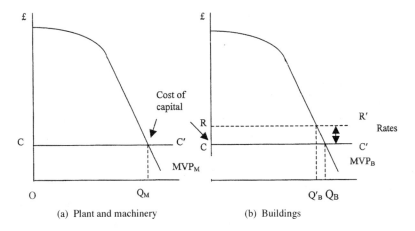

(a) Plant and machinery          (b) Buildings

**Figure 18.1**

average 'error' made by valuers if their valuations are compared with sale prices is of the order of 10%. Further, in the UK, if not in the US or elsewhere, valuations are infrequent. Thus the connection between small capital improvements to a property and the level of property taxation may not be seen as very direct, indeed may not be perceived at all. And if the rate of taxation is low, as, again, it is in the UK, the distorting effect of a property tax or of the rates may in practice be negligible.

## Site value taxation

Site value taxation avoids this problem because it is intended to be a tax on the value of the land alone, and therefore not a tax on the buildings on the site. As well as a tax on the value of the land alone, site value taxation (SVT) differs from a property tax in that it is meant to be a tax on the value of the land in its 'highest and best' use, and this may not be its current use. While the use of property taxes is widespread, the use of site value taxation is not and this is curious since its use has been widely advocated. For example, for most of the last century, along with proportional representation, it was one of the central tenets of the Liberal Party.

Site value taxation has its ancestry in the old single tax movement. Its beneficial effects include, as we have said, the fact that it does not distort the capital market in the way that a property tax might. It is further argued in its favour that it discourages speculation. This is because it is a tax based on the income from a piece of land in the use which would yield the highest current income, not on its income in its current use. Thus, it is argued, SVT imposes an additional cost on land owners who use their land inefficiently and so causes the available land to be used efficiently. In particular it would make it more expensive for land to be left vacant or idle.

These arguments in favour of SVT are, of course, correct so far as they go. Nevertheless, the reader will remember that in earlier chapters discussing the theory of the supply of land, we put forward various reasons why land might not be used for the use which would yield the highest current income, reasons which did not seem to be unsocial. To consider the most extreme case, the elderly owners of a bungalow with a large garden might have an attachment to their house. Would we wish to impose taxes on them to force them to move so that two or three terrace houses can be constructed on the site, or maybe merely a larger house for someone more wealthy? Again, it is not clear why speculation *per se* is to be discouraged. Suppose the reason why a piece of land is left idle is because it is anticipated that a future use would be profitable, but that it would be unprofitable to develop it in one way, say as housing, only to demolish the houses after a short time to replace them by, say, shops. Why should the latter be encouraged? It would not only be unprofitable but it would also be socially inefficient. If it is inefficient why should the taxation system discourage long-run efficiency in the interest of efficiency in the very short run? And finally, as we also noted earlier, if the future is uncertain, not to do anything may be best until the situation is resolved. There seems no reason to suppose that there are social advantages in discouraging delay and encouraging an earlier, but possibly wrong, development.

There are further arguments against the 'rose tinted' view of the advantages of SVT. For the tax to function as it is intended to function the valuers who are carrying out the site valuations must be expected to know what the optimal use for each piece of land would be. We know anyway, as we noted in Chapter 4, that the average error made by valuers in the valuation of existing properties is about 10%. The valuation of a piece of land in some expected better use, with different buildings must have a significantly larger margin of error. Moreover, the thrust of the argument runs against the whole economic theory of the advantages of a decentralised price system. This argues that as against a centrally planned economy the various participants in a market economy will have an accumulated but dispersed knowledge which will allow better decisions to made than if decision making were centralised. It seems unlikely that a valuation office could have the resources and the ability to accurately estimate the site values of every piece of land in the city. It would appear obvious that, to avoid arguments and appeals, in practice they would tend to assume that the current use is the best use.

This will occur not only because of lack of knowledge but also because of lack of time and resources. For example, when the valuers in the UK valued all residential properties for the new council tax, they appear to have tended towards the mean. So, comparing actual sale prices with valuations, the more expensive properties on a street tended to be undervalued and the less expensive properties tended to be overvalued (Stabler 1996).

Finally, whatever might be the merits of the arguments for using SVT in a property market which was free of controls, it is difficult to see how it would operate in a land market affected by planning controls, particularly one with a 'non-zoning' system such as that operated in the UK. If planning permission has to be obtained for any change of use, and the grant of permission is not certain, there would seem to be a possible conflict between what the district valuer might envisage as being the current 'highest and best' use, and what the planning system provides for. It would seem that the valuer would generally have to assume that the highest and best use is that which is currently permitted, since permission for change cannot be taken for granted.

To understand the nature of the problem it is worth noting that in many areas of Britain a third of the new housing is provided on so-called 'windfall' sites, land which had not been previously identified by the planners as suitable for housing but which was put forward by the owners or by developers, found to be suitable and therefore given permission. These sites could not have been subject to tax at a high rate beforehand because of their high site value, first, because if the planners did not know of their existence there seems no reason to suppose that the district valuer's officials would do any better, and, second, because they need not have been given permission so the valuers, if they had thought that the land should be used for housing, would have to second guess the planning officers and the elected planning committee.

But if the value of the site is simply that which is currently permitted, then the value of the site in its current use becomes indistinguishable from its value in its highest and best use. SVT then cannot deliver its vaunted objective, that of ensuring that land is used most efficiently, because it is the planning system which is controlling the use of land, not, primarily, the owners. SVT is then left without a role to play. The only argument for its use would be that, as a tax on land rather than a tax on both land and buildings, it could not distort the pattern of investment of capital in buildings, plant, and machinery in the way described in the previous section.

Finally, we may note that when SVT has been used in practice there has been little evidence that it has had any significant effect on the use of land. Prest (1981) reported that SVT had been used in Auckland, New Zealand, alongside other types of property taxation, and appeared to have made little difference to the use of land. As regards the claim that it could be used to generate significant revenues for the government, an argument used by the single tax movement, SVT has been used in Taiwan as the main means of taxing land and property, but raised relatively little revenue, only some 2%–3% of total government revenue. Thus, despite the claims made on its behalf, it appears neither to have any significant effect on the pattern of development nor is it, in practice, a substantial revenue raiser.

## Land nationalisation

Advocates of SVT would probably argue that the reason why SVT has not been a significant revenue raiser where it has been used is that the rate of taxation has not been set high enough. This would certainly be the view of followers of the Single Tax Movement, and often they are the same people. If, in fact, the rate of tax were raised to more significant levels, then this would have two noticeable effects. First, as intended, the high level of SVT would tend to ensure that the owners of the land would seek to obtain the highest possible income from it, and, second, the value of the land to the land owner would fall as the after tax return fell, relative to the net of tax return on other forms of capital investment. In the end, of course, as the rate of tax tended to 100% the capital value of the land would tend to zero. As this point is approached the owner is faced with two contradictory incentives. The first is to maximise the income from the property, the second is not to bother, because little, if any, of this increased income would remain in the owner's hands. The point that Herbert Morrison made with respect to the British 100% betterment levy is just as true of very high rates of annual taxation – 'we are in danger of getting ... private ownership without the incentives which a system of private ownership needs to operate'.

In the same way, if the rent from the land were taxed at a rate of 100% any value attributable to the land would arise solely from the possibility that the rate of tax would be relaxed in future and that the owner has some control over who uses the land and how it is used. That this kind of situation is not implausible is illustrated by the situation which arose in Vienna, though because of rent controls rather than explicit taxation. In the fourth quarter of the last century the rents of housing were still fixed at 1919 levels. In 1970 someone I know well inherited a one-third share in a block of flats located in the second district near to the city centre. No income was derived from the ownership of the property since the rents paid did not cover the cost of running the property. If repairs needed to be done an application was made to the court on behalf of the tenants to allow a loan to be obtained to pay for the repairs, and for the rents to be raised for a fixed period in order to cover the cost of borrowing the money and repaying the loan. At the end of this period rents would revert back to 1919 levels.

In effect the property had been expropriated in favour of the tenants. There was no expectation that rents would be raised to market levels. What value the ownership of the property might have lay in the fact that if vacancies occurred the owner could control who filled the vacancy. After 18 years of ownership, from which no income was derived, the owner sold the one third share for a paltry sum.

When rates of site value taxation of 100% are proposed it is the government in whose favour the property is being expropriated rather than the tenants. It follows that rather than high rates of taxation it would seem logical to consider the possibility of nationalising land, and this has been frequently suggested, most recently in the 1970s, in the UK, by a committee which included the noted economist Nicholas Kaldor. The arguments for the nationalisation of land mirror and extend the arguments for the differential taxation of land (Brocklebank *et al.* 1974). All increases in rents and in land values would go to the community, therefore the equity problem, so resented by Mill, that the land owners grow rich while they sleep, is completely solved. Furthermore the problem which high tax rates create, that the owners of the land have no incentive to use the land efficiently, is also solved. Since the land is now owned by the state it is now up to the state, or to its representatives and managers, to ensure that the land is used efficiently.

There is a third advantage which relates to the planning system. Planning systems in capitalist economies which respect the ownership rights of land owners tend to be negative in their operation. Developments proposed by land owners or construction firms can be refused permission, but land owners cannot be forced to propose developments which might be thought desirable from the community's point of view. The owners of land cannot be made to use their land in ways which seem to them to be unprofitable. If, on the other hand, land is nationalised, then *positive* planning, instead of *negative* planning, becomes feasible. The state, or its officers, can plan and ensure that their plans are implemented.

Finally, some advocates of land nationalisation have seen one of the benefits as being that the price of land to local and national government can be reduced below the market price, indeed may be reduced to zero. Government can therefore be more active as a developer since its land costs are significantly reduced, if not completely eliminated.

The disadvantages of land nationalisation arise as correlates of the advantages. Taking the last first, the function of price is to ensure that factors of production are used efficiently. If the price of land to government is low then it is likely, indeed virtually certain, that land will be used inefficiently. More land may be used than otherwise would be, or activities are located in the wrong place. For example, a study of the use of land in Moscow at the end of the Communist era showed that higher density apartments had been constructed at the edge of the city leaving low density land uses, particularly lower density housing and manufacturing, occupying sites nearer the centre. The result was that the average journey to work was much longer than it would have been in a capitalist city (Bertaud & Renaud 1997). However, in the Communist era, given a Marxian labour theory of value, land was considered to have no value since it was not produced by labour.

As regards the second argument, that all rents go to the community, it may be that the officials responsible for allocating land uses fail to understand the price incentives to which they are required to respond. If all land is nationalised there is no land market and therefore no market price. There is only a shadow price which must be guessed at from the rents which might be paid for the use of the land. The new owners of the land, the state and its officials, do not face the same incentives as the private owner and may fail to respond to 'shadow' incentives. So, as was mentioned above, in the former communist countries differences in location were not seen as a factor generating price differences between sites and therefore differences in the intensitivity of use. Land near the city centre might be used less intensively than in a capitalist city, and land near the edge more intensively.

Governments may fail to respond to price incentives with respect to the land that they own even in the absence of complete land nationalisation. We do not have to study the former communist countries to find evidence of the nature of the problem. In the UK in the 1980s there was considerable concern expressed about the existence of vacant inner city sites, and the view on the left was that this was a failure of capitalism. But empirical studies showed that local authorities and publicly owned utilities were most probably the owners of these sites. Kivell (1993) notes that 'the 1988 Survey of Derelict Land in England showed that over 60% of urban dereliction in known ownership was the responsibility of the public sector' (p. 163). It would appear that they did not seek to develop sites because they had no incentive to do so, and were ready to purchase sites well ahead of any proposed road or housing scheme and leave it idle for the same reason. The cost was an opportunity cost, i.e. the income foregone, and was not recognised and acknowledged for that reason. It appeared in no sets of accounts as a cost.

The final argument against land nationalisation is the standard argument in favour of the market and against central planning. An economy, particularly a modern economy, is complex, and information is dispersed amongst the participants. A market economy can respond to changes as the participants recognise these changes and themselves respond. Indeed change can be promoted in unforeseen, and unforeseeable, ways, as firms and individuals generate and implement new ideas leading to competition and emulation. An economy which cannot respond to price signals because there are none is doubly handicapped. First, those responsible for land use have less information to guide their decisions than does the market. This may be regarded as acceptable. Indeed, the ubiquity of land use planning in market economies where the planners' failure to respond to price signals may be regarded as a virtue, as in southern England, suggests that it is widely accepted. With respect to the perceived trade off between a lack of information and a chaos of environmental externalities, the former appears to be preferred to the latter. Nevertheless, the lack of price signals may conceal the second and equally important handicap. If those responsible for land use receive no signals to suggest that changes in land use would be efficient then those changes will not be made.

The above arguments suggest the reasons why land markets were introduced not only in the former Communist countries of eastern Europe, but also, and with more difficulty, in the People's Republic of China. There the problem was one of trying to determine the prices at which land should and would be traded when the land market came into existence. With no evidence to go on this was extremely difficult, but it was necessary to try to minimise the windfall gains to buyers which seem to be the inevitable consequence of privatisation.

## Summary and conclusions

In this chapter we began by reviewing the ways in which land may be taxed on an annual basis. We showed that taxes imposed on real estate as a whole may distort the way in which capital is invested, since the tax is imposed on capital invested in buildings but not on movable plant and machinery. A way of avoiding this is to impose a tax only on the land. Such a tax may be imposed on the assessed income from the land in its current use or on the income which it is assessed could be obtained from the land in its 'highest and best use'. These may not be the same. Advocates of site value taxation, as it is called, have frequently been allied with, or the same as, supporters of the Single Tax Movement of Henry George. The view of the latter has been that land should be taxed differentially at a high rate of tax. But if this occurs then such high taxation removes any incentive for the owner of the land to try to maximise income.

Site value taxation would re-establish this incentive, it is argued, because the owner of the land is driven to maximise income in order to cover the tax which has to be paid and which is based on an assessment of this highest income. Questions arise, however, as to whether the local valuer can assess better than the owners of the land what might be the most profitable use for their land, and as to the problems which might arise when the uses of the land are controlled by the planning system. Thus three parties would seem to be required to express a definitive view as to the optimal current use of a piece of land, the owner, the valuer, and the planner. If the valuer simply follows the views of the planner, as would seem inevitable, then the introduction of SVT would have a negligible effect on the use of land.

If it is difficult to tax heavily the rent from land without removing the incentives necessary to motivate the land owner, then an alternative policy stance would be the nationalisation of land. Indeed, if land is so heavily taxed that its value becomes negligible, then nationalisation becomes a virtual necessity. Nevertheless, while nationalisation might solve the distributional or equity problem, there seems no reason to suppose that the state as an owner of land would use it more efficiently even than a 'disincentived' land owner. Indeed, both theory and empirical evidence suggest that in practice the state will use land inefficiently. In the longer run this would seem too high a price to pay to stop land owners becoming richer while they sleep.

# 19

## Conclusion: Themes and Changes in Perception

### *'Here comes the sun'*

---

### Recapitulation

In this book I have attempted to set out the economic theory of the land market. In so doing I have brought together a number of separate contributions to the theories which have been published over the last few years. Bringing them together has meant that I have had to think through the way in which they are connected, and, I hope, to present them together in a way which draws out the connections between somewhat disparate pieces.

These connections make up the themes, the *leitmotivs* which have run through this book, of which the main themes, it seems to me, are four. The first is the need to detach the theory of the land market from the handicap posed by Ricardian theory as it has been half-remembered by economists. The remembrance of this theory has been like a lumpen weight dragged around slowing progress in the field.

For apart from the fact that it is usually half-remembered and mis-remembered, as importantly, the assumptions of Ricardian theory induce a mindset, a way of thinking, which is both misleading and wrong. All other theories of factor supply, whether of labour or of capital, are presented in terms of the supply of the factor to a firm or firms in a period. We do not start from the presumption, with respect to labour, that the supply of labour to an economy can be regarded as fixed in the short and medium term, even though this is true, and even though we have been happy to make the equivalent assumption with respect to the supply of land.

A change in this mindset, in this way of thinking, is essential to a better understanding of the land market. With other factors we are concerned with their supply for a use within a period. So with respect to the supply of land we should be concerned with the supply of land for a particular use, for development say, within a given period or sequence of periods. Thus we should stop thinking always of land as a stock and instead think in terms of a flow. I recognise that this is difficult, even odd, because land is immovable and therefore 'flows' nowhere. But whatever may be true physically, in economic terms there is a movement as pieces of land 'flow' from one use to another.

This brings us to the second theme. Once one has jettisoned the imprisoning mindset that land is always to be thought of as a stock, a whole new approach to the economic theory of land is opened up. In particular, once one thinks in terms of the supply of land for a use then the land owner has a role to play. The theories of Ricardo, as of Von Thunen, as of Alonso, assume that the use of land is determined wholly by demand. Land is there, its supply is fixed, its use is determined by what activity can pay the highest rent. These are demand side theories. But once one thinks in terms of the supply of land, then the owner of the land has to make decisions as to whether the land should be put to this use or not, should be developed or not, should be let or not.

Thus the owner has to make choices. There are alternatives, indeed one may say that there are always alternatives, one of which will be continuing as before, and the owner has to decide what to do. Some half-a-dozen chapters at the core of this book look at these alternatives.

Which brings us to the third theme. Once it is seen that decisions have to be made, that the land owner is not an automaton responding only to the stimulus of the 'highest current rent', then the role of the market changes. For once it is recognised that things are not so simple, that the landowner has to choose amongst alternatives, then questions arise as to the extent to which the necessary information is available, and the way in which these choices are made. And we have argued that a distinctive feature of the land market, indeed of the market for real estate as a whole, is that information is not freely available, and is often costly to obtain. The property market is very inefficient, informationally. This means that the choices which are made may be the result of decisions reached in the absence of full information. And that time and resources have to be spent in acquiring information to try to reach a decision. This lack of information means that prices are not fully determined by and in the market, but are only determined within a fairly wide range. This means that other extraneous factors help to determine the price in the case of each transaction, the bargaining positions and abilities of participants, whether an agent is employed and so on.

Which brings us to the fourth major theme of the book, the heterogeneity of the properties available for sale, a major cause of which is the fixed location of each piece of land. In terms of market efficiency this means that each piece of land cannot be brought to be traded, and compared, at a single market site. Conversely, this means that in terms of acquiring land for development the relative location of sites, in particular their contiguity, may be of overriding importance. And it is this feature which makes the land market different from any other. In other factor markets one may simply advertise for labour or for capital. The capital provided by different people can simply be put together to form a single capital sum. Workers can be recruited to form a labour force with no interest being taken in where they come from. But if a large site is required then it has to be formed from a number of contiguous sites.

This feature of the land market accounts for various policies which otherwise appear anomalous. It accounts for the almost universal existence of powers of compulsory purchase or eminent domain. It also accounts for the existence, in some countries, of policies for the reallocation of land ownership. And it interacts with the features of the market we have recapitulated above, the ownership of land and the imperfection of the market. For the owners of land may take advantage of the quasi-monopolistic position which the need for contiguity can give. While, on the other hand, it may be the objective of a developer to conceal the information that a large development is needed, so as to try to price discriminate between possible sellers, so as to purchase the land at the lowest total cost.

## Coda

The theory of the land market which has been set out in this book should result in a change in the way the market is perceived, a paradigm shift, with two important implications.

The first is one that is spelled out in the previous two chapters. The received, demand-oriented, theory of the land market has the implication that most forms of taxation of land do not distort in the way that other taxes do. The price of land and the use of land is unaffected, the tax is borne only by the landowner. But the more supply-oriented theory presented here does not have this implication. Indeed the reverse is true. Most forms of land taxation can and will be passed on in the form of higher land prices, and the use of land will almost certainly be affected. Land taxes can and do distort.

The second implication of the theory relates to the way land use planning systems operate, and has itself been a theme running through the book. Most systems for planning land use operate negatively. Development may be allowed in one area, but not allowed in another. One type of development may be permitted in an area but no other. The received, demand oriented, theory implies that since land owners simply use their land for the use which yields the highest current income, then whatever kind of development is permitted will occur. There are, in effect, no choices to be made.

But the implication of the supply-oriented theory presented in this book is that the owners of land do have a choice and can choose that their land should not be developed. For numerous reasons, even though they could sell out at a profit, they will still carry on using it for the same use that they have before. One result, as we have shown, is that land prices, where development is permitted and does occur, will be higher than they would otherwise have been. The other, which we have only alluded to, is that the process of development, where it is allowed, will take longer than received theory would suggest.

Evidence of this, in terms of the UK planning system, is the existence of what Bramley has called an 'implementation gap'. Local authorities may designate increased amounts of land for development in their plans, but there will be a time lag of variable and unpredictable length before development takes place and the houses, offices or factories come onto the market. And the implication is that tighter restrictions on the availability of land for development have a more immediate effect on market prices and the availability of properties than any relaxation in the tightness of the constraints. But discussion of the implications of the theory for the perception of the way a land-use planning system may operate takes us further than we have pursued the topic in this book. The economics of land use planning are analysed in another book (Evans 2004).

# References

Adams, David (1994/2001) *Urban Planning and the Development Process*. Routledge, London.

Alonso, William (1960) A theory of the urban land market, *Papers and Proceedings of the Regional Science Association*, 6.

Alonso, William (1964) *Location and Land Use*. Harvard UP, Cambridge, MA.

Ave, G. (1996) *Urban Land and Property Markets in Italy*. UCL Press, London.

Ball, Michael (1977) Differential rent and the role of landed property, *International Journal of Urban and Regional Research*, 1: 380–403.

Ball, Michael (1983) *Housing Policy and Economic Power*. Methuen, London.

Barrett, S., M. Stewart & J. Underwood (1978) *The Land Market and the Development Process*. Occasional Paper No. 2, School of Advanced Urban Studies, Bristol University.

Bertaud, A. & B. Renaud (1997) Socialist cities without land markets, *Journal of Urban Economics*, 41: 137–151.

Black, Fisher & Myron Scholes (1973) The pricing of options and corporate liabilities, *Journal of Political Economy*, 81, (May/June): 637–659.

Blaug, M. (1997) *Economic Theory in Retrospect*, 5th edn. Cambridge University Press, Cambridge.

Blume, Lawrence, Daniel L. Rubinfeld & Perry Shapiro (1984) The taking of land: when should compensation be paid? *Quarterly Journal of Economics*, 99(1): 71–92.

Bristow, Roger (1984) *Land-use Planning in Hong Kong: History, Policies and Procedures*. Oxford University Press, Hong Kong.

Bramley, G. (1993a) The impact of land use planning and tax subsidies on the supply and price of housing in Britain, *Urban Studies*, 30: 5–30.

Bramley, G. (1993b) Land use planning and the housing market in Britain: the impact on housebuilding and house prices, *Environment and Planning A*, 25: 1021–1051.

Briggs, Asa (1999) *England in the Age of Improvement 1783–1867*. Folio Society, London.

Brocklebank, J., N. Kaldor, J. Maynard & O. Stutchbury (1974) *The Case for Nationalising Land*. Campaign for Nationalising Land, London.

Brown, James H., Robyn S. Phillips & Neal A. Roberts (1981) Land markets at the urban fringe. *Journal of the American Planning Association*, 47(2) (April): 131–144.

Brownstone, David & Arthur De Vany (1991) Zoning, returns to scale and the value of undeveloped land, *The Review of Economics and Statistics*, 73(4): 699–704.

Buchanan, Daniel H. (1929) The Historical Approach to Rent and Price Theory, *Economica*, Vol. 9, 123–155. Reprinted in *Readings in the Theory of Income Distribution*, pp. 599–637, (eds) W. Fellner & B.F. Haley (1950). Allen & Unwin, London.

Capozza, D.R. & Helsley, R.W. (1990) The stochastic city, *Journal of Urban Economics*, 28: 187–203.

Case, K.E. & Shiller, R.J. (1989) The efficiency of the market for single family homes, *American Economic Review*, 79(1): 125–137.

Chamberlin, E.H. (1933) *The Theory of Monopolistic Competition*. Harvard University Press, Cambridge, MA.

Cheung, Steven N.S. (1969) Transaction costs, risk aversion, and the choice of contractual arrangements, *Journal of Law and Economics*, 12(1) (April): 23–42.

Chisholm, Michael (1968) *Rural Settlement and Land Use*. 2nd edn., Hutchinson, London.

Cobin, John M. (1997) *Building Regulation, Market Alternatives, and Allodial Policy*. Avebury, Aldershot.

Colwell, Peter F. & C.F. Sirmans (1978) Area, time, centrality and the value of urban land, *Land Economics*, 54 (Nov.): 514–519.

Cullingworth, J.B. (1975) *Environmental Planning 1939–69, Vol. 1. Reconstruction and Land use Planning 1939–47*. HMSO, London.

Department of the Environment (1987) Report of the Inspector – Appeals by Consortium Development Ltd, Application Nos (A) THU/370/85, (B) THU/583/85 and (C) pp. 1789–85. DoE, London.

Department of the Environment (1992) *The Relationship between House Prices and Land Supply*, London.

Dieterich, Hartmut, Egbert Dransfield & Winrich Voss (1993) *Urban Land and Property Markets in Germany*. UCL Press, London.

Duncan, S. (1985) Land policy in Sweden: separating ownership from development, in: S. Barrett & P. Healey (eds) *Land Policy: Problems and Alternatives*, Chapter 15, pp. 308–344. Gower, Aldershot.

Dynarski, Mark (1986) Residential attachment and housing demand, *Urban Studies* 23(1) (February): 11–20.

Dyos, H.J. (1961) *Victorian Suburb: a study of the growth of Camberwell*. Leicester UP, Leicester.

Eckart, W. (1985) On the land assembly problem, *Journal of Urban Economics*, 18: 364–378.

Evans, Alan W. (1973) *The Economics of Residential Location*. Macmillan, London.

Evans, Alan W. (1975) Rent and housing in the theory of urban growth, *Journal of Regional Science*, 15: 113–125.

Evans, Alan W. (1983) The determination of the price of land, *Urban Studies* 20: 119–129.

Evans, Alan W. (1985) *Urban Economics*. Blackwell Publishing, Oxford.

Evans, Alan W. (1986) The supply of land: A pedagogic comment, *Urban Studies*, 23: 527–530.

Evans, Alan W. (1991) On monopoly rent, *Land Economics*, 67(1): 1–14.

Evans, Alan W. (1992) On differential rent and landed property, *International Journal of Urban and Regional Research*, 16(1): 81–96.

Evans, Alan W. (1995) The property market: ninety per cent efficient? *Urban Studies*, 32: 5–29.

Evans, Alan W. (2000a) On minimum rents: Part I, Marx and absolute rent, *Urban Studies*, 36(12), 2111–2120.

Evans, Alan W. (2000b) On minimum rents: Part II, a modern interpretation, *Urban Studies*, 36(13): 2305-2315.

Evans, Alan W. (2004) *Economics and Land Use Planning*. Blackwell, Oxford.

Evans, A.W. & C. Beed (1986) Transport costs and urban property values in the 1970s, *Urban Studies*, 23: 105–117.

Eversley, David E.C. (1986) Tillingham Hall Inquiry: Proof of Evidence on behalf of the Council for the Protection of Rural England. CPRE, London.

Fama, Eugene (1970) Efficient capital markets: a review of theory and empirical work, *Journal of Finance*, 25: 383–417.

Festinger, Leon (1957) *A Theory of Cognitive Dissonance*. Stanford UP, Stanford, CA.

Frayn, Michael (1999) *Headlong*. Faber and Faber, London.

Froot, K.A. & E. Dabora (1999) How are stock prices affected by the location of trade? *Journal of Financial Economics*, 53: 189–216.

Gatzlaff, Deon H. & Dogan Tirtiroglu (1995) Real estate market efficiency: issues and evidence, *Journal of Real Estate Literature*, 3: 157–189.

GB Commission on the Third London Airport (1970) *Papers and Proceedings, Vol. VII*. HMSO, London.

George, Henry (1879) *Progress and Poverty*. Centenary edition (1979). Robert Schalkenbach Foundation, New York.

Gerald Eve, with Department of Land Economy, Cambridge (1992) *The Relationship between House Prices and Land Supply*. Department of the Environment Planning Research Programme, HMSO, London.

Glaser, R., P. Haberzettl & R.P.D. Walsh (1991) Land reclamation in Singapore, Hong Kong and Macau, *Geo Journal*, 24(4): 365–73.

Goodchild, R. & R. Munton (1985) *Development and the Landowner*. George Allen and Unwin, London.

Gosling, J.A., Geoffrey Keogh & Michael J. Stabler (1993) House extensions and housing market adjustment: a case-study of Wokingham, *Urban Studies*, 30(9): 1561–1576.

Grigson, W.S. (1986) House Prices in Perspective: A Review of South East Evidence. SERPLAN, London.

Grossman, S. & J. Stiglitz (1980) On the impossibility of informationally efficient markets, *American Economic Review*, 70: 393–408.

Hager, D.P. & Lord, D.J. (1985) *The Property Market, Property Valuations and Property Performance Measurement*. Institute of Actuaries, London.

Hardin, Garrett (1968) The tragedy of the commons, *Science*, vol. 162 (December 13): 1243–48.

Harrison, Fred (1983) *The Power in the Land*. Shepheard Walwyn, London.

Harvey, David (1973) *Social Justice and the City*. Edward Arnold, London.

Haurin, D. (1988) The duration of marketing time of residential housing, *AREUEA Journal*, 16: 396–410.

Hebbert, M. & N. Nakai (1988) How Tokyo grows: land development and planning on the metropolitan fringe. Suntory – Toyota International Centre for Economics and Related Disciplines. Occasional Paper No. 11. London School of Economics, London.

Hibbert, Christopher (1969/1980) *London: The Biography of a City*. Penguin Books, London.

Hoskins, W.G. (1955) *The Making of the English Landscape*. Hodder and Stoughton, London.

Imrie, Rob & Huw Thomas (1997) Law, legal struggles and urban regeneration: rethinking the relationships, *Urban Studies* 34(9) (August): 1401–1418.

Jevons, W.S. (1911) *Theory of Political Economy*, 4th edn. Macmillan, London.

Jones, T. (2003) *The Dark Heart of Italy*. Faber and Faber, London.

Jud, G.D. & J. Frew (1986) Real estate brokers, housing prices, and the demand for housing, *Urban Studies*, 23: 21–31.

Kaucz, J. (1976) Residential location: the application of the social physics model and the behavioural model to Edinburgh. Unpublished MSc dissertation, Edinburgh College of Art.

Kim, K-H. (1993) Housing policies, affordability and government policy: Korea, *Journal of Real Estate Finance and Economics*, 6: 55–71.

Kim, K-H. (1994) Controlled development and densification: the case of Seoul, Korea. *Discussion Paper, Department of Economics*. Sogang University, CPO Box 1142, Korea.

Kivell, Philip (1993) *Land and the City*. Routledge, London.

Knaap, Gerrit, J. (1985) The price effects of urban growth boundaries in Metropolitan Portland, Oregon, *Land Economics*, 61: 28–35.

Lin, Robert (1993) Urban Land Policy Issues in Taiwan, in: B. Koppel & D.Y. Kim (eds) *Land Policy Problems in East Asia – Toward New Choices, A Comparative Study of Japan, Korea and Taiwan*. East West Center and Korea Research Institute for Human Settlements, Hawaii and Seoul.

Lin, Tzu-Chin (1999a) Empirical and Theoretical Aspects of Land Supply. PhD Thesis, Centre for Spatial and Real Estate Economics, The University of Reading.

Lin, Tzu-Chin (1999b) Land Owners' Decision Making in the Face of Compulsory Purchase. *Discussion Papers in Urban and Regional Economics*, No. 137, Centre for Spatial and Real Estate Economics, The University of Reading.

Lin, Tzu-Chin & Alan Evans (2000) The relationship between the price of land and size of plot when plots are small, *Land Economics*, 76(3) (August): 386–394.

Lipsey, R.G. (1975) *An Introduction to Positive Economics*, 4th edn. Weidenfeld & Nicolson, London.

Loyat, J. (1988) Rente foncière et métayage, *Revue d'Economie Régionale et Urbaine*, 5: 733–750.

Maclennan, Duncan & Gavin Wood (1982) Information acquisition: patterns and strategies. *Modelling Housing Market Search*, ed. W.A.V. Clark, Ch. 6. Croom Helm, London.

Marriott, Oliver (1967) *The Property Boom*. Hamish Hamilton, London.

Marshall, Alfred (1890) *Principles of Economics*. Macmillan, London.

Marx, Karl (1894/1962) *Capital: Volume III*. Foreign Languages Publishing House, Moscow.

McAllister, P. (1995) Valuation accuracy: a contribution to the debate, *Journal of Property Research*, 12: 203–216.

McCarthy, Kevin (1982) An analytical model of housing search. *Modelling Housing Market Search*, ed. W.A.V. Clark, Ch. 2. Croom Helm, London.

Meacham, A. (1988) Applying regression analysis to real estate appraisals, *Real Estate Appraiser and Analyst*, 54(2): 23–27.

Mills, E.S. (1970) Urban density functions, *Urban Studies*, 17: 5–20.

Munch, P. (1976) An economic analysis of eminent domain, *Journal of Political Economy*, 84: 473–497.

Muth, Richard F. (1969) *Cities and Housing*. University of Chicago Press, Chicago.

Needham, B. (1992) A theory of land prices when land is supplied publicly: the case of the Netherlands, *Urban Studies*, 29(5): 669–686.

Nelson, Arthur, C. (1985) Demand, segmentation, and timing effects of an urban containment programme on urban fringe land values, *Urban Studies*, 22(5): 439–443.

Nelson, Arthur C. (1988) An empirical note of how regional urban containment policy influences an interaction between greenbelt and ex-urban land markets, *Land Economics*, 54: 78–184.

Neutze, Max (1973) *The price of land and land use planning*. OECD, Paris (mimeographed). Also in Bendixson, T. (ed.) (1977) *The Management of Urban Growth*. Environment Directorate, OECD, Paris. The relevant part is reprinted in McMaster, J.C. & Webb, G.R. (eds) (1976) *Australian Urban Economics: A Reader*. Australia and New Zealand Book Co., Brookvale NSW.

Neutze, Max (1987) The supply of land for a particular use, *Urban Studies*, 24(5) (October): 379–388.

Newburger, Harriet (1995) Sources of difference in information used by black and white housing seekers: an exploratory analysis. *Urban Studies*, 32(3): 445–70.

Perry, Gregory M. & Lindon J. Robison (2001) Evaluating the influence of personal relationships on land sale prices, *Land Economics*, 77(3): 385–398.

Piccinato, G. (2000) Intervista/Interview. Section 4, *Acquarello Italiano*, 9(3): 4–6.

Pissarides, C.A. (1985) Job search and the functioning of labour markets, in D. Carline, C.A. Pissarides, W.S. Siebert & P.J. Sloane (eds) *Surveys in Economics: Labour Economics*, Chapter 4. Longman, London.

Pissarides, C.A. (2000) *Equilibrium Unemployment Theory*. MIT Press, Cambridge, MA.

Porter, W.G. (1982/1998) *England in the Eighteenth Century*. Folio Society, London.

Prebble, John (1963) *The Highland Clearances*. Secker and Warburg, London.

Prest, A.R. (1981) *The Taxation of Urban Land*. Manchester UP, Manchester.

Rayburn, W., Devaney, M. & Evans, R. (1987) A test of weak form efficiency in residential real estate returns, *AREUEA Journal*, 15: 220–33.

Riganti, Patrizia (1997) *Valuing Cultural Heritage*. University of Reading, Centre for Spatial and Real Estate Economics, Discussion Paper in Urban and Regional Economics, No. 124.

Rosen, S. (1974) Hedonic prices and implicit markets, *Journal of Political Economy*, 82: 35–55.

Rydin, Y. (1998) *Urban and Environmental Planning in the UK*. Macmillan, London.

Shleifer, Andrei (2000) *Inefficient Markets*. Oxford University Press, Oxford.

Simon, H.A. (1959) Theories of decision making: economics and behavioural science, *American Economic Review*, 49(3), June: 253–283.

Smith, Adam (1776/1910) *An Inquiry into the Nature and Causes of the Wealth of Nations*, Vol. 1. Everyman Edition, Dent/Dutton, London/New York.

Stabler, M.J. (1996) Time to review Council Tax valuations: A case study investigation of their accuracy and the implications of the housing market recession, *Journal of Property Tax Assessment and Administration*, 2(1): 41–70.

Staley, Samuel R. (1994) *Planning Rules and Urban Economic Performance*. The Chinese University Press, Hong Kong.

Stevenson, Glenn G. (1991) *Common Property Economics: A General Theory and Land Use Applications*. Cambridge University Press, Cambridge.

Stigler, G.J. (1961) The economics of information, *Journal of Political Economy*, 69(3): 213–25.

Stigler, G.J. (1962) Information in the labour market, *Journal of Political Economy*, 70(5), October: 94–105.

Tabuchi, Takatoshi (1996) Quantity premia in real property markets, *Land Economics*, 72 (May): 206–217.

Titman, S. (1985) Urban land price under uncertainty, *American Economic Review*, 75: 505–514.

Valuation Office (2002) *Property Market Report, Autumn 2002*. Valuation Office Agency/Estates Gazette, London.

Von Neumann, John & Oskar Morgenstern (1944) *Theory of Games and Economic Behaviour*. Princeton University Press, Princeton.

West, D.S., Von Hohenbalken, B. & Kroner, K. (1985) Tests of intraurban Central Place theories, *Economic Journal*, 95 (March): 101–117.

White, Paul (1986) Land availability, land banking and the price of land for housing, *Land Development Studies*, 3: 101–111.

Wilcox, J.P. (1979) Implementation of a computer-assisted appraisal system: Multnomah County, Oregon, *Assessor's Journal*, 14: 179–92.

Wilde, Oscar (1899/1961) *The Importance of Being Earnest*, in *Five Plays by Oscar Wilde*. Bantam Books, New York.

Willis, K.G. & M.C. Whitby (1985) The value of green belt land. *Journal of Rural Studies*, 1(2): 146–162.

Willis, K.G., N. Beale, N. Calder & D. Freer (1993) *Paying for Heritage. What Price for Durham Cathedral?* Countryside Change Unit, Working Paper 43, Department of Agricultural Economics and Food Marketing, University of Newcastle-upon-Tyne.

Wiltshaw, D.G. (1985) The supply of land, *Urban Studies* 22: 49–56.

Wiltshaw, D.G. (1988) Pedagogic comment and the supply of land for a particular use, *Urban Studies* Vol. 25, No. 5 (October): 439–447. Witte, Ann D. & James E. Bachman (1978) Vacant urban land holdings: portfolio considerations and owner characteristics, *Southern Economic Journal*, 45(2) (October): 543–558.

Wingo, Lowdon (1961) *Transportation and Urban Land*. Resources for the Future, Inc., Washington DC.

Witte, Ann D. & James E. Bachman (1978) Vacant urban land holdings: portfolio considerations and owner characteristics. *Southern Economic Journal*, 45(2) (October), 543–558.

# Index